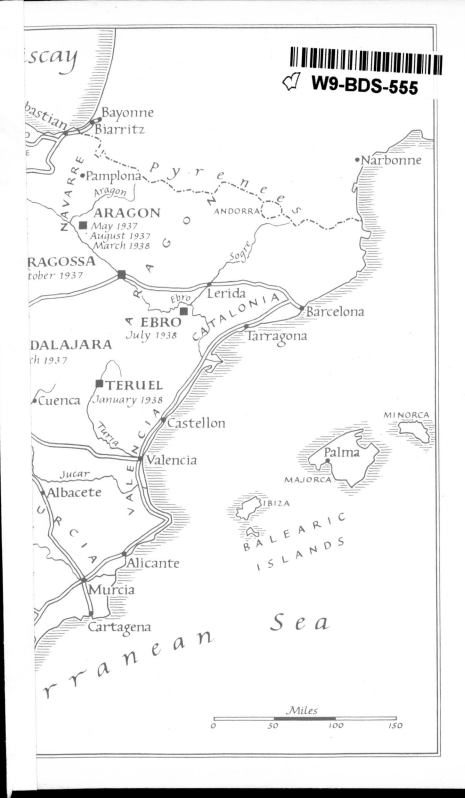

THE INTERNATIONAL BRIGADES

The International Brigades

Spain 1936-1939

Vincent Brome

1966
WILLIAM MORROW & CO.
New York

Contents

Illustrations

Acknowledgements

Thanks are due to the following for permission to quote copyright material:

Blandford Press Ltd (*Reason in Revolt* by Fred Copeman); Curtis Brown Ltd (*Boadilla* by Esmond Romilly); Chilton Books (*American Commissar* by Sandor Voros); Eyre & Spottiswoode (Publishers) Ltd and Harper & Row, Publishers (*The Spanish Civil War* by Hugh Thomas); Faber & Faber Ltd and Random House Inc ('Spain 1937' from *Collected Shorter Poems* by W. H. Auden); Faber & Faber Ltd (*English Captain* by Tom Wintringham); Rupert Hart-Davis Ltd and Miss Joan Daves (*The Owl of Minerva* by G. Regler); Lawrence & Wishart Ltd (*Britons in Spain* by William Rust and *Volunteers in Spain* by John Sommerfield); Edwin Rolfe (*The Lincoln Battalion*).

Many have heard it on remote peninsulas,
On sleepy plains, in the aberrant fisherman's islands,
In the corrupt heart of the city,
Have heard and migrated like gulls or the seeds of a flower
They clung like burrs to the long expresses that lurch
Through the unjust lands, through the night, through the
* alpine tunnel;*
They floated over the oceans;
They walked the passes: they came to present their lives.

W. H. AUDEN

Introduction

ANY attempt to name and thank all the people who have helped me with this book would make a tedious recital. In an abbreviated and unsatisfactory account I must acknowledge first both Hugh Thomas's distinguished book, *The Spanish Civil War*, from which I drew considerably, and his personal help with a number of questions, bibliographical and otherwise. I have also drawn on the memoirs of many people in a number of different countries, details of which are given elsewhere.

Inevitably, the present book involved research abroad and I have to thank Alvah Bessie, Sandor Voros, James Norman, Marvin Karpatkin, Arnold Krammer and Bert Levy for their help in America; Marguerite Rubens, Herbert Southworth and Raymond Rudorff for research in Paris; Dalmacio Negro in Madrid; and the Anglo-German Society in East Berlin. Ludwig Renn also gave me his views on a number of points and Luigi Longo in Rome made available certain material. A. Salazar and Pedro Schwartz were very helpful about the general Spanish scene, and the Office of Information in Madrid made available their own pamphlets on the International Brigades. Not unexpectedly, when I approached the Spanish Embassy for access to any captured Republican records, they refused under the rule common to most Western European countries which bans access to state papers for fifty years, and even specific questions, quoting the numbers of specific trial documents, could not be answered. I have taken into account evidence from Spain, Germany, Italy, France, England, America, Sweden and Norway, and newspaper and periodical reports in many languages. There were also a number of diaries and letters.

I have interviewed many survivors from the International Brigades and am especially grateful to Dr Ernst Adam, who was Chief of Staff to General Kléber, and to Fred Copeman, one-time Commander of the British Battalion, who spent many hours answering questions. Dr Tudor Hart who was surgeon to the XIVth Brigade, Dr I. Königsberg, George Aitken, Miles Tomalin, Walter Greenhalgh, Sefton Delmer, John Sommerfield, Peter Elstob, Richard Bennett, Roland Gant, Arthur Jenkins, Nan Green, Ilsa Barea, Kitty Wintringham, Bob Edwards, Jack Watson, Geoffrey Cox, Reed de Rouen, Will Paynter, Charlotte Haldane, Michael Young, Paul Tabori, Jerzy Pietrkiewicz, F. Smieja, Istvan Gal, Dr Skwarczynski and Françoise Basch were also very helpful. A talk with Albert Digges, secretary of the British International Brigades Association, was revealing, and I have been in touch with the equivalent organizations in New York and Berlin. Gerald Brenan, Manuel Aznar and Professor Nadal kindly answered a number of questions. To my many translators from the Norwegian, Dutch, Polish, Swedish and Danish I offer thanks for their patience when, time and again, they sat opposite me reading page after page. I am extremely grateful to Egbert Faas who did a great deal of similar work, to Ester Minetto and A. Busja. The French, German, Italian and Swedish Institutes were very persistent in tracing books for me, and the Spanish Institute made available its interesting collection on the International Brigades. As always the staff of the British Museum Library were tirelessly efficient in finding book after book and I particularly appreciated the help of Ian Willison. The Royal Institute of International Affairs gave me access to its collection of newspaper cuttings about the Brigades in several languages. *Reynolds News* also carried an interesting series of articles by Walter Greenhalgh. I made some use of a fairly extensive collection of material in the New York Public Library, placed there by the Abraham Lincoln Veterans Association. I have also drawn on a number of newspapers and periodicals produced by the Brigades during the war. The Hemerotica Nacional has a collection of these in Madrid.

One important point remains to be made clear. Any attempt to give a detailed account of all the battalions drawn from fifty nationalities would obviously involve a twelve-volume work and I have concentrated mainly upon the British and Americans with considerable reference to the Germans, French and Italians and to a lesser extent the Poles.

This is, I think, the first general account of the International

Brigades from their beginning until the end, in which an attempt is made to clothe the skeleton of history with the living flesh and blood of what it meant to be involved in such a remarkable experience.

For the rest, anyone interested in a more detailed bibliography will find it at the end of this book. It remains to say that considerations of length have made it necessary to exclude all but passing reference to the International Air Force and Medical Services.

The International Brigades[1]

Brigades	Battalions	Principal initial composition
XI (formed October 1936) (Hans Beimler)	I Edgar André	German
	II Commune de Paris (later transferred to the XIVth Brigade)	French-Belgian
	III Dabrowsky (later transferred to XIIth, 150th and XIIIth Brigades)	Polish Hungarian Yugoslav
XII (formed November 1936) (Garibaldi)	I Thaelmann (transferred to XIth)	German
	II Garibaldi	Italian
	III André Marty (Franco-Belge) (transferred to 150th, XIIth and XIVth)	French-Belgian
XIII (formed December 1936) (Dabrowsky)	I Louise Michel (transferred to XIVth)	French-Belgian
	II Tchapiaev (transferred to 129th Brigade)	Balkans
	III Henri Vuillemin (transferred to XIVth)	French
	IV Mickiewicz, Palafox	Polish
XIV (formed December 1936) (Marseillaise)	I Nine nations Battalion (transferred to Commune de Paris)	
	II Domingo Germinal (mostly Spanish Anarchist youth)	
	III Henri Barbusse	French
	IV Pierre Brachet	French

[1] *L'Épopée de l'Espagne* (2nd ed.), p. 249.

XV (formed February 1937)	I Dimitrov (transferred to 129th and then XIIIth)	Yugoslav
	II British	British
	III Lincoln, Washington Mackenzie-Papineau	U.S. Canadian
	IV Sixth of February (transferred to XIVth)	French
150th (formed June–July 1937)	I Rakosi	Hungarian
	II (transferred to XIIIth)	
	III	
129th	I Mazaryk (attached to 45th Division)	Czechoslovak
	II Dajakovich	Bulgarian
	III Dimitrov	Yugoslav Albanian
(in the 86th Brigade)	An international Battalion commanded by Colonel Morandi	

Chapter 1

The Background to the Brigades

How did it come about that in the year 1936 there gathered a modern crusade of men from America, England, Germany, France, Italy, Poland and half of Europe to submit voluntarily to a life of danger, hardship and death, in a mixed-up, brutal, and sometimes romantic war, which did not directly concern their own countries? The story of the 40,000 men who came over the seas and mountains to break through the barriers of international law, mixing thousands of ordinary working men with intellectuals, seamen with occasional criminals, soldiers with the unemployed, had all the elements of a film epic, but the reality was sometimes a confused nightmare and the motives sometimes complicated. If you shared the vision of many who fought in the International Brigades during the Spanish Civil War it was the last of the great crusades. 'It seems hardly believable that in the 'thirties of our century such a great and unique wave of brotherhood and self-sacrifice could rise from the depths of the people. Allegiances were pledged in those days not with signatures, not in words, but in blood.'[1] Modern conditions and weapons tend to ridicule the old chivalries. The upsurge of the individual driven by conscience to fight, the intellectual driven to become man of action, the rallying of a class to answer the call of the blood are now military anachronisms; but it is easy to romanticize this very remarkable episode. What was the truth about these men and where did the story really begin?

It is commonly supposed that every period has its own distinctive flavour and the years 1935–37 were certainly charged with events which produced a series of closely related crises. In England the great Hunger March of 1934 when thousands of unemployed poured into London from many parts of the country, relying for food and shelter on wayside charity,

[1] Ilya Ehrenburg, *Eve of War, 1933–41*, p. 167.

distressed and alarmed the Government, but it was a Labour Prime Minister,[1] the golden-voiced and Machiavellian Ramsay MacDonald, who refused to see the marchers' delegates. A bigger demonstration followed in 1935, and once again the reports in the newspapers gave a day-by-day account of what became a mass pilgrimage to that old shrine of English grievance, Trafalgar Square.

There, the early beginnings of the Popular Front were apparent with Clement Attlee, the Labour leader, speaking on the same platform as Wal Hannington the Communist. These were days which stirred men like Aneurin Bevan and McGovern to brilliant invective against a situation which they regarded as intolerable. It was cold, bitter weather. Thousands of marchers had come hundreds of miles, the newspapers relayed their story dramatically step by step, and there was something disturbing to the conscience of England in the spectacle of a hunger march which led inexplicably to impassable barriers at the door of the House of Commons. McGovern lost his temper in the House and described the situation as a 'damnable outrage'. There were cries of 'Order! Order!' and McGovern shouted back 'To hell with you and your order. . . . If these people are not fit to be admitted to the House I may as well leave the House. . . .'

The biggest piece of pomp and pageantry which Britain had witnessed since the coronation of King George V presently gripped the imagination of all classes, as preparations went forward on a huge scale for the celebration of King George V's Jubilee. A nation still haunted by unemployment, poverty and hardship was not the best material to respond to royal celebrations, but the Labour Party decided to co-operate and the East End districts of London put their feelings concisely in the slogan draped across one main street in crimson lettering – 'Lousy but Loyal'. The sixth of May 1935, the key day, was a flawless spring day of blue skies and brilliant sunshine and the great processions and marches mounted to the climax of the royal family driving in state to St Paul's, rapturously received by surging crowds which sometimes burst their banks and overwhelmed the police. Some deeper consciousness, some mystical fusion of patriotism, pageantry, prayer, worship and even gaiety stirred people inexplicably and for many ordinary millions the

[1] After 1931 Prime Minister of a National Government.

hardships of the poor and unemployed momentarily sank into the background.

Simultaneously, Ramsay MacDonald soared into the empyrean with one speech after another and his words came echoing back from outer space touched with lofty confusions. 'Society goes on and on. It is the same with ideas.' Society must 'keep in touch not only with the progressive but also with the retrograding movements in our advance'.

The General Election of 1935 gave the Conservatives some ten million votes and the Socialists eight million, but the Socialists held only 151 seats against the Conservatives' 438. Ramsay MacDonald lost his seat at Durham by 20,000 votes and was immediately smuggled back to the House again from the backwaters of the Scottish Universities. The Left Book Club, founded in May 1936 on the model of the American Book of the Month Club, chose an advisory committee composed of Harold Laski, Socialist professor of political theory, John Strachey, who had momentarily deviated to support Mosley but now brilliantly professed Marxist economics, and the not-yet-venerable but already widely known Victor Gollancz. As Robert Graves and Alan Hodges remarked in their fascinating mosaic of nineteen-thirties life, *The Long Week End*: 'The existence of the Club embittered the controversy between Labour and the extreme Left. Labour was invited to participate but refused unless its point of view was adequately represented on the Selection Committee. . . . Labour groups tried to counter this by setting up a Labour Book Club and a Socialist Book Club: the Diehard Conservatives already had their Right Book Club and the Liberals were forming a Liberal Book Club. None of these rivals, however, was ever successful enough to challenge the supremacy of the Left. . . .'[1]

An extraordinary upsurge of political awareness among intellectuals, poets, writers and artists, created an atmosphere in which well-to-do middle-class people passionately embraced left-wing views, and the guilt of a privileged upbringing converted many an academic to a brand of Marxism which regarded the proletariat as the chosen people.

There was no doubting an equivalent moral questioning of the old liberal views, and strong pressures were brought to bear

[1] Robert Graves and Alan Hodge, *The Long Week End*, p. 334.

for more drastic measures to prevent two million unemployed persons from slowly rotting away in a society which too easily surrendered to commercial expediency. If every other poet and writer did not commit himself to the Labour theory of Value or dialectical materialism, many of the most talented men of the Left, men like Stephen Spender, Arthur Koestler, and Richard Wright, were temporarily members of the Communist Party. As Stephen Spender wrote much later: 'I was driven by a sense of social and personal guilt which made me feel firstly that I must take sides, secondly that I could purge myself of an abnormal individuality by co-operating with the workers' movement. . . . Socially conscious liberals were confronted with the old conflict between means and ends in much sharper form. It was argued that in order to gain power you had to use bad means while indignantly denying that you were doing so.'[1]

These men saw that what was called Collective Pacifism in the League of Nations, Coolidgism in America, and Baldwinism in Britain, was really a woolly liberal attempt to contain forces too strong for such beliefs. Crossman referred to them as 'lazy intellectual shams which blinded most of us cautious, respectable democrats to the catastrophe into which we were drifting'. It was necessary to find a philosophy which analysed and exposed these shams and the obvious answer for many intellectuals was Marxism. Its great attraction lay in its power to explode liberal fallacies, but its substitution of religious by secular disciplines, and the projection of private problems into public places, also played a part.

In the everyday outer world, the same superficial preoccupations which have protected people against harsh reality down the centuries persisted, and the ugliness of unemployment, the first startling news of the abdication, and the outbreak of violence in a far-off country called Spain, were not of great consequence to many people. Superficially the London scene seemed secure enough with some streets still gas-lit, occasional hansom cabs still available for those who liked novelty, a number of buses still open-topped and great lumbering tramcars lurching down steel tracks. If you went out into the city on a normal day and saw its life deeply engrossed in small everyday habits, there was little sign of the great events which, one after another, were

[1] *The God That Failed*, ed. R. H. S. Crossman, p. 271.

to convulse the international scene. Mickey Mouse, Pluto the Hound, and Donald Duck filled the crevices of many leisured hours and where they failed there were Cochran's Young Ladies dancing in perfect unison, or the cynical sophistications of Mr Noël Coward to explain the impermanence of human relationships, or Walter Greenwood's *Love on the Dole* where the heroine saved herself and her family from starvation by becoming a bookmaker's mistress.

These parochial niceties were quickly overwhelmed by the tremendous clash which occurred in Spain. When news reached England of a military uprising against the Republican Government, it split the Labour Party into a number of factions with Aneurin Bevan characteristically leading the most rebellious and vociferous, while many Conservatives, by ancient prescription, shared the views and aims of General Franco. There were some perceptive politicians who knew that the civil war in Spain represented a cleavage in European thought too deep and universal to remain confined to the Iberian peninsula. The world had recovered reasonably well from Manchukuo and Abyssinia, France had survived the Stavisky scandals and even Hitler's penetration of the German Rhineland, but what now became known to Bevan and his group as the emasculated diplomacy of non-intervention, left Blum, premier of France, visibly weeping and shocked the radical Left throughout the world.

It was the belief of Aneurin Bevan that Spain and its elected Government were about to be sacrificed to a medieval Catholic hierarchy, aided and abetted by Fascist Governments ready to try out their armies and equipment, but the Conservatives were equally convinced of the threat of Russian Communism overrunning Spain and possibly Europe. Winston Churchill had the vision to see the meaning of the ghost armies steadily rising in Germany, as a vast war potential absorbed more men and more materials and the fever of Nazi ambitions began to run high. Churchill was one of the few people in 1936 who fully appreciated that the first twilight of a particularly black and hellish night was coming down on Europe.

Meanwhile every intellectual became interested in Spain.

Men who had never had any qualms about Gibraltar being kept by the British could no longer bear the idea that Mussolini might keep Ibiza. Men who had ignored the exploitation of the Spanish workers for years suddenly became eloquent about the misery of the Spanish land proletariat. Men who had never taken part in the vulgar life of a political demonstration now appeared before large crowds raising clenched fists. Among the Oxford Communists many talked uneasily about the guilt of safety, and if few went to the actual seat of the war because it was not local party policy to send them, many organized petitions, marches and demonstrations.

Spain and the civil war were the big issues at the Labour and Conservative conferences of that year. The Conservatives defended the policy of non-intervention on the obvious ground that whatever hidden aid was reaching insurgent and Republican Spain would, if we openly supplied arms, swell into a tide capable of converting a localized war into an international nightmare. The militants in the Labour Party believed it was better to challenge the growing forces of what was generally referred to as Fascism, now in their infancy in Spain, where they could be 'nipped in the bud', than to wait for a world war of catastrophic proportions. Official Labour policy endorsed non-intervention and a violent split developed which left the Socialist radicals deeply depressed. Men like Aneurin Bevan felt that a vital spark had gone out of the Left-Wing movement in Britain. The old crusading zest which took in half the world had dwindled to a series of polite local gestures at a number of conferences where men met together in far greater numbers and greater power than ever before, but produced in the end a dowdy and highly diplomatic mouse.

What, in fact, was happening in Spain, and where exactly did the civil war begin? For many years the enemies of the Republic had been gathering their forces and, as Hugh Thomas said in his excellent book, 'the first shot in the contest . . . was the grave but violent pastoral letter of Cardinal Segura, Archbishop of Toledo and Primate of the Spanish Church – made at the beginning of May 1931. This proud and uncompromising prelate combined intelligence with intense fanaticism.'[1] A man

[1] Hugh Thomas, *The Spanish Civil War*, p. 29.

approaching fifty, still at the height of his powers, his letter began with a eulogy of Alfonso XIII and rose to this peroration: 'If we remain quiet and idle, if we allow ourselves to give way to apathy and timidity, if we leave open the way to those who are attempting to destroy religion or if we expect the benevolence of our enemies to secure the triumph of our ideals, we shall have no right to lament when bitter reality shows us that we had victory in our hands, yet knew not how to fight like intrepid warriors prepared to succumb gloriously.'[1]

The political situation in Spain was complicated to the point of absurdity and in 1931 a multiplicity of parties or groups were all aligning and re-aligning themselves, some with a readiness for violence which growing tensions made all too possible. Any brief account of the situation must suffer serious shortcomings, and those interested in the full details should read Hugh Thomas's analysis. A mere list of some of the leading parties gives some idea of the fierce fragmentation of political ideals which went far beyond anything known in Britain or America and automatically created explosive possibilities among a nation where passions, when stirred, ran high.

CEDA, a Catholic party was the Confederación Española de Derechas Autónomas; the CNT an Anarcho-Syndicalist Trades Union, the Confederación Nacional del Trabajo; the FAI, an Anarchist secret society, the Federación Anarquista Ibérica; the JONS, the Fascist Party, the Juntas de Ofensiva Nacional-Sindicalista; the POUM, said to be a Trotsky Party, but refusing to accept the definition, the Partido Obrero de Unificación Marxista; the PSUC, the United Catalan Socialist-Communist Party, the Partido Socialista Unificado de Cataluña; the UGT, the Socialist Trade Union, the Unión General del Trabajadores; the UME, a Right-Wing officers' group (Unión Militar Española) and the Republican Officers' group UMR (Unión Militar Republicana). These factions changed and interchanged as the Left, Right, Communist, Socialist and Anarchist movements struggled to gain ascendancy and the situation in the Church deepened the complications within each party.

In the 1930s there were 31,000 priests, 60,000 nuns and 20,000

[1] Quoted by Hugh Thomas, ibid., p. 30.

monks in Spain but it was estimated by the Church authorities that no less than two-thirds of the population failed to confess or go to Mass although the Church remained the spiritual sanction for baptisms, weddings and funerals. The Church authorities exercised power out of all proportion to the numbers of practising Catholics and automatically aligned themselves against any Republican Government, but their association with other parties was complex and variable.

The adult population of Spain in 1936 totalled some eleven million with two or three million industrial workers and miners, four and a half million agricultural workers, two million tradesmen and small artisans and two million middle-class people. The industrial workers and miners had recently achieved a reasonable standard of living but three-quarters of the agricultural workers in Andalusia, Estremadura and the two Castiles had an income of less than 1 peseta (or 6d) a day in 1936.

Agriculture and its workers remained the central problem in the social scene and was a source of great strength for the anarchist CNT party. Moreover, as Hugh Thomas wrote, the Agrarian Law of 1932 'only applied to Andalusia, Estremadura, three provinces of Castile . . . and Albacete in Murcia', where 'all unworked estates over 56 acres would be taken over by the Institute of Agrarian Reform. . . . Land secured would be controlled by the State and distributed either to selected individual peasants or to co-operatives of peasants. In both cases the State would be the new landowner.'[1] Geographically limited as they were, these reforms had revolutionary characteristics but, surprisingly, they met with little opposition in the Cortes, perhaps because they left large areas of Spain untouched and failed to come to grips with the bigger question of agricultural credit.

Meanwhile the Army could easily disdain land reform and economic interference as it waited in the background, with over 200,000 men and 20,000 officers – one officer for every ten men. Traditionally the Army was more concerned with enforcing law and order within its own boundaries than with challenging any enemy abroad, and now the usual proliferation of small plots and conspiracies multiplied, as it watched the growth of Left-Wing power.

[1] Hugh Thomas, *The Spanish Civil War*, p. 51.

The Left Wing in Spain had come through every vicissitude from the assassination of some of its members to plots, burnings and internecine strife within its own parties. In 1931 a series of strikes organized by the CNT had finally developed into a general strike in Seville, to crush which the Government brought up artillery. Thirty people were killed and 200 wounded in the 'battles' which followed. There had been the October revolution in Madrid and Barcelona, and the tragic affair in Asturia when the miners successfully established a revolutionary Soviet throughout the province only to be overwhelmed by the Foreign Legion directed by Generals Goded and Francisco Franco. Early in 1936, the quarrel between the two vast trade unions, the CNT and the UGT, which centred around the best means of strike action, reached a climax and resulted, dramatically, in many gun battles between them. Simultaneously the ancient quarrel between the Socialist leaders Prieto and Caballero came to an even fiercer head. Thus, while the Left suffered from terrible internal divisions, the Right closed its ranks and presently included in those ranks what remained of the Centre. The Constitution of the Spanish Republic had unwisely included savagely anti-clerical clauses which amounted, in effect, to the disestablishment of the Church and served to stiffen the Army's resistance even when Azaña thundered: 'Do not tell me that this is contrary to freedom. It is a matter of public health.'

In the 1936 elections the parties of the Left formed a Popular Front in accordance with the policy laid down by the Bulgarian Communist Dimitrov, then General Secretary of the Comintern, and its repercussions in Spain were more profound than elsewhere. The aggregate votes for each group were: Popular Front 4,176,156; National Front 3,783,601; Centre 681,047; and Basque Nationalists 130,000. Thus the country was too closely divided between Left and Right for anyone's peace of mind.

General Franco, Chief of Staff at the Ministry of War, had given an assurance that he would not take part in any plot against the new Republican Government, but three weeks after the election, while the caretaker Prime Minister Portela Valladares was still holding a precarious balance under explosive conditions, Franco called on him and urged him 'to declare a state of war and thus prevent – at any cost – the

Popular Front from taking effective power.' Portela recoiled from any such action, pointing to the dangers of revolution which Franco said were negligible providing he had the support of the caretaker government. The following day, Portela relinquished power to Manuel Azaña, the most balanced among the Socialist leaders.

With the Left Wing reaffirmed in office there were tremendous outbursts of popular enthusiasm and great crowds massed before the Ministry of the Interior in Madrid crying 'Amnistia'. The prisons in Oviedo were opened and most of the prisoners taken in the Asturias Revolution released. Among rapturous scenes, with passions running high, Azaña, once more Prime Minister, maintained a State of Alarm which included a rigid press censorship, and Generals Franco, Fanjul, Varela and Emilio Mola took no immediate counter-revolutionary action.

Franco, in some disgrace, was next sent off to semi-banishment in the Canaries, where he not merely continued to brood on the fate of Spain but actively conspired against the Government. On 23 June he wrote once more to the Prime Minister of the Republic protesting against the arbitrary dismissal of Right-Wing officers in the Army, which he said was liable to undermine discipline and must lead to serious doubts and disturbances in the minds of the rank and file. It was unfortunate that the Prime Minister did not reply. Franco thereupon finally made up his mind. Already a rising had been planned and it needed only agreement with the Carlists to fix the date.

It was claimed, at this stage, by the Right Wing that chaos threatened from strikes, disturbances and political murders, but although shootings and assassinations were reported almost daily in July, and the capital was in the grip of a complicated building strike with a series of lesser strikes among waiters, bullfighters and lift attendants, there was no sign of widespread general disorders.

And then on 12 July, a very hot Sunday, Lieutenant José Castillo of the *Asaltos* was shot dead in Madrid by four men who quickly melted into the surrounding streets. At three o'clock in the morning on the following day, 13 July, the Monarchist leader Calvo Sotelo (Leader of the Parliamentary Opposition) was roused from his bed by Captain Condés, a member of the Civil Guard, a man called Cuenca and a number of Asaltos. When Calvo Sotelo had examined Captain Condés's papers he agreed to accompany him to police headquarters and told his family that he would be in touch with them immediately he knew the charges against him – 'unless', he added, 'these gentlemen are going to blow my brains out.' Lurching away at 70 miles an hour in a storm-trooper's military car, the men were all silent, despite Calvo Sotelo's attempts to talk, and then, suddenly, Cuenca drew a revolver and fired two shots into the back of Calvo Sotelo's neck. It is said that he died at once, but remained sitting upright wedged firmly between two Asaltos as the car raced on into the night. Finally they handed over his body to a local cemetery as the corpse of some stranger found dead on the street.

Within a few days half of Spain was aghast at the murder of the Leader of the Parliamentary Opposition by what were, in effect, members of the regular police. In the Cortes Committee, Gil Robles, the sleek young leader of the Catholic Party, paid tribute to the memory of Calvo Sotelo, reminded the Assembly of sixty-one murders all committed in the course of one month, and concluded that the Government had reduced democracy to a travesty which permitted blood, shame and violence to overwhelm its true nature.

Something else had become much clearer to those in touch with both sides in Spain. After two years of Right-Wing Government and two years of Left-Wing, the opposing parties were agreed upon one thing – they could not coexist amicably. From the point of view of the Right, the Left were forming their own private armies in the shape of workers' militia and the Left regarded the activities of the Army itself with the highest suspicion. The voting had given the Popular Front a majority, but it was too slender to discredit the theory that the country was equally split between Left and Right into completely intransigent forces.

Against this background, away in England, a certain English pilot, Captain Bebb, had already been hired by Spanish Falangists to fly a plane from Croydon to Las Palmas, close to Franco's place of exile, and on 11 July Douglas Jerrold, the English Catholic publisher, 'procured' Hugh Pollard, his daughter, a friend and Major Bolin to play the role of normal passengers, thus giving the flight a routine air.[1] The plane was in fact intended to fly Franco from the Canaries to Morocco to take over command of the Army of Africa. Captain Bebb successfully landed at Las Palmas without papers, the Under-Secretary and the Ministry of War gave Franco permission to leave Tenerife to attend the funeral of a military dignitary, and Colonel Valentín Galarza, in the War Ministry of Madrid, passed a message from Mola to Goded in Majorca that he should proceed to Barcelona. On the night of 16–17 July, General Romerales toured the city of Melilla, found nothing suspicious, joked with the local Socialist leaders at the *casa del pueblo* – 'the masses at vigil I see' – and the following day was forced to resign at the revolver-point. At Tetuán, next day, Colonels Asensio, Sáenz de Buruaga and Beigbeder demanded the resignation of the High Commissioner by telephone from their headquarters. Meanwhile, General Franco easily took over Las Palmas, and at a quarter-past five on 18 July he issued a Manifesto claiming a special patriotic mission for the Spanish officers of the Army and eloquently promising a new, sane and quite different order in Spain, once the rising was complete.

In the great heat of the night of 17 July, the streets and cafés of Madrid were full of wild rumours and counter-rumours, people choked the roadways, arguing passionately and clamouring, in many cases, for arms, but a group of Left-Wing officers were still in control in the War Ministry and the leaders of the Madrid uprising held quick, furtive and very anxious meetings in their own homes. At last, in the stifling dawn of 18 July, the rising on the mainland really began. Everywhere the pattern was similar. Military garrisons led by Right-Wing officers rose, took over the town hall and where available the radio, supported by the Falange and in many cases the Civil Guard. Proclamations were read from the balcony of each town hall declaring a state of war, and military law was quickly imposed. With civil rights suspended the Army proceeded to apply its powers ruthlessly and brutally, committing a number of atrocities calculated to keep any reasonably imaginative human being firmly in his place.

On 19 July Spain had three successive governments in one day. Señor Casares Quiroga, the then Prime Minister, threw

[1] *News Chronicle*, 7 November 1936, article by Captain Bebb.

in his hand and resigned. Three hours later Señor Martinez Barrio, who proposed a compromise with the military rebels, took over and was in turn replaced by Señor Giral, who threw open the public arsenals to the militia.

During the nightmare of the civil war which followed, leaving Spain torn and traversed by hatred, murder and atrocities on both sides, it is chastening to remember that Franco himself would have hesitated had he realized what a prolonged and bloody struggle lay ahead, and the Republican Government in Madrid could certainly have put down the uprising in a few weeks if they had chosen to arm the workers quickly.

But the die was cast and as the rebels swept forward and split Spain in two, with Republican resistance hardening everywhere, this microcosm of a division which was beginning to split the world created the conditions for the birth of the International Brigade. Some governments in the outer world reacted to the catastrophe according to the laws of international diplomacy; others with a Machiavellian absorption in the experimental possibilities of new weapons; some were horrified at the tragic waste of human effort and achievement and all were driven by a desire not to burn their fingers uselessly. In February 1936 the policy of non-intervention was conceived with the ostensible purpose of stopping the war from spreading, and those foreigners who wanted to fight on one side or the other were forced back on subterfuge, until a means was found of organizing the first units of that strange band of volunteers, at first sight romantic and later cold-bloodedly realistic, which became known as the International Brigade.

Chapter 2

Origin of the Brigades

ONE of the men involved in the early beginnings of the International Brigade was W. G. Krivitsky (alias Ginsberg), for a number of years Chief of the Soviet Military Intelligence in Western Europe. Living in The Hague, Holland, disguised as an Austrian antiquarian, he travelled extensively throughout Europe, ostensibly buying and selling antiques. Immediately the Spanish Civil War broke out he dispatched an agent to Hendaye on the Franco-Spanish border and another to Lisbon, where they were to establish contact with Franco's Spain and organize a secret information service. Stalin was already playing a waiting game, anxious not to commit himself before he discovered whether Franco would achieve a quick and easy victory, and for some time Krivitsky received no special instructions from Moscow.

His action in Hendaye and Lisbon was routine and even when he read reports from Russian agents in Berlin, Hamburg, Rome, Genoa, Bremen and Naples stating categorically that Franco was receiving powerful aid from Italy and passed these details on to the Comintern, there was no reply. It has to be remembered that the Spanish Republic had existed for some years without recognizing the Soviet Government and any diplomatic relations between the two countries were highly unofficial. Stalin argued that the old Spain was gone forever, but he still did not know whether the new Spain would eventually join the Italian-German bloc and he did not merely move cautiously but tried to conceal every step he took until late in August of 1936. Three representatives of the Spanish Government then set out for Russia intent on buying war supplies. 'They offered in exchange huge sums in Spanish gold. Even now, however, they were not conveyed to Moscow but kept incognito in a hotel in Odessa. . . . Stalin doubly cautioned his commissars that Soviet aid to Spain must be unofficial and

J. B. S. Haldane, heard the door open and there stood her sixteen-year-old son Ronald. He was a lanky, serious-minded boy who had been brought up in the Marxist tradition and now, with the Spanish Civil War emblazoned across every newspaper, a not-unexpected crisis suddenly arose. 'His enormous velvet-dark eyes blazed from his thin angular face which was pale as cheese and on which the acne spots stood out vividly. He had the pathetic nobility and panache of the adolescent completely vowed to any cause. . . .'[1]

Ronald Haldane now quietly informed his mother that he not merely wanted to volunteer for Spain, but had already joined the International Brigade and was leaving England almost at once.

An intellectual of no mean order, Mrs Haldane did not follow the conventional formula and plead with him not to go; she masked her alarm and simply barked at him: 'You silly little fool, what use would you be? Why, you can't even shoot.'

'Oh yes I can', he said, squaring his shoulders. 'I did P.T. at school.'[2]

Mrs Haldane was momentarily silenced. In the outer world the Spanish Civil War had divided one country after another into viciously opposed camps with an intensity unknown since the far-off days of the Inquisition. Those who felt that General Franco's uprising against the Republican Government was necessary in the interests of law and order referred to the legitimate government of the day as incompetent and tyrannical Reds. Those who believed that the Republican Government represented a splendid but shaky attempt to infuse some of the principles of democratic socialism into a ramshackle feudal system called the insurgents an army of Fascists, whose preparedness for violence at any cost was characteristic of their creed. Mrs Haldane wholeheartedly supported the Republican Government. She and her husband, in company with a large number of Communists, Socialists, idealists, liberals and democrats, had thrown all their energies into propaganda for the Republicans, and one of the people involved in their arguments had been her own sixteen-year-old son. He had listened and absorbed the gospel. He had gone away deeply imbued with its ideals and now he had acted upon the very message his mother

[1] Charlotte Haldane, *Truth Will Out*, p. 93.   [2] Ibid., p. 94.

---

handled covertly in order to eliminate any possibility of involving his government in war.'[1] He crystallized his policy in a phrase which was handed down from one committee to another, 'Podalshe ot artillereiskovo ognia!' which roughly translated meant: 'Stay out of range of the artillery fire!'

It was against this background, one day in August, that a special courier arrived from Russia at The Hague with a message for Krivitsky, which, according to Krivitsky, read: 'Extend your operations immediately to cover Spanish Civil War. Mobilize all available agents and facilities for prompt creation of a system to purchase and transport arms to Spain. A special agent is being dispatched to Paris to aid you in this work. He will report to you there and work under your supervision.'[2] This special agent turned out to be a man called Zimin.

There followed a meeting in the Lubianka on 14 September when Yagoda discussed the idea of foreign volunteers joining the Republican Army and it was agreed that any movement of volunteers to Spain must be 'secretly policed by the Ogpu'.[3]

Several people are credited with originating the idea of the International Brigades. On 22 September, Thorez, leader of the French Communist Party, visited Moscow and supported the arguments of Rosenberg, Russian Ambassador in Madrid, for direct military aid to Spain. 'He also suggested that aid should be given to the Republic in the form of volunteers raised internationally by foreign Communist Parties (though they would welcome non-Communists). . . . Tom Wintringham, in Spain with the British medical aid unit, had also suggested the idea.'[4] Dimitrov, the Bulgarian head of the Comintern, came out in favour of the scheme, and certain leading Russian generals saw an opportunity of learning important military lessons by sending a shock force, camouflaged by international colours, into the Spanish War.[5] Already the Germans were taking a sharp interest in every detail of the Spanish War and the military papers *Wissen und Wehr* and *Kriegskunst* reported and analysed each action closely. Presently, their Russian equivalents,

[1] W. G. Krivitsky, *I Was Stalin's Agent*, 1940.   [2] Ibid., p. 101.   [3] Ibid.
[4] Hugh Thomas, *The Spanish Civil War*, p. 296.
[5] Manuilsky's Report to the Eighteenth Congress of the Communist Party of the Soviet Union, 10 March 1939.

Krassnaya Armii and *Krassnaya Zvezda*, took up the analysis in even greater detail.

The non-Communist Italian Republican, Randolfo Pacciardi, next went to Madrid and offered to found an international brigade, but Largo Caballero turned down the idea. Later, an anti-Fascist delegation, consisting of the Italian, Luigi Gallo, the Pole, Stepan Wizniewski, and the Frenchman, Pierre Rebière,[1] was received by Martinez Barrio and asked for official recognition of an International Force. Barrio said, 'Under what conditions would you be prepared to take part in the struggle?' and received the answer, 'Under any conditions.'[2] It now became the main purpose of the Comintern to organize the International Brigades, and men like Togliatti in Spain and Josip Broz (later Marshal Tito) in Paris threw themselves into the work. Broz lived in a small hotel in the Latin Quarter under a false name and devised what was known as his secret railway 'which provided passports and funds for East European volunteers', but the main offices of the Brigade were in the Rue de La Fayette, Paris. It was decided to cover the actual recruiting activities by selecting trade union offices as their centre and the Maison des Syndicats at No. 8 Rue Mathurin-Moreau became the core of the campaign with a network of similar trade union offices throughout Paris, France and Belgium. Over 1,500 Yugoslavs including many intellectuals were sent through Tito's secret railway via Austria and Switzerland, but a proportion had no idea that they were responding to a call with, in many cases, Communist origins.

According to Krivitsky the original nucleus of the Brigade consisted of five or six hundred men expelled from their own countries for revolutionary activities. They had sought refuge in Russia and become something of an embarrassment to Stalin, who welcomed the Spanish Civil War as a means of employing them. Now they were sent to form the kernel of the Brigade but – once more according to Krivitsky – not a single Russian appeared amongst them. Krivitsky claimed that 'an impenetrable wall was deliberately erected between this force and the units of the Red Army detailed for service in Spain.'

Krivitsky, himself a renegade from Soviet Russia, tends to exaggerate the effective control exercised by Russian sources:

§ *L'Épopée de l'Espagne*, pp. 50–1.   § Ibid.

'When a volunteer offered himself he was dire[cted to] enlistment bureau. Here he filled out a questio[nnaire and] told to await notification. Behind the scenes th[ey investi-]gated his political record. . . . In Europe w[ere a large] number of secret control points where each app[licant was] thoroughly reinvestigated. . . .'

The Ogpu's control of those volunteers found [loyal to] the cause 'was continued in Spain, where i[nformers were] planted among them to weed out suspected spie[s, to remove] men whose political opinions were not strictly or[thodox, to] supervise their reading matter and their convers[ation.]

Some of this is exaggerated. As will be seen [a high] proportion of those who volunteered and serve[d were adven-]turers, neurotics, and even criminals and razor b[oys who could] have passed Ogpu scrutiny on one ground only – t[hat] they were quite beyond the pale. But Krivitsky is [right when he] says that: 'Practically all the political commiss[ars in the] International Brigade were stalwart Communists.[']

It would be false, none the less, to convey the im[pression that] the early beginnings of the Brigades were a carefu[lly planned] Communist plan. Without formal Communist [planning] there would have been many volunteers pouring i[n to] fight; indeed there *were* many volunteers who [actually] fought before any official recognition or planning wa[s complete.] Various international centuria went into action in [and near] the Tagus valley very early in the war, and men [like Ludwig] Renn, Hans Beimler, Rosselli, John Cornford and [many others] travelled to Spain on their own initiative as pure v[olunteers.]

The birth of the Brigades, then, was confused. Wh[at are the] facts of early recruitment? Who were these men? H[ow did they] break through so many international barriers to re[ach Spain] and how, exactly, were they trained, organized, pa[id and – at] such emergency speed – thrown into battle?

It was one of those November evenings when all th[e elements] combined to make winter the special experience it is i[n the fog-] enshrouded British Isles. Lying in bed with a serio[us attack of] influenza, Mrs Charlotte Haldane, wife of the famou[s scientist]

[1] W. G. Krivitsky, *I Was Stalin's Agent*, p. 113.

had instilled into him, and come to her with a *fait accompli*. He was going to Spain to fight for Democracy against Fascism. Mrs Haldane wrote: 'I was helpless, trapped. You cannot have your cake and eat it. . . . But he was sixteen years old, I was his mother. Was I perhaps sending this child of mine to glory, death, wounds, mutilation, disfigurement? It was a heinous responsibility I had piled up for myself.'[1] She decided to talk over the matter with her husband, J. B. S. Haldane. She could easily exercise her rights, as the legal guardian of a boy of sixteen, and simply stop him from launching into an adventure the exact nature of which, at his age, he could hardly know. The romantic glow of taking up arms in defence of democracy might wither and die under the mutilation of machine-gun bullets more certainly than any slip of a boy, unaccustomed to pain, could imagine. But these were emancipated parents with austere beliefs in private freedom of choice even for a boy still in his teens, and Mrs Haldane wrote: 'His fight for his own personal and private freedom was my fight for mine, at his age, against my own mother, against all the frustration of my own childhood and adolescence.' Her husband, when she finally consulted him, shared these views. The boy must make up his own mind.

Determined to discover the Party's reaction to her son's romantic gesture, Mrs Haldane next staggered up from her bed of sickness, dressed, went down to her car and drove round to the propaganda bookshop behind which lay the headquarters of the British Communist Party in King Street, Covent Garden. She asked to see the secretary and was shown up a flight of narrow, creaking stairs into a business-like office with a vast portrait of Lenin looking down from the mantelpiece. Underneath sat the thickset, virile figure of Harry Pollitt. Mrs Haldane did not know then that this squat figurehead of a ruthless political creed was, in fact, a little scared of the forceful, intellectual woman now confronting him, with a brain probably twice as good as his own. She has recorded the following conversation between them: 'Well,' he said in a dour, north-country accent, but a pleasant baritone voice, 'Ah suppose ye've come to tell me 'e can't go.' 'No,' she said, 'I haven't. I don't feel I've the right to stop the boy if he wants to go.'

[1] Charlotte Haldane, *Truth Will Out*, p. 94.

A combination of relief and surprise showed in Harry Pollitt's face. Relief because he had expected a tough argument with Mrs Haldane, and surprise because bourgeois mothers did not normally have the courage of their convictions.

Mrs Haldane insisted on one thing, however emancipated she might profess to be. If Ronald followed through this gesture he must take with him a gas-mask. In the light of subsequent events this stipulation seemed of little consequence beside the enormous decision her son had taken, but in those days the preoccupation with the horrors of poison gas haunted the minds of scientists, intellectuals and military alike.

Mrs Haldane returned home, went back to bed and ran a high temperature. Whatever torment she now underwent is not recorded, but unlike many of her counterparts, whose resolution quailed when self-imposed principles threatened to destroy someone they loved, she did not allow the conflict to change her mind.

Some days later, she summoned sufficient strength to drive Ronald to Victoria Station to catch the night train for Dieppe en route for Spain. Ronald Haldane had one hallmark of his class not possessed by the rank and file who were then being recruited for the International Brigade. He had a passport. He could also speak French and knew his way around Paris. The complications which made recruitment such a tortured undertaking for the average individual and led into all kinds of subterfuge as the movement gathered force did not trouble Ronald Haldane.

But the power of mother-love and intellectual conviction were now equally matched in Mrs Haldane, and she wrote: 'We drove away from the station and I needed a drink. I needed a great number of drinks. J.B.S. was good to me. We did a pub crawl until the pubs shut. Then we went home and attacked a bottle of whisky. Around three-thirty in the morning I had absorbed sufficient alcohol to enable me to sleep.'

But that was not the end of it. She developed pleurisy and what at first sight seemed a matter of two weeks in bed became a prolonged struggle in which her temperature would not return to normal. Meanwhile, J. B. S. Haldane was fretting about the situation in Madrid as reports came back of Hemingway and other Left-Wing intellectuals 'having a lot of fun and frivolity and pseudo-military excitement in that heroic city.' Finally the urge to go to the front and discover for himself what was happening became compulsive, but for some reason the trip could only be undertaken in an extraordinary garb consisting of a black leather jacket and breeches and a motor-cyclist's cap with a visor.

Christmas came round. Even those protected by the most rigorous intellectual detachment had been known to soften at Christmas, and Mrs Haldane was no exception. 'A friend came to help me eat Christmas dinner. There was an enormous sirloin, a regular Christmas Scotch sirloin cooked to perfection. It was my first day up and I was a little silly with physical weakness and emotion. I started to carve it and the tears began pouring down my face into the gravy.'

In the spring of the following year, 1937, Mrs Haldane found herself on the way to Paris bent on a mission of her own, no less valuable to the International Brigades than her son's. She had been selected by the Party to play an official role in a Paris recruitment centre for International Brigade volunteers. The address of the office she was to visit remained at this time a secret, its secretary and organizers all worked incognito, and a whole smoke screen of security surrounded every operation. The Non-Intervention Pact had rendered every step taken under the Brigade's auspices illegal and the Paris police wavered between austere attempts to enforce every detail, and a casual indifference which refused to notice flagrantly suspicious conduct under its very nose.

As for Mrs Haldane, there could be no possible reason for suspecting this distinguished but sensible-looking Englishwoman, clearly anxious to renew a life-long acquaintance with the art treasures and graces of the most beautiful city in the world. The emerald Bois de Boulogne, the glittering Champs Elysées, the white dome of Sacré Cœur and the sparkling café life all combined with elegant shops, clothes and people to preserve the illusion of a romantic Paris which was denied by the news headlines, the glum faces in the Métro, the peeling walls, the ancient *pissoirs* and a tatterdemalion air in the quarter of the city towards which she moved. She arrived by

Métro at the Place du Combat, the working-class district where tall houses crowd above narrow streets, the cafés are dingy, sweat and garlic mingle their odour with the ancient smells from old drains and people talk a Parisian argot alive with coarse vitality.

She crossed the Place to No. 10, and found herself 'outside a door in the entrance gate to a group of office buildings behind an extensive high wall that completely screened them from the street.'

A porter stared impassively at her from his lodge until she said: 'I am looking for Max' – and the arranged password immediately changed his manner. He escorted her through the gate with fresh instructions. She entered an open courtyard and saw a notice board which said that these were the district administrative offices of certain French trade unions. She entered the gloomy, dilapidated building, turned down the corridor, counted the doors on the left and knocked on the third. A voice called '*Entrez*' – she pushed open the door and there, to her surprise, was a group of six men gathered round a battered deal table, obviously absorbed in some sort of conference. She automatically selected an intellectual-looking young man whose chair was tilted back against a wall, because his face and bearing had that mark of a man of purpose which makes a leader. In fact their eyes met, as she stood there – 'with one of those lightning flashes of recognition, as of a man and woman who had waited for this precise moment all their lives.' Once more, this romantic encounter turned out to be a delusion. When Mrs Haldane addressed him in French – 'Comrade Max?' – he shook his head and the man next to him said: 'I am Max. What can I do for you?'

She explained that she had been sent from London on a special International Brigade mission and he replied, 'Just wait outside, Comrade. We're in conference.'

Ten minutes later the meeting broke up. Comrade Max emerged, beckoned to Mrs Haldane and led the way to a nearby café. Max now explained what seemed to her in doubt before: that he was very glad indeed to see her because she spoke French fluently and they desperately needed an interpreter for the casual English who were coming into Paris en route for Spain without a word of any other language.

Max quickly revealed a number of characteristics which seemed admirable to Mrs Haldane. Externally he had 'the stunted body of the typical city slum-child, a dead-pale face with two tiny, twinkling light blue eyes', but his intelligence was quick and vivid, his spirit vivacious and his sense of humour a stimulating compound of cockney and Jewish wisecracks. This man had taken charge of the Combat District International Brigade recruitment centre and now, volubly, he explained that Mrs Haldane's appearance was heaven-sent. She must stay and join the staff. 'I suppose I can if it's arranged between yourselves and London,' she said.

Half an hour later they were walking down the Boulevard Jean-Jaurés, through the grim Métro arches alive with touts from the brothels which catered for every sexual taste and perversion. Superfluously, Max explained the inevitable problem which the brothels created, especially for British and American recruits who came to Spain with more money than other nationalities.

Not unexpectedly, these men felt the need for a final fling before they left for the front and the garish attractions of the brothels were irresistible. Some emerged with venereal disease of one kind or another and this meant being jailed in Spain, a humiliating end to high adventure.

Max next led the way into one of the new co-operative restaurants where the ordinary worker could get a reasonable meal and a bottle of pinard for a few francs. It was bursting with men and women all eating away ferociously, and at first sight there was no room for any newcomer. Ignoring the crowd, the waiters and the gesticulating assistant at the cash desk, Max made his way towards the stairs. A casual stranger tried to follow them up the stairs, but the cashier intervened. 'Sorry – it's full upstairs now.'

At the top of the stairs Max led the way into a long room with big tables ranged down either side, and gathered round these tables was the most cosmopolitan crew Mrs Haldane had ever set eyes on. The majority bore the stamp of working men – miners, seamen, navvies, labourers – but here and there were men of frailer constitution with white hands and soft cheeks, the intellectuals, the writers and the artists who now shared a common cause with men remote from their normal way of life.

An extraordinary babel of tongues gave the scene the polyglot air of some international anarchists' conspiracy, and the quick concise sound of the French language was broken into and overlaid by half the languages of Europe from English and German to Latvian, Dutch and Walloon. This upper floor of a public restaurant, so thinly protected from the outside world and the Paris police, held enough evidence to condemn its owners to long terms of imprisonment and here were gathered, talking, laughing, exchanging quips in argot, broken English and bad French, one of the nuclei of the International Brigade.

Max passed between the tables and made his way to a second room beyond the first, which was reserved for the couriers and organizers of the Brigade. Immediately Mrs Haldane picked out, at a side table, the distinguished young man who had exchanged the lightning flash of recognition with her when she first burst into the conference room that morning. Max now introduced this man as Jack, using the single Christian cover-names under which they operated. Mrs Haldane suddenly realized that the three men sitting at the table were all Americans. Her own description of the second man, called Lee, is worth quoting:

'Lee was a fat, dumpy little Jew, with large, dark, cow-like eyes, magnified by enormous horn-rims . . . squat, lazy, good-tempered, madly homesick and secretly terrified to find himself in this illegal *galère*. His inferiority complex and his guilty fears caused him to assume a phoney aggressive manner. He was one of those inconspicuous aspiring literary types, semi-journalist, semi-dramatist, whose personal frustrations and disappointments are constantly jumping them, to their deep distress, into a life of romantic political adventure.'[1]

The second American, who went under the name of Eric – his full name was Eric de Witt Parker – came from Connecticut and looked the part of the long lean American with a prematurely bald head. Born into an immaculately bourgeois family, the son of a well-known Harvard professor, he had been educated as an engineer and seemed vaguely ashamed of his privileged origins.

During the next few hours Mrs Haldane discovered the roots of the relationship between these three men. Jack, who had

[1] Charlotte Haldane, *Truth Will Out*, p. 105.

once edited the American paper, *New Masses*, unashamedly Communist in policy, had fluent Spanish but spoke no French, and yet the French had quickly recognized him as a born leader. Lacking higher education himself, he had developed an exaggerated respect for intellectual people and first chose Lee as his lieutenant, but this had not worked very well because Lee revealed a tendency to panic in emergencies. Eric then arrived with a later group of Americans and Jack at once saw in this stoical, physically very strong man, a substitute for Lee, with many of the qualities which Lee lacked. Not the least of Eric de Witt Parker's attractions was a highly developed sense of humour which continuously expressed itself in that kind of subtle gaiety which even the French police could appreciate.

Max explained to Mrs Haldane how the recruitment centre worked, and the role of each of these men. Her own work began in earnest the following morning, which happened to be a Saturday. The British were able to ship over scores of men under cover of week-end excursion tickets, because no passports were required in those days for 48-hour trips, and it was always on Saturday that the British volunteers began to pour in.

Recruitment in England took many forms. Sometimes officials from the C.P. headquarters in King Street talked to young Communists and hinted broadly that perhaps they should go to Spain, but there were many reasons for exemption. Student Party Members in their final year at L.S.E. and those who had special propaganda skills were not encouraged to go. Many more were genuine volunteers quite free from propaganda pressures. There were said to be 'recruiting centres' at the Twentieth Century Café in the Mile End Road, at a house in Cook Street, Liverpool, and in Trafalgar Square.

Once the volunteers were across the Channel they were met at the Gare du Nord by people like Mrs Haldane, and escorted to nondescript and sometimes broken-down hotels in the Combat area. The hoteliers had a network of intelligence which kept them fully informed when the police threatened to take too deep an interest in the register of any particular hotel. It was legitimate for Englishmen to visit any part of Paris during their week-end trip, and on Saturday and Sunday they made no bones about being British, but as the Sunday developed into

Monday some crude attempts at disguise were made, with French berets and workmen's blue dungarees.

It came as a considerable shock to the individualistic Englishmen who constituted a high proportion of the British volunteers to have their spare cash confiscated on arrival, but this policy was the only effective antidote to the combined lures of drink and brothels. Each man had ten francs a day doled out to him, enough to buy cigarettes and possibly two bocks.

Such treatment was even more dismaying to the Americans. They included a proportion of young men who came over as tourists, richly equipped with leather suitcases, clothing and small luxuries, and at this stage, according to Mrs Haldane, 'regarded the whole thing as an adventure'. They were led by a few professional Communists but they did not easily yield their casual ways to the demands of Party discipline or the seemingly outrageous confiscation of money.

If there were days when the recruitment routine seemed as normal as an ordinary working day, filtering ragged bands of volunteers through a great and watchful metropolis like Paris created a state of continual tension in the lives of the organizers. They lived in comparative poverty. They worked hard. Some amongst them were never free from a sense of being shadowed in the streets of Paris, and one at least – a Czech from Prague – was arrested and hurried away for interrogation, but it would be false to exaggerate these working difficulties. The French Government, under its Socialist leader, M. Blum, may have signed a non-intervention pact but it sometimes concealed a private liking for volunteers under a public show of vigilance.

Peter Elstob, among the early English volunteers, was less fortunate than most. An American-educated Englishman, he had thrown up college life and come to England in search of adventure and excitement. Too young to know much about the technicalities of politics,[1] he received instructions from a bookshop in Covent Garden to call on another bookshop near the Gare du Nord, with the password, 'I have a letter from Comrade Le Gros', and when he arrived in Paris no one met him at the station. Operating alone, he traced the French bookseller who,

---

[1] One ex-Communist who recruited volunteers in England claimed that frequently the volunteers had no political background whatsoever. Douglas Hyde, *I Believed*, p. 62.

on their first encounter, behaved like an agent in a schoolboy's thriller, ssh-ing him to silence as he uttered the magic password. He then told Elstob, in whispers, to leave the shop, take the first door on the right and ask again for Comrade Le Gros. The second door confronting Elstob was heavily protected by iron bars and as he rang the bell he became aware of a man watching him by means of an inside mirror. Asked what he wanted, he repeated the password. A small buzz was followed by the door creaking open under electrical control, and the man proceeded to give him another address, instructing him to ask for Room Twenty. This address turned out to be a big block of offices and Elstob found and entered Room Twenty without knocking. His entrance and the words 'I am looking for Comrade Le Gros – is he here?' caused pandemonium. One man jumped to the door and locked it and another, a grey-haired, distinguished-looking person, instantly said: 'We know nothing about him – he is not here.' Then came the question: 'Are you alone?' Elstob indicated that he was and one man went outside to check his statement. Slowly they relented. The grey-haired man asked a number of questions about the Covent Garden bookshop, read the letter and finally directed him to yet another address.

The third address proved very obscure and difficult to find, but at last Elstob reached it and was directed downstairs to a room where he discovered 'the choicest selection of Parisian sewerdregs that I had ever seen'.[1] From this room a guide took him deeper still into the cellars and there, as he entered, were two hundred men yelling support to another man who stood on a table, gesticulating violently. Almost at once they began singing the Internationale, made a rush for the ladder and tore up it, through the outer room into the street again.

At last Elstob received his papers and instructions. Some time later he was sitting quietly in a café when a hand descended on his shoulder. 'I am sorry but I must ask you to come with me to the police station to answer a few questions.' His arrest was quite without fuss, noise or violence.

The British and Americans were, in fact, a small part of the tide which, as the months slipped by, continued to bring men

[1] Verbal evidence from Elstob.

from Germany, France, Italy, Poland, Ireland, Mexico, Latvia and Yugoslavia, to swell the volunteer ranks until the several Parisian recruitment centres were choked with men and the process of weeding out the undesirables became more complicated as deceptions became more sophisticated. Perhaps unaware of the terrible hardships and painful deaths to which they opened themselves, there were men prepared to lie and deceive their way into the ranks of this volunteer army, but as the number of unemployed men, adventurers, mercenaries, scientists, intellectuals, writers, poets, idealists, Communists, sailors and soldiers, and thousands of ordinary working men grew, the dark forest of motives thickened to the point where any clear-cut analysis became very difficult. The clarion call of democracy versus Fascism had echoed splendidly through Europe and America as the Civil War in Spain reached a new intensity, but there now gathered under a new banner the most contradictory company whose first attempts at military discipline resulted in a new, more colourful version of Fred Karno's Army.

Chapter 3

Some Early Recruits

THE ship was late docking at Le Havre and the six Americans arrived in Paris at one o'clock in the morning when only the late-night cafés, the prostitutes and the taxis still gave the city that fascinating half-life which never seems to cease throughout the night. They went to an hotel near the Gare St Lazare, climbed the twisted dusty stairs and entered three rooms, each with a double bed. Proios, the Greek, looked at Merkel, the huge German-American seaman, and indicated that for his part he was ready and willing to sleep on the floor. Proios had performed the remarkable feat on the boat crossing the Atlantic of playing poker and cleaning out the pockets of one third-class passenger after another, without having a single word of English at his command. Words, in his case, were substituted by laughter. He could introduce an infinite variety of meaning into a smile, and when he won yet another round of poker his hands apologized with eloquent gestures, his teeth gleamed in a gold-filled smile and the smile broke into eloquent laughter.

On board ship, the party had consisted of nine men: Alvah Bessie, a writer who later left a fascinating account of his experiences; Merkel, a sea-cook from the West Coast; three Americans from California, Hoover, Garfield and Earl; two Cubans, Prieto and Díaz; a New York student known to the others as López; and the gentle, charming, wordless Greek, Proios. Three of the party – Hoover, Garfield and Earl – had temporarily broken away when the ship docked but the others now settled down to sleep in an hotel whose dusty plush furniture was the height of fashion in the late nineteenth century. Before he went to sleep in a bed shared with López, Bessie examined the room in detail, from its threadbare red carpet and push-button light switch, to the gilt clock which had long since ceased to function under its glass bell.

At seven-thirty the next morning he descended the stairs,

went out into the street and joined the throng of early morning workers 'who looked just the same as other people going to work all over the world – dejected, tired, defeated but content.'[1]

Still comparatively rich beside other volunteers, he took a taxi to the Place du Combat, reported to the offices where Mrs Haldane worked, appeared before a small committee, answered its questions satisfactorily and came away with six food tickets for a co-operative restaurant, a few hundred francs to keep the group going, and instructions to report again at two o'clock in the afternoon.

Still spendthrift in the first flush of Parisian excitement, he taxied back to the hotel near the Gare St Lazare and found the other five sleepy, grumbling and not too anxious to hurry into anything – even their clothes. Bessie, who knew his Paris, wanted to show them the chastity belts in the Musée de Cluny, the great dark mass of Notre Dame and the Sainte Chapelle, but time was short and some of the group did not share his cultural enthusiasms. Bessie's main preoccupation was with the same old problem: how to merge into the Parisian scene six men whose clothes, walk, talk and gestures marked them out not only as immutably foreign but unmistakably American. Max had told Bessie the first and most important maxim: Keep your mouth shut and do not attract attention. But now it seemed laughable that these six men, loping down the boulevards, could possibly escape detection.

Bessie did not like the food in the co-operative restaurant, López became tangled up in sending an extraordinary cable signed Hy to someone the other side of the world, and they finally reached the offices off the Rue du Combat again in a mixed mood. They were directed into a room full of hard wooden benches and settled down with twenty other volunteers to wait for what they believed would be instructions, but turned out to be a lecture. Now, for the first time, they reencountered Garfield, Earl and Hoover, flipped ironic greetings at each other and sat gossiping quietly. Near by sat a man with a leather glove covering an obviously artificial hand. 'You guys just get back?' he said. 'No,' Bessie said, 'we're just going.' 'Oh,' he mumbled, 'more suckers.' It wasn't the best form of encouragement to encounter on the first day of real business,

[1] Alvah Bessie, *Men in Battle*, p. 5.

and several eyes kept coming back to the cold, immobile hand with its flat rigidity.

Someone – probably Max – now rose to address them. It seemed straightforward, obvious advice which he gave about caution and the border being closed and non-intervention meaning more than a legal fiction.

Bessie was looking at Garfield, Earl and Hoover who had been steadily drunk the whole way over on the ship from the States as Max said: 'I advise you guys to watch your step. Don't drink too much and avoid whores. There are plenty of Fascist spies in Paris who are very interested in what we're doing. You guys came here to go to Spain, not to paint the town red; keep that in mind at all times and I'm sure we won't have any trouble.'

Finally they were all instructed to be waiting in their hotel rooms at four o'clock that afternoon with a small paper parcel containing nothing more than absolute essentials. Suitcases and other gear, including clothes and small personal belongings, would be picked up, numbered and carefully preserved for the day of their return. At this point the man with the artificial hand suddenly got up and left. The day of return seemed too much for him.

Garfield and the three Californians also disappeared once more in search of a drink. With the lecture over, one by one the remainder filtered back into the Paris streets and now began those small purchases of a petty but significant kind – a flask of brandy, a pack of cigarettes, a slab of chocolate. They wrote last letters, packed a few fundamental clothes, made more purchases and kicked around waiting until the three Californians came back once more. Garfield now looked haggard, with all the bounce gone out of him. On the verge of leaving the friendly soil of civilized France the adventure looming ahead assumed proportions which brought a new sobriety into the behaviour of many recruits. Seen from the skyscrapers of New York, there was a glamour about volunteering to fight on foreign soil for the high principles of democracy. Now, cold reality, all too vividly symbolized by the man with the dead, rigid hand, was creeping in.

By four o'clock nothing happened. By four-thirty everyone was very restless, mutiny threatened and then at last, at five, a

man came knocking on their respective doors to distribute
money and tickets for the 9.10 train from the Gare de Lyon.
Two more men appeared and one, a stocky, thick-set person, was
introduced as their guide. They were to look for him at the
station, follow him faithfully, board the same train but never,
on any account, to speak to him.

They travelled to the station by three separate taxis and the
steady persistence of a suspicious-looking car in their tracks
convinced Bessie that they were being followed. They picked out
the guide at the appointed place in the Gare de Lyon and
against all the rules it seemed to them that he nodded greetings.
The next half an hour had elements of comic opera. What
possessed a committee of fanatically efficient men to create a
badge for the very recruits which they wished, at all cost, to
remain anonymous, is beyond understanding, but the simple
fact of each man carefully carrying his belongings in a brown-
paper parcel meant that the 9.10 train from the Gare de Lyon
was alive with foreigners all self-consciously silent, all staring
stonily away from one another and all nursing their brown-
paper insignias. Bessie and his four companions fulfilled their
small part in the pattern. Finding an empty third-class compartment, they sat away from one another and preserved a
fixed silence.

It was winter, the coach poorly heated, the atmosphere
stale, and the seats hard. The ordeal of waiting in silence prolonged itself minute by minute. 'Merkel lit his pipe and winked
at me; López blew his nose; Garcia and Díaz sat staring through
each other; Proios had been left, temporarily, in Paris to get
treatment for an infected eye. The whistles blew and I thought
again of my two little kids back in Brooklyn and of the postcard
I had sent them from the ship.'[1]

As the train at last drew out of the station, the guide came
ambling down the corridor and again gave a faint nod as he
passed their compartment. Repeated at intervals, his nod could
not more obviously have given the game away, but it speaks
eloquently for the Paris police that every possible clue was
placed under their noses and they disdained to notice.

At last the train slid away and now, confined in one compartment for eighteen hours, they began the usual process of

[1] Alvah Bessie, *Men in Battle*, p. 8.

personal discovery about one another. The most colourful, the Cuban Díaz, had once played a dashing role in the Cuban cavalry, and his legs were permanently bowed by too much acquaintance with horses. He still wore high boots under his city overcoat, he spoke no English and had two personalities which he interchanged with bewildering rapidity. One was the big, powerful, cheerful cavalryman with flashing white teeth, who sang a lot when ordinary conversation failed him, and the other a sullen, surly fellow whose view of the world was hopelessly jaundiced.

Merkel, they discovered, had served for four years in the German Army.

'What was it like?' Bessie asked.

'It ain't bad,' he answered, 'it ain't bad at all. You get used to it. You never see the enemy; you shoot and you shoot and you never see 'em. It ain't bad at all.'

As the train reached high speed and shrieked along the tracks, the windows steamed up, the air became foul and all attempts at sleep were broken by one interruption or another. At one point the guide came boldly in, shut the door and sat talking to them. He spoke many languages in a broken sort of way, and three quite well, but English was not amongst them. It was extraordinary to hear him switching from vernacular Yiddish when he talked to López, to French for Bessie, Spanish argot for Díaz and German to Merkel. He explained, under questioning, that he made this trip three times a week and claimed, extravagantly, that there were over a hundred recruits on the train, 'mostly Poles, Rumanians and Czechs'.

Many hours later, as the train swung through Valence, Avignon, Nîmes and Montpellier they were cold, hungry and still sleepless. At last the train slowed as it approached Béziers and the guide hurried down the corridors indicating, with hopeless indiscretion, that this was the first stop for all recruits. Once again the revealing pantomime was repeated as scores of men climbed down from the train wearing oddly similar clothes, carrying the same pathetic brown-paper parcels, carefully observing a silence which still made them suspect.

Béziers was a delightful little town built on a hill with houses gleaming in the morning sun from soft blue to faint pink, from dark mauve to primrose yellow, and the narrow cobbled streets gave on to a main boulevard with palm trees sprouting their foliage. The air was sweet, silent, peaceful. It seemed impossible that this was the first serious link with a bloody, bitter civil war already intensified to the point where terrible atrocities were within the capacity of both sides.

They quickly dispersed to various small working-class hotels and later in the day Bessie with his group sat down at long tables to a solid unimaginative meal of soup, bread, sausage, vegetables and beer. Few spoke a common language but they served a common cause and this overrode national barriers. There were Americans, English, French, Germans, Poles and Rumanians scattered round the table and they pieced together, in fragments of five languages, a conversation highly original and sometimes hilariously funny. By now the cross-section of people already included dock-workers, farm-hands, students, engineers, soldiers, clerks and labour-organizers. Thrown together in the enforced community of the tiny hotel, their knowledge of one another deepened, and many contradictory motives came to the surface. As Bessie wrote, some 'were among the first soldiers in the history of the world who really knew what they were about, what they were going to fight for.' Others were plain adventurers, some branded from early beginnings with the death-wish, others again eager young idealists, and some simple members of the unemployed.

The Americans contrasted sharply with most of the group, especially Earl, Hoover and Garfield, now reunited in the hotel with their original unit. Earl had once earned a living as a small-time boxer before becoming, like Hoover, a sheet-metal worker in a Californian aircraft factory. Garfield, a one-time small-part Hollywood actor, in turn stood out as different among the Americans. He was one of those drifting characters who had been mixed up in the artistic world of Greenwich Village, and had never really come to terms with himself. Barely twenty-five years old, he seemed far removed from the stereotyped Hemingway hero, having a feminine streak in his make-up, which made him talk about hospital work rather than front-line fighting. Fully aware of the womanliness in his appearance, when asked why he had volunteered for Spain he replied: 'To make a man of myself.'

Bessie, as a Communist, had the clear-cut motive of wanting

to fight Fascism, and unlike many others he could give a close definition of what he meant by that fiercely emotive word, but there was a secondary motive – to achieve self-integration.

Hoover seemed as loud as Garfield was quiet. Earl and Garfield quickly took a dislike to Hoover. There was too much big talk about being a pilot, and one day he produced a picture of an ex-girl-friend killed in an accident, with the flamboyant comment: 'I haven't cared whether I lived or died since. I hope to get killed.' By the end of their stay in the hotel Earl remarked: 'We hope he does too. It's no great loss.'[1]

Events now moved rapidly. A series of taxis arrived the following morning, and they drove out to a farmhouse. Scores of men slowly collected in a big stone barn until the walls rang with tongues as different as Japanese and German, Danish and Polish, English and Russian. Garfield found a cask of wine, managed to tap it with a metal tube and as the blood-red wine spurted into his mouth sang 'La cucaracha – la cucaracha ya no puede caminar!' between gulps. Others drank and sang too. Presently the barn echoed to the song 'Arise! Ye wretched of the earth!' sung in every kind of language, and a peasant farmer came hurrying in to tell them that they must be quieter.

There followed a nightmare ascent of the Pyrenees with the brown-paper parcels disintegrating into soggy messes, the wind becoming so strong that they were forced to turn sideways and lean against it, and their feet beginning to bleed from the stones, boulders and every kind of torment which nature could devise. The rain increased, the crude tracks became steeper and the night so pitch-black that they had to move with 'one hand outstretched before [them], like elephants in a circus procession holding on to each other's tails.'

Four hours from starting time, the guide announced that they were one hour from the frontier and they staggered on encouraged, only to find that after another two hours the interminable crests still rose round them, the flints were sharper, the wind shriller and now, to make the scene grandly austere, snow lay crystal-hard and white in the folds of the hills. One man's face streamed with blood, two men were carrying another and every other man seemed to limp. As the dawn came up 'the brilliant light hurt our eyes . . . you could feel the grit in the corners of

[1] Alvah Bessie, *Men in Battle*, p. 14.

your eyes . . . the men's clothes were the colour of the earth.'
When the last, uttermost crest rose splendidly against the sky
it was necessary for the ragged, exhausted band to make a final
superhuman effort and run quickly across it because here was
the danger point where figures silhouetted against the sky could
easily be picked out. Stumbling, running, heaving, with breath
coming in great painful gulps they groaned aloud as they
struggled to keep up with the guide. And then, at last, they were
over, and there, far below, cool and beautiful in the clear
morning air, with silver rivers threading its flatness and no
sound other than the wind to greet them, was Spain – rich,
sunburnt, superstitious Spain, emptied it seemed of life or
movement, a deceptively virgin land.

Several hours later, the fifty men were roaring along in army
lorries escorted by Spanish Republican soldiers with the red
five-pointed star of the Republic on their caps. They laughed,
shouted, and greeted every stray peasant on the road with
'Salud!' or 'Viva la Republica!' The driver was a tremendous
Spanish driver pumping away at his horn, determined to keep
the lorry hurtling at violent speed over the appalling roads,
scaring burros, people, everything out of his path. Once they
were stalled beside another truck full of Spanish soldiers travelling in the opposite direction and they threw across bottles of
something labelled *Coñac*. 'Viva los extranjeros!' they shouted.
'Vivan las Brigadas Internacionales!' The Americans sent
back wild 'Vivas!' But the coñac, when they drank it, tasted
'like a mixture of paint-remover and vanilla'.

In the end more than three thousand Americans volunteered
for the International Brigade, but each group encountered a
different set of difficulties. The experiences of Bessie's group were
straightforwardly successful. Steve Nelson's story was another
matter. A man brought up to the tough life of a Philadelphia
slaughter-house where he had stacked great slabs of meat on
racks thirty feet high, day after day, he volunteered with twenty-
five other men for Spain, and quickly ran into trouble.

Joe Dallet was among his group and a more unlikely volunteer for Spain it would be difficult to find. An accomplished
pianist, a man who had once sported a goatee beard, spats and a

cane, he had lived the bohemian life in the Latin Quarter of Paris, but was the kind of rebellious son of wealthy New England parents who idealized the working class to such a pitch that he tried to pass himself off as one of them. Once a Dartmouth graduate, he had become a steel workers' organizer and 'the Spanish business seemed to crystallize the struggles I had with the so-called bosses. To go there seemed the obvious thing to do.'

In Paris, the group led by Nelson and Dallet encountered the usual uneasy wait, but in their case it lasted almost three weeks, and time and again one of the group nearly gave the game away to the Paris police. Then, at last, they set out not to climb the Pyrenees secretly, by stealth of night, but merely to travel down to the tiny summer resort of Perpignan, on the French coast. There, at ten o'clock one evening, they lay hidden in the sand-dunes waiting for the fishing boat which would carry them along the coast to Spain.

They remained in hiding all that afternoon, with a cold fresh wind which brought small flurries of white sand to sting their faces, to seep into clothing, eyes and ears, and the sun was fierce enough to burn the toughest skin. As the hours dragged by, they became restless, slipped out of hiding and began openly to play a form of American baseball. After all, they might be American tourists enjoying the sea and the sand, but a Frenchman who came riding down the coast road on a bicycle was so staggered at the apparition of twenty-five obvious foreigners all locked in a form of sport which seemed to him to resemble a particularly brutal battle, that he wobbled off the road and nearly fell from his bicycle. Straightening himself, he puffed out his cheeks, tapped his forehead to describe the lunatic Americans, and shot away at double speed.

The sea remained relatively empty all that afternoon. By 10.30 in the evening Joe Dallet became uneasy. Eleven o'clock and still there was no sign of a boat. The thought constantly recurred in Dallet's mind – 'What do I do with this little lot if our boat turns up and there is nowhere capable of concealing twenty-five hulking, energetic, restless, schoolboy Americans?'[1]

Eleven o'clock gave place to twelve and the black midnight horizon remained unbroken by anything resembling a ship. As

[1] Verbal evidence to the author.

Nelson wrote: 'Joe paced the veranda of a beach cottage and groaned and struck his hands together and strained his eyes towards the black void of the sea.'[1] Nothing. The tideless sea pressed against the white sand as it had done down the centuries, quite unchanged by the thousand different dramas played out within its reach.

One among the twenty-five recruits was a totally unexpected person already nicknamed the Professor, a slight, gentlemanly little man with a goatee beard. A mining engineer from Canada, the Professor had several times performed mysterious technical tricks for the benefit of the group and now, when a small jewellery of lights appeared out at sea and the bored, tired, rebellious group rose excitedly to stare and whisper, he ran back and forth setting up two stakes. The men watched with ribald whispers. A groan went up when he announced his verdict. The lights were moving south-east at about eight knots which was certainly not in their direction. After a while the lights diminished and died away.

At 2.30 they sent out scouts again and they were kicking their way back through the sand, cursing, when Nelson said, 'How long since you took a look at the pier?' It seemed absurd to reconnoitre the pier again when no boat had been detected approaching it, but they stumbled down in the darkness and a moment later came back excitedly: 'The boat! It's here! Waiting. . . .'

With infinite cunning, two thin, wiry Frenchmen had brought their fishing boat silently into the pier under cover of darkness without drawing the attention of even those who were watching for it. Swearing, stumbling, the men rushed down to the boat and piled on board. It was a modern and larger version of one of the fishing boats painted by Van Gogh, thirty feet long with a pointed bow and stern painted in two colours, and a single-cylinder engine. It seemed hopelessly inadequate to cope with the twenty-five big Americans who stumbled over ropes and gear, crumpled into hatches, and generally behaved as if they were mixed up in a mock football scrum. Presently 'water boiled under the stern . . . we felt the boat move under us . . . the black line of the pier and the shore faded and disappeared. . . . France was behind us.'

[1] Steve Nelson, *The Volunteers*, p. 38.

Shortly after dawn the next day, the atmosphere in the tiny hold of the boat was compounded to almost suffocating proportions of stale breath and the smells from bad fish, onions, urine, tar, cigarette smoke, sweat and gasoline. Twenty-five bodies crushed together, some sleeping, some snoring, some still talking, were cramped and irritable when the excited voice of a man called Shorty Friedman yelled, 'Boys, I can see Spain.' He had his eye glued to a crack in the ribs of the boat and immediately half a dozen men struggled towards him, trying to get a glimpse of what they had almost come to regard as the promised land. 'Step up, gents,' someone called, 'see the Pyrenees, see Spain for a dime, ten cents, one-tenth part of a dollar only!'

They were still excitedly taking turns to glimpse Spain through the spy-hole, when suddenly one of the French fishermen leaned over the hold and shouted something. A moment later the hatch-cover slid into place and in the semi-darkness they all held their breath as a deep throbbing became louder and louder. The ever-ready Professor guessed that it was a diesel engine, and a big one, belonging, he thought, to a patrol boat of some kind. Five minutes later the hatch-cover slid open again, a gold-braided cap appeared above a heavy-jowled face, a question was followed by a knowing grin, and the game was up.

Arrested, they were taken ashore and marched under heavy guard through the cobbled streets of Collioure to the local jail, where they proceeded to drive the officials into a fury by their complete inability to remember dates and places of birth, and the stupidity with which one name became confused with another. Chained together, two by two, they were next driven off to Perpignan, and on the way a man called Bill Dimmer astounded everyone by ingeniously escaping from his handcuffs and offering them, with a half-bow, to his janitor.

The American consul was waiting in the prison warden's office at Perpignan. Addressing them in what seemed to Nelson a very pompous manner, he said he would give them every help possible within his power, but he insisted that he must first collect their passports. They were breaking the non-intervention pact between Western European powers and their behaviour was heavily frowned on by Mr Cordell Hull, then

Secretary of State. Steve Nelson, who had eaten nothing but stale bread and drunk nothing but *ersatz* coffee for three days, looked at the well-dressed, immaculate consul with unconcealed hostility. Setting the example, he refused to give up his passport, declined to argue the matter and presently led the procession back to the big stone cell with two small windows high up near the vaulted roof, which held eighty prisoners, some criminals and petty thieves, others renegade soldiers and the rest volunteers for Spain brought to this unspectacular impasse.

In the next few days, they drove the warden of the prison close to despair. On the third day, he summoned six Americans to his presence and pointed to the man called Dallet. 'You,' he said, 'you . . . appear to be educated and yet you give us a bad time. You are many times worse than our criminals . . . without shame, without humility you show not the slightest respect for the officials of French law, the dignity of French justice. . . . You hammer on doors, you shriek for the warder, you make demands impossible of fulfilment . . . you corrupt our routine.'[1]

Dallet's answer was simple and straightforward. 'We did not ask to be thrown in this pest-hole,' he said.

Matters improved on the fourth day, when baskets of food from the French Popular Front Committee were allowed into the jail and simultaneously M. Gregory, the very young and very militant local Popular Front lawyer, arrived to prepare the case for their defence.

The French prosecution quickly discovered that it was a mistake to underestimate the wits of this rough-looking crowd and particularly those of its leader Dallet. The police tried to break up the main group into smaller units for separate examination but Nelson briefed everyone on an elaborate stalling procedure, and when three men from Ohio were summoned to appear separately before the court they simply refused to leave their cell. The warden then went down to the cell himself to reason with them, and Nelson, who was called in as a witness, recorded the conversation which followed.

'Is Joe going?' the men asked the warden.

'No – it is not so ordered.'

'We won't go without Joe to translate for us.'

[1] Steve Nelson, *The Volunteers*, pp. 55–6.

'There is an interpreter there. An official – believe me you may have confidence. Also there will be present your lawyer.'

'The lawyer can't speak English. And the interpreter won't understand our English. We speak working-class English. We want Joe alone.'

The warden made a delicate gesture of near-despair, rolled his eyes to heaven, turned to Joe Dallet and said: 'Tell them to come. I implore you, as man to man, tell them! The interpreter is an honourable man. You can be confident. But tell them!'[1]

It was then arranged that Joe Dallet should accompany each group for interrogation. At last, the day came when the whole contingent appeared in court for the final hearing, and the French Popular Front Committee mobilized the townspeople to give them a great reception. The streets of the approaches to the court house were lined with men, women and children. When the prison buses came charging up at breakneck speed they roared in unison: 'Vive l'Espagne! Vivent les Brigades Internationales!' Over three hundred people crowded into the small court room, and almost at once M. Gregory, counsel for the Americans, asked permission for Joe Dallet to speak for the entire group, which was granted. The prosecution then put two questions to Dallet:

'You are American?'

'Americans and Canadians, yes.'

'Why did you come to France?'

'In order to reach Spain to fight in the Loyalist Army against Fascism.'

The whole court room sent up a roar of cheers and jeers at this statement, and when the judge demanded silence and the gendarmes went in among the people bellowing and threatening, it was of no avail. Several minutes passed before order could be restored. Since there was no attempt to dispute the facts, and the niceties of non-intervention were not debated, since the prisoners fully admitted their crime and the law was clear-cut, the case resolved itself into simple statements from the prosecution and defence. M. Gregory acknowledged the Americans' guilt, but concentrated on pleading for what in England would be called mitigation. 'There are laws and laws

[1] Steve Nelson, *The Volunteers*, p. 62.

. . . there are crimes and crimes. Theirs is a political crime – that they loved liberty, democracy and peace. Before this court I wish to pay homage to these Americans, who left homes, jobs, families and friends to fight for their ideals. . . . I beseech this tribunal to temper justice, the letter of the law, with mercy in this case, for the honour of France and of humanity.'

There was another great burst of applause. It then became clear that the American consul had asked for all passports to be confiscated before sentence was passed, but M. Gregory claimed that they were part of the papers necessary to the case which must be retained, and the judges upheld him. At last came the verdict: 'For violating French laws and an international agreement to which France is a signatory . . . you are sentenced to twenty-one days in prison.'

Since they had already been in prison eighteen days, there remained only three to serve, and back in the great barren cell they laughed and sang, embraced each other and excitedly plotted another attempt to get across the border.

Many days later they, in their turn, underwent the ordeal of dodging the border guards, of negotiating impossible mountain paths, moving through the midnight darkness of a countryside where one false step could topple a man a thousand feet to serious injury or death. They, too, reached the border close to the point of collapse with the guide dancing ahead, and the ragged line of men stumbled on, in Nelson's words 'like spavined horses'. Nelson recorded his own ordeal: 'The muscles in my thighs danced wildly, uncontrollably, as they had danced for hours; there was a slimy, sour taste in my mouth and my throat and lungs were on fire, my blood was roaring in my ears.'

And then, at last, the guide stopped at a small pile of stones and performed a little caper of delight. 'España!' he shouted. 'España!' They too were across.

The focal point in Spain upon which the ragged lines of volunteers from all over the world converged, was the small town of Albacete, where a gimcrack machinery for training raw recruits had long been planned rather than realized. To this town came many more Americans. Men like Robert Hale

Merriman with a lumberjack father and an authoress mother, who worked his way through the University of Nevada, majored in economics and joined the American Reserve Officers' Training Corps. Later he won the Newton Booth Traveling Fellowship in Economics, and became head teaching assistant in economics at the University of California. While he was travelling in Europe to complete a study of European agriculture, the war broke out in Spain and – as a good Communist – he abandoned everything to get across the French border and join the International Brigade. A man who stood six foot two and a half inches, his presence was made commanding by a military bearing and a high scholarly forehead. A supreme example of the intellectual as man of action, his name will recur in these pages because he was destined to become Major Merriman, Chief of Staff of the XVth International Brigade.

Then there were men like twenty-year-old Paul Sigel who came from New York and had hardly finished his final examinations at New York University School of Engineering when the struggle in Spain seized his imagination and he felt compelled to board a ship and join the volunteers.

A young man of indomitable good cheer, one single worry troubled him on a rough trip across the Atlantic – had he passed his finals in Thermodynamics? Approaching England his anxiety and impatience reached breaking-point and he spent a large sum from his small and rapidly dwindling capital to send what was then called a wireless to his sister back in New York. 'Did I pass?' The answer came back 'Yes', and with this anxiety removed, he set out to face the hazards of a civil war with complete equanimity. That his equanimity did not survive undisturbed was inevitable, but the details of his disillusionment occupy a later and different part of this very long, confused and in some senses tragic story.

John Murra, another volunteer, was remarkable for being able to converse, instruct, and blaspheme in five languages other than English. Granted his baccalaureate at Chicago University, he was just about to launch into work as an archaeological graduate when the call came, in his case resolving a conflict between an idealized belief in the necessity of saving democracy from Fascist damnation, a youthful restlessness and the demands which academic training imposed on him. In the end Spain won, and he left America on 20 February 1937 to join the growing tide of recruits.

John Gates, another name to become famous in the history of the Brigades, came of Polish-Jewish extraction and entered the College of the City of New York simultaneously with the Wall Street crash which left chaos and ruin among thousands of American families. As a youth he saw what it meant to be unemployed for months at a time, and later he realized the truth of Edmund Wilson's words – 'between 1929 and 1933 the whole structure of American society seemed actually to be going to pieces.' His father went down with the crash, became a waiter for a time, and then bought another candy store and returned to the drudgery of a sixteen-hour day and a seven-day week in a struggle to support a wife and four children. Gates himself quickly joined the Young Communist League and once the Spanish Civil War broke out – 'I was determined to get there come hell or high water.'

As he later wrote: 'In Paris the headquarters of the committee was rocking with activity; volunteers were being processed from all over the world. . . . I fell into a great piece of luck – I found 10,000 francs in a taxicab. Every last franc was soon gone.'[1] His entry into Spain was simplicity itself. He took a train from Paris to Perpignan, boarded a bus for Figueras and in fifteen minutes crossed the border – 'and that was all there was to it.'

Men like these came together from many corners of the United States to serve a common cause; some driven by fanatical Communist beliefs like Steve Nelson, some innocent of any vestige of political sophistication like Roger Murray, some bums and drifters whose unemployment record did not stand close examination, and many ordinary working-class idealists.

Deeper than these surface characteristics lay, according to Edwin Rolfe – the poet who came out of the Brigade with a fine record – a general conception which fused the identity of widely different personalities: 'their profound anti-Fascist convictions, so profound and so deep-going that they were ready to die to stop the advance of Hitler's and Mussolini's invaders.' In the event this proved untrue of – well – a number.

Whatever the detailed truth of the matter, in the course of

[1] John Gates, *The Story of an American Communist*, p. 43.

one year nearly two thousand Americans crossed the border
from France into Spain and passed through the training centres
in and around Albacete, a small provincial capital with a
population of 40,000. Albacete was famous for the manufacture
of steel blades and at least one poetic spirit among the tide of
men which poured into its narrow cobbled streets, overwhelmed
its cafés and transformed its rural life into a military camp, saw
a shining Toledo sword hanging in the air as an emblem.

When the very first contingents of the International Brigade
arrived at Albacete late in 1936, according to the Belgian
volunteer Nick Gillain, the preparations made to receive them
were hopelessly inadequate if not non-existent. These first
contingents were quartered in the barracks of the Republican
Guard (formerly the Civil Guard), a comparatively modern
building in Libertad Street near the bullfighting arena and the
feria pavilions. The Spanish Information Office of the present
Government issued a pamphlet in 1952 claiming that 'the
rooms of the lower floor had their walls stained with the blood
of the people that had been murdered there when the city was
occupied by the Republicans on July 25th.' Gillain's account
said: 'Sinister stories were told. . . . It was evident that men had
been killed there but no agreement was reached on the nature
of the victims. The majority believed that they had been
Fascists. . . . In spite of everything the volunteers showed a
marked repugnance to sleeping on the lower floor and preferred
to crowd in the upper domitories.'

Gillain himself was representative of a certain type of French
and Belgian recruit who drifted into the International Brigade
with no special convictions. His first answer when asked why he
volunteered was: 'I happened to be in Ostend at that time and
was bored to desperation. I had the desire to do something out
of the ordinary and decided to go to Spain.' This, he later
elaborated: 'I left for Spain out of a spirit of adventure, out of
boredom and because of the autumn rain, the grey sea and the
sky charged with clouds. . . . When questioned about my motive
I say it is simply – a sense of adventure.'

Anyone suspected of being a volunteer for Spain was stopped
at the Belgian frontier and Gillain suffered this first check. He

had to disguise himself as a casual daily worker to get across, and then he proceeded to Lille where he sought out the Spanish consul. The consul received Gillain courteously, but having serious doubts about his real intentions, refused officially to grant his request for a permit to enter Spain. 'However, while walking along the corridor [on the way out] he whispered: "Go to the House of the Syndicates . . . You will surely get what you want there!"'[1]

Gillain gave this description of the House of Syndicates in Lille: 'A former convent [it] was in that period of strikes as lively as a general headquarters on the day of a great battle.'

A man known as Comrade Dumoulin received him and passed him over to another comrade – Burneton – who said bluntly: 'So you want to go to Spain?' Receiving the answer – yes – he provided money and tickets for the journey to Paris. When they reached Paris they went to another House of the Syndicates in Mathurin-Moreau Avenue, where a mob of volunteers were collecting in a dirty square and that same night they left for Perpignan. 'We were five hundred men like in the Cid, the majority of us unemployed workmen and foreigners. . . . In Perpignan the labour organizations gave us documents of identity duly stamped and full of names. If they ask you why you do not know Spanish, I was told – say that you left the country when you were a baby. . . .'[2]

Armed with one flimsy piece of subterfuge after another they at last boarded a train en route for Valence. Gillain found himself in a compartment with eight other Belgians and as conversation developed into fierce argument he discovered that each had different reasons for volunteering. Speaking with dangerous frankness, Gillain found himself the target of attack, and within an hour the whole compartment concentrated its hatred on him, describing him as a 'dirty bourgeois'. The train seems to have been under the control of the Volunteer organization to a remarkable degree, because it halted at deserted wayside stations, the volunteers poured out to eat and rounded off each meal with a wild rendering of the Internationale 'heard only by indifferent shepherds'.

At Valence they sent a delegation to the local Spanish agent asking for permission to parade in the streets, but he bluntly

---

[1] Nick Gillain, *Le Mercenaire*, p. 16.   [2] Ibid.

refused this request, explaining that it was necessary to conceal every kind of troop movement. Gillain did not believe it. He thought the Spanish authorities were worried by the dirty, dishevelled air of the recruits which might disillusion the civilian population about the nature of the help which was beginning to pour in from abroad. This particular group of French and Belgians had expected an enthusiastic welcome, with crowds lining the streets, women hanging on their necks and old people blessing them, but as they passed through Catalonia and Valencia they were met only by hostile or indifferent faces.

At last they reached Albacete and were quartered in the blood-stained barracks. 'The following day we were taken into a neighbouring field, numbered and identified, a simple and short operation. A clerk then read out the list and asked if there were officers, non-commissioned officers, cooks, stenographers, artillerymen, and machine-gunners amongst us. The answers were what one would have expected because there being no control there was no need to be bashful and each one ranked himself according to his own private ambitions.'[1]

Gillain became part of an embryo cavalry squadron with an Italian as captain, a Belgian political commissar, and volunteers of such mixed origin that they even included a Mongolian. He quickly found that the idea of dedication to duty, or a crusading spirit determined to overwhelm the enemies of democracy, did not exist in this unit. It seemed to be united only by the desire to do nothing, and 'it was impossible to get more than 50 per cent to do any work'. As the first few days went by, he became more and more disillusioned. As yet if anyone fell ill there was no means of getting proper medical attention, and the two principles by which the squadron lived – that discipline should be freely given and that military officers took orders from a political hierarchy – led, in his experience, to the whole 'organization being riddled by hypocrisy'.

Their horses were old, their equipment almost non-existent, their morale low, discipline pitifully inadequate and far too many cavalrymen spent most of their time in the cafés. Arms and uniforms were of all kinds and nationalities, with the one common factor of being old. Some revolvers came from Austria,

[1] Nick Gillain, *Le Mercenaire*, p. 18.

machine-guns from France, ammunition from America, shoes from Russia and uniforms – if they could be described as such – from many countries. Already a number of prostitutes had sprung up to 'service' the army, and travelling merchants of all kinds were ready to provide anything from a woman, properly equipped with her french letter, to drink, cigarettes, watches or lucky charms.

As the Americans, French, Belgians, Germans, Poles and English became more familiar with Albacete it revealed the shortcomings of a small town accustomed to play the role of a central clearing house for wheat crops, and now overrun by a multitude of strangers unfamiliar with the strict codes of Spanish behaviour, or even the Spanish tongue. There was one large main street bisected by a smaller 'business' street, and here they could buy salty goat cheese, marmalade, coffee, vermouth, malaga, cognac, dried fruits, marzipan and endless trinkets. Skirmishes between men who spoke no Spanish and the shopkeepers sometimes became hilariously funny, and sometimes threatened physical violence, but as the numbers of recruits swelled, Albacete could no longer contain them. Public buildings, including the bullfighting square and the *feria* pavilions, were requisitioned and converted into storehouses and offices, and the Church of La Concepcion became the Brigade prison, the secular revolution overwhelming religious scruples.

The arrival of new volunteers continued throughout the last golden days of October, until the civil barracks were overflowing and now began the redistribution of men among different towns in the same province. The Italians went to Madrigueras, the Poles and other Slavs to Tarragona de la Mancha, the French to the outskirts of La Roda and the Germans to Mahora.

It would be false to assume that a high proportion of the recruits had a similar background and outlook to Nick Gillain. Among the Italians there were simple and devoted anti-Fascists like Bocchi, a man who had served as a sergeant in the First World War and become a builder's mate in Paris after the war. He volunteered for Spain as a duty 'to fight the evil growth of Fascism'. Brignoli, too, was a Communist from Lombardy, a man once a carpenter, who had enormous common sense and offered his services not with any lofty commotion about ideals, but simply because it was necessary to combat the forces which he thought were gathering to overwhelm the rights of the working man.

Also among the Italians was a very good-looking man known to his fellows as Antonio, a person with dark-blue, bell-bottomed trousers, a blue flannel windjacket and a bright white cap. Antonio was the essence of Latin vitality and claimed – performing a little dance of delight – that no less than one thousand Italian recruits had already arrived.

Among the French, Jean Berger represented another ordinary working man. Once a metal-worker in Paris, he lost his job after a policy disagreement with his employers, and his wife left him because, in the depression, he could not get work. She took with her their only child. In desperation one day, Berger went to enlist in the Foreign Legion, and outside the recruiting office met another unemployed worker who said he had volunteered to fight for Republican Spain. Berger, too, in due course arrived at Albacete.

John Cornford, the English intellectual and poet, travelled to Albacete with two more French recruits whose background was not so commonplace. They were, in fact, Paris toughs and Cornford said of one, Michel: 'His threadbare clothes and horribly worn shoes told a story of long unemployment that was borne out by his emaciated face and sunken eyes.' Marcel, the second Frenchman, spoke the argot of the toughs who frequented the Place de la République and had 'a tremendous shock of reddish-brown hair, freckles and a grin.' He was fond of pulling up his trousers to show a long red, newly-healed scar on his right thigh, where, as he put it, he had been 'knifed by a Fascist'. When asked what finally happened he replied: 'Oh, I shot the swine.' Also with this group came a Belgian, Albert, a small man with a cheerful alcoholic's face who, on the way from Paris in the train, kept getting to his feet to begin a speech about 'how he was a Belgian aviator and was going to Spain for various noble and important reasons', but no one would let him finish.[1]

At the other extreme, among the French recruits was an ex-officer of the French Army, a man with a clipped moustache and military manner, who wore a woollen-collared trench coat

[1] John Cornford, *Volunteer in Spain*, p. 15.

with something of the swagger of the dandy. 'I came of a middle-class family. I went to a military academy. I secured promotion young. I was keen on my work. In 1923 my regiment was sent into the Ruhr. One day in the streets of Düsseldorf there was a workers' demonstration against us. I was told to charge with my company against the unarmed crowd. I refused and was cashiered out of the army. . . .'[1] Now he had come to put his military skill at the disposal of the cause he believed in – 'the cause of the people'.

These men joined the growing French battalion and were quartered in a nunnery where some recruits proceeded to write and draw on the walls the most fascinating obscenities about its previous occupants. The food was rich Spanish food, cooked in rancid olive oil and full of pimentos. Within forty-eight hours, diarrhoea reached epidemic proportions and the four lavatories serving eight hundred men quickly seized up, until a shock brigade of volunteers became necessary to clean them out.

Shortly after this episode, Cornford heard the sound of men marching down the street one afternoon and rushed upstairs to the nearest window. 'Down the road comes a long column of men that stretches endlessly into the distance. . . . It turns out that this is the second lot for the International Column; there are eleven hundred of them, French, Hungarians, Czechs. Also there are a few English. . . .'[2]

Like the great majority of volunteers, most among the British were ordinary working men, but as they increased in number they included intellectuals, writers, poets, and one at least came of aristocratic lineage – the wild-cat nephew of Winston Churchill, Esmond Romilly.

[1] Geoffrey Cox, *Defence of Madrid*, p. 85.
[2] John Cornford, *Volunteer in Spain*, p. 35.

Chapter 4

Nephew of Sir Winston Churchill

AN original young man full of a sense of adventure, Esmond
Romilly had 'been educated up to the school certificate stage
at a famous public school (Wellington College) and having
left rather rapidly and suddenly . . . decided it was preferable
to support [himself] on [his] own labour.'[1] He was just seven-
teen at the time, but his fair-haired, red-cheeked youth did not
inhibit his confidence. Without any specialized knowledge of
any particular profession 'and not being troubled with an over-
quantity of honesty or scrupulousness, he went into salesman-
ship because he belonged to that very large class of unskilled
labourers with a public school accent.'

He sold silk stockings for a time, but the patent dishonesty of
half the patter required to persuade a housewife to accept a
dozen trial pairs of musquash troubled even his diminished sense
of conscience. After a brief excursion into advertising and
publishing, he next joined a paper called *Film Review*, and
pounded away at a typewriter drawing eloquent attention to
the fact that this was a top-exclusive advertising medium, but
the *Film Review* in turn dissolved into nothingness, and he at
last succumbed to that classic temptation of all bohemian,
well-educated young gentlemen, freshly down from Wellington
– night-club life.

The Spanish Civil War penetrated even these sophisticated
purlieus and was widely and wittily discussed far into the night.
Romilly found himself sympathizing with 'the cause of the
Spanish people' but his motives for doing so were complicated.
'The reasons would be much the same as those of the other
English members of the Thaelmann Battalion, but I do not
think anybody ever does anything just for one clear-cut logical (in this case political) motive. However strongly I sympathized with the cause of the Spanish people, no doubt if my

[1] Esmond Romilly, *Boadilla*, p. 21.

circumstances in London had been completely satisfactory I should have gone no further than sympathy. I am assuming it will be taken for granted that everybody who joined the International Brigade had "political convictions" but these were not necessarily the only reasons why they joined.'[1]

The idea of volunteering had occurred from the very beginning of the Spanish Civil War, but his military illiteracy did not encourage him. 'I did not even know how to load a rifle. At Wellington College I had been a pacifist and had refused to join the O.T.C. so I lacked even that experience.'

When, finally, he made up his mind to go to Spain, he decided to camouflage his real intent by telling his friends that he was off to work on a Belgian farm, in case his hopeless inadequacy should be detected too quickly by the Brigade organizers and his imediate return became ignominious.

Esmond Romilly was not a Communist. Any member of the Ogpu who took the trouble to discover his connection with the illustrious family of Winston Churchill would have denounced him either as a spy or as thoroughly unsuitable material for the International Brigade. Neither of these obvious stigmas prevented him from boarding a ship without complications of any kind, and arriving at the Marseilles recruiting office where an elementary cross-examination completely failed to discover his shortcomings. Numerous forms were filled in, some with false information, and he quickly learnt that the proliferation of documents did not mean very much. The second part of his journey to Spain aboard the *Mar Caspio* 'proved more interesting'.

Romilly quickly attached himself to a small Polish and Italian group aboard the ship, and shared a bunk with a Pole who looked sixteen but was in fact twenty-eight. The Pole had worked in the French coalmines for seven years and then qualified for French citizenship by completing two years' military service. 'There were [also] two German boys from Toulouse – one was twenty, the other twenty-three; two of their brothers had been murdered by the Nazis. . . .' After the French, the Germans were one of the largest groups.

When the ship finally left Marseilles, simply sliding away from the shore in a routine manner, a tall, fair-haired, 25-year-old

[1] Esmond Romilly, *Boadilla*, pp. 26–7.

Frenchman, an acknowledged member of the Central Executive of the Communist Youth International, took charge of the party and addressed everyone in the dining-room, calling for the strictest discipline.

Once outside Marseilles, the ship dropped anchor again and waited in a rising sea until four o'clock in the morning. Then abruptly, in pitch darkness, with all lights out, she changed course and set out for Spain. By the following evening the ship was heaving and groaning her way through heavy seas, hugging the Catalonian coast, and at ten o'clock the blaze of Barcelona became visible and slowly slid by, a great revolving fairyland of lights, people and subdued gaiety.

They reached Valencia without incident the following morning, and as they came to anchor and began disembarking, a great crowd gathered, roaring 'Vive la République!' and sending up great huzzahs. The procession which followed seemed to Romilly lengthy out of all proportion to its numbers, stretching down the main road out of sight, and the air rang to cries of 'No pas-ar-an!' and 'Vive le Front Populaire!'

'That is the only impression I have of Valencia – a huge, cheering crowd, a hot and tiring march down interminable streets, slogans and posters and military flags and badges everywhere. Some of the Frenchmen shouted "Les Soviets Partout!" Others reproved them: "No Sectarianism".'

When Esmond Romilly, in his turn, reached Albacete, he at once entered the crazily disorganized world of a gathering volunteer army where White Russians met Red, Turks rubbed shoulders with Rumanians and a smattering of Americans and English had not as yet come to terms with one another. Romilly became part of a group of 14 Russians, once White émigrés, and now led by a man called Sokolinoff who 'looked like a character from *Anna Karenina*'. Six years before, the 14 Russians were given the chance to regain Russian citizenship, but they were known as White Russians and feared the consequences of returning to Russia even though officially encouraged to do so. Six long years of exile with crazily unsuitable jobs in Paris – one played the role of clown in a small local circus – had driven fear into the background, and the steadily mounting desire to

smell, at any cost, the air of Russia again, had brought them
into the incredible situation where they volunteered for a 'Red'
Army fighting against all the principles for which they themselves had once stood.

The maddest character among them was known as Nono,
a huge, fat old man whose face had gone back to the puzzled
expression of childhood, as if he could no longer understand
why life should have brought him to this sorry pass. Nono
spoke hardly at all. Another Russian called the Little Latvian
fastened himself on Romilly and never stopped talking. Forever
popping peanuts into his mouth he professed to love the English
above any other form of life but when asked why he did not go
and live among them he told the sad story: 'You see they say
No. I can't come in. When I got to Southampton I clapped my
hands. I knew I would like England though I never go there
before; and I thought I could do more – how do you say? –
trade with Englishmen. But the police he say no. So I had to go
back. . . .'

Fascinating at first, his story repeated endlessly with little
variation became boring in the end. A fierce rivalry developed
between the Latvian and Nono, and whenever Romilly set
off with the Latvian on a shopping expedition, Nono followed
lamely ten yards behind like a poor retainer. 'Hee's crazy,' the
Little Latvian would say. 'I don't know what we do about
heem – he follow us always.' Sometimes Nono dared to catch
up with them and sometimes sat down at the same café table
to drink, but whenever he could get Romilly alone, he constantly warned him against the Latvian.

There were some among the Russians who seemed normal
enough, but Nono and the Latvian apart, at least three others
were tall, broken-down wrecks who might have been taken for
'slobbering old women'.

Such was the company Romilly first encountered in the
International Brigade and he wondered, with some reason,
what it could ever amount to as a fighting force. Now began a
dreary routine of marching from the Barracks No. 1 where they
slept to Barracks No. 2 where they ate; swallowing the same
monotonous midday meal of soup, hash and fruit, and marching back to Barracks No. 1 once more. Looking along the line
as they marched, Romilly would see Nono start off in step and

quickly fall out of step, and the strange old men who looked like women soon found the pace too hot for them and sweated and panted along, losing all pretence to discipline. The ragged, inconsequent marching, the comic attempts at drill, the panting collapse which followed physical exercise among the Russians, sometimes reduced Romilly to a state of hysterical giggling which puzzled Nono, the big fat Russian, who flew into rages if he thought anyone was baiting him.

On the third day the ragged band was solemnly marched, like would-be soldiers, to a big open space outside the town, and there they found to their astonishment a tremendous gathering of 'serious volunteers' from fifteen different nations. A Frenchman in uniform, the famous André Marty, Commander of the International Brigades Base at Albacete, addressed them. It was disgraceful, he said, that with at least 11,000 volunteers in Albacete only 700 had turned up for this meeting, and group leaders who were incapable of instilling more discipline into their men must immediately be replaced. Yes – he knew everyone was impatient about haphazard arrangements, he knew everyone was anxious to 'get going', but feeding, clothing, organizing and arming 11,000 recruits was no mean undertaking. Immediately rifles and equipment arrived everything would change. Meanwhile there was no call for idleness. Tomorrow morning at seven o'clock they would assemble in the same place to begin hard physical training. One important fact became clear at this meeting. The majority of volunteers were working-class men seriously concerned with meeting the Fascist challenge in Spain.

Romilly now found himself assigned to a small group numbering only 50 out of 11,000, who were unwise enough to admit that they had no military training whatever, and once again the farcical marching, counter-marching and exercising began, but now fresh complications arose because the English, French, Germans and Latvians all had their own method of answering the commands – about turn or form fours – and the result sometimes resembled a battlefield.

Drink, too, introduced slap-happy episodes. Marching back from the barracks where they fed, to the barracks where they slept, the group sometimes swayed off the pavement one side of the road on to the pavement the other side, because a number had drunk too much strong Spanish wine, and one uncorked bottle might still be seen passing from man to man as they marched. But no one particularly cared what happened to this small and impossibly inadequate group who were, according to Romilly, playing a part in a comic opera.

Each morning the front page of the *Mundo Obrero* was posted on the barrack walls and beside it, permanently in place, a reproduction from a Russian newspaper article which proclaimed that Leningrad was in greater peril in 1918 than Madrid today. Reactions varied from ribaldry to respect, but the Russians found the German notice exalting – Discipline! Discipline! – alongside a French notice calling upon recruits to avoid V.D. in the brothels, far more interesting.

On Romilly's fourth day in Albacete, some rifles and equipment were suddenly distributed to a few hundred men, and they actually paraded, complete with pots, pans and knives, in the main square with some approximation to military precision. The following morning the Little Latvian burst in on Romilly full of excitement. 'You see, I say there were Engleeshmen here.' He gestured at a group of men who were distinctive on the barrack square because they wore khaki uniforms. 'You ask them', the Latvian said, 'if I can come too.'

The first Englishman Romilly spoke to was Lorrimer Birch, a man of very different calibre from those he had so far met. Birch was a 24-year-old graduate of Cambridge who had abandoned his job as a research chemist to come to Spain and join the International Brigade because his profound belief in Communism permitted no alternative when the Spanish Civil War broke out. One of the early members of the English Tom Mann Centuria[1] led by the famous Nat Cohen, he himself had quickly revealed remarkable qualities of leadership. A man of high intelligence, he did not allow his Communism to interfere with his judgment of non-Communists and he was quite prepared to co-operate with people he did not like.

He had stayed with the Tom Mann Centuria in Barcelona for six weeks' training as a machine-gunner, and unlike some of his comrades he did not fritter away his spare time drinking in the

[1] Which had been in action earlier.

cafés. Birch was a Communist first and last, a man drilled and dedicated to the fulfilment of the Communist vision. He it was who organized the Group Meetings which became a centre of dispute. They were run on political lines with a chairman, an elaborate agenda and a strong Communist faction, and they might last anything from two to five hours, involving complicated debating procedures which baffled men less politically conscious than Birch.

This, then, was the first Englishman Romilly encountered in Spain. 'Can you give us any low-down on this place?' Lorrimer said and Romilly told him what he knew of Albacete.

'Well, what the devil's going to happen here?' Birch went on. 'It looks as if we're going to be kept waiting about like we were in Barcelona.'

'Ay,' said Bill, an Irishman, 'we'd ha' done much better to stay in Barcelona.'

Over the next few days Romilly got to know several of the English, among them a colourful character called Aussie. An Australian by birth, Aussie had wandered over half the world and now, at 30, looked at least 40. Before he came to France and Spain, his wanderings had taken him to Mexico and there, where the peasants' creed insisted that food must be given to any casual stranger who knocked on the door, he had picked up a reasonable living, but he had no friends, he could not find work and at last he signed on as one of the crew of a cargo boat bound for Le Havre where, they told him, there were as many jobs vacant as women. It did not work out that way. His complete lack of French proved his undoing. The French had no time for a man who could not communicate volubly and easily, and when he knocked on French peasant doors they received him less warmly than the Mexicans, and offered him nothing more than hunks of grey bread.

By every kind of cunning and subterfuge he managed to reach Paris, but here the sophistication of the café life, quite without spontaneous warmth for the distressed, turned his thoughts to England. August in Paris in 1936 was very hot, and Aussie slept on the benches of the boulevards of Montparnasse, but he knew no one, he still spoke hardly any French, he had no money and the French seemed to regard him as just another drifting bum who should have been conscripted into the Renault factories. The name England spelt mist, fog, snow, and ice in the very near future, and Aussie had it on good authority from fellow bums that for all its human reputation, tramps did not touch the hearts of the average English citizen. Lying one night on a harsh bench beside the Seine, feeling at his very lowest ebb, he thought suddenly of the war in Spain which had penetrated even his limited awareness of the outer world. He saw it in the sharp terms of a clash between the exploited worker and the privileged capitalist, and suddenly the idea took hold of him that he should go to Spain and do something for the people of Spain, who were fighting for his and their precarious rights.

A Catholic welfare society, fully aware that he wanted to 'go and fight for the people in Spain', provided him with ten francs and a ticket to Marseilles. In Marseilles he met Jerry Fontana and Harry Addley. Fontana was an American who had worked as a longshoreman but having no politics – except to take care of himself – he decided to volunteer because 'there might be something in this Spanish idea'. Harry Addley, an Englishman, had been a sergeant in the Buffs in World War One, and was so tiny in person that wherever he went men automatically dubbed him Tich. His size, however, was sometimes his fortune. Bullets, he said, found difficulty in seeing him. Certainly, in the battle of the Somme, when men were dying round him in hundreds, a piece of shrapnel managed to lodge in his diminutive thigh, but he crawled into a shell-hole which would have afforded scant protection for anyone else and lay there for four days unattended. He survived to go back to England and after the war opened a restaurant in Dover with Arthur Ovenden, an ex-R.A.F. pilot. When the Spanish war broke out the restaurant was flourishing, but both by now were Communists and they decided that their military experience would be of value to the International Brigades. They turned over the restaurant to friends, dug out their old uniforms and boots and set out for Spain.

These and men like Joe Gough from Westmount, Province of Quebec, Canada, Jock Gillan, a lorry driver from the Gorbals, Glasgow, and Keith Watson were all part of the English group which Esmond Romilly now came to know in detail. He found that he had a few London friends in common with Keith Watson, and over the same old soup and hash lunch

Watson suddenly said to him one day: 'Are you one of the faithful?'

'Faithful? How do you mean?'

'Member of the Communist Party, I mean – you know – see the holy light.'

Romilly confessed that he was a mere milk-sop member of the British Labour Party and Watson went on: 'It's a religion, you know. You'll have enough of it in the next few weeks.'[1]

Romilly told him about the Russians. 'Do you think I could join with that lot too?' Watson said. 'Nono sounds heaven.'

When it came to the point Romilly was easily admitted to the English group but the Little Latvian, in his anxiety not to be left out, overdid his enthusiasm for the English and greeted Birch, the cool Communist, so effusively that Birch whispered quickly to Romilly: 'Is there any way of telling him in Latvian to fuck off?'

Romilly now had his first taste of the way in which a People's Army was trying to introduce true democracy into the natural autocracy of military life. A Group Meeting consisting of ten Englishmen unanimously elected Romilly a member of the English team, but the unanimity broke down when it came to deciding which section he should join – the French or German. Romilly, who spoke French, wanted to join the French, but the remainder were in favour of the Germans. There followed a long discussion on discipline and whether Birch, their natural leader, should have the power to decide what punishments should be meted out to offenders in all categories from the delinquent to the criminal. Finally they agreed to appoint a tribunal of three, and one of the three was Keith Watson, who commented in private to Romilly – 'That's a good thing. I am one of the chief offenders and can be relied on to deal thoroughly with others.'

Later the same day Watson confided his distaste for the whole business: 'These people are absolute dictators . . . on the way in a train I met a very nice girl so I went and sat with her in her compartment and everything was going fine you know and then that great silly Sid comes barging in and says: "Oh, you can't sit there – you've got to come in the same compartment with us", so I said fuck you; and what do you think they did – put me under military arrest – military arrest! All this stuff about

[1] Esmond Romilly, *Boadilla*, p. 62.

"being in a state of war" because they haven't found someone to get off with themselves.'[1]

On his eighth day in Albacete Romilly was one of hundreds who were ordered to parade in the barrack square to listen once more to a long harangue from André Marty, a big bear-like figure with a huge beret, a walrus moustache and a voice of thunder. The speech went on for nearly thirty-five minutes and Romilly made notes and translated for the British group afterwards.

'The Spanish people and the Spanish People's Army', André Marty said, 'have not yet conquered Fascism. Why? Is it because they lack enthusiasm? A thousand times no. Is it because they lacked courage? I say ten thousand times no. But they have not won. There are three things that they have lacked, three things that are essential for victory, three things which we must have – which we will have. The first is political unity; the second is military leaders; the third is discipline.'

Marty, himself an avowed Communist and member of the central committee of the E.C.C.I., went on to make a statement in keeping with the Popular Front policy at that time, a policy embracing help from all Left-Wing organizations. The men assembled before him might be Communists, Socialists, Radicals or Republicans – that did not matter, he said – what mattered was their common cause against Fascism. He then introduced a number of military leaders beginning with 'General Emilio Kléber!' As the short, stubby, powerful figure of Kléber rose to his feet and gave the clenched-fist salute there was the customary roar of applause. Kléber wore a grey lumber jacket, with no badges of rank, khaki breeches and dark blue puttees. Marty enlarged on Kléber's fighting record in Russia, China and now Spain, and again the crowd of recruits in their wildly different clothes rose to the occasion with a suitable outburst of cheering. Marty then concluded: 'There are those who are impatient, those who wish to rush off to the front at once, untrained, without proper arms. I say those people who spread those ideas – though they mean well – are criminals. We are preparing for war, not for massacre. When the first International Brigade goes into action they will be properly trained men with good rifles, a well-equipped corps. . . . Comrades,

[1] Esmond Romilly, *Boadilla*, pp. 65–6.

tonight you are leaving for the training camp; if you wish to be good soldiers in this fight, train well, learn well.'

By now the Germans had accepted the English group into the growing Thaelmann Battalion which was already divided into companies and zugs, each zug consisting of 30 men. The English joined a dozen or so Flemings with a number of Germans and became the 3rd Zug of the 1st Company, led by a 'tall tough Prussian . . . with a gangster face.'

Presently they received an official issue of clothing, plates, knives, spoons and mugs. The clothing consisted of brown corduroy trousers which all came in one enormous size, a number of thick khaki coats, and underwear of startling variety. There followed the slapstick comedy of dressing in trousers far too long, while friends with an enormous pair of shears marked the surplus length – sometimes as much as eighteen inches – debagged the victim and sliced off the required portion. There was still time for comic relief, still situations where the complete lack of any real efficiency became quite hilarious, but as each step took them deeper into the military machine the sense of fun diminished and the sense of a cold, implacable purpose increased. Meanwhile, in the background, away at Alcantarilla, the distinguished French novelist, André Malraux, was busy organizing the first units of the volunteer air force.

Chapter 5

Early Training

TOM WINTRINGHAM was one of the chief instructors for those early units of the International Brigade which carried out a series of sketchy exercises with a handful of outdated weapons under impossible conditions in the overcrowded town of Albacete. A solicitor's son of middle-class origins, Wintringham had gone through public school and Oxford University, become a Communist and found himself convicted at the Old Bailey for his part in the General Strike of 1926. A natural rebel against capitalist society, it was inevitable that he should play a part in the Spanish Civil War and put his O.T.C. training at the disposal of the International Brigades. When he arrived at Albacete in November 1936 it had become what he described as a menagerie with 'an incredibly expansive old sea-lion' at the top, with 'the biggest beret ever worn by man.' This, of course, was André Marty. 'The next in power, the heads of departments and brigades . . . almost all wore shaggy sheep-skins. Their hurrying lope down the narrow streets of that little town, through the winter mud of daylight or the black lampless dark, made them seem wolves in sheep's clothing. And like wolves they raided, got things . . .'

The Grand Hotel had received this influx with Spanish courtesy, but the age-old custom of delaying dinner could not be shaken by the most imperious military demands and it was nothing for the commanders and commissars, a 'seething crowd in khaki, and wool, with the most imposing boots and pistols in Spain and the most curious semi-military hats', to be kept kicking their heels for over an hour in semi-darkness waiting for dinner.

Within a fortnight of his arrival, a lorry took Wintringham out to the first military training camp – Madrigueras. Its semi-derelict condition did not surprise him. The cross-roads were marked by an abandoned petrol station, the cottages had their windows shuttered, the barns looked broken down and only the sudden appearance of a small, limp flag with a bored French sentry in a khaki cape, gave any indication that this was a military camp. 'Under the cape showed a pair of trousers which ended in light yellow puttees apparently only long enough to wrap twice around the ankles.' This had become the head-quarters of the 12th Battalion of the first developing International Brigade.

The 12th Battalion was made up of French, German, English and a few American recruits, each having a half-concealed scorn for the national idiocies of the others. A fat, puffing Frenchman known as Alexandre was commander of the 12th's machine-gun company, and on the first morning of training 'he jumped about round the guns as if he was an incredibly agile brown bear, three-quarters of him good yellow grease and cunning, and one-quarter unconsolable melancholy.' The second day's machine-gun drill revealed a puzzling feature of French behaviour. On the order 'Action!' one of each machine-gun crew flew off in almost any direction to a distance of twenty yards, and there fell flat on his face. Later, Wintring-ham discovered that this was the French method of placing observers, but the German and English complaints about the wildly erratic behaviour of French crews seemed without foundation when they emerged from a furious muddle around each of the Colts in exactly the place where they were required. But comment remained sarcastic. The English were scornful of the Frenchmen's rifle shooting, the Frenchmen of the Ger-man's fighting by numbers, and the Germans of English implied superiority.

Within the national groups themselves there were the usual troubles. The English, now nearly half a company strong, were very resentful of one of their number, a boy still in his teens known as Tommy, a member of the Young Communist League from the East End of London who had absorbed the doctrine that a revolutionary army should achieve discipline by agree-ment. Thus, to refuse to obey orders was, to him, not necessarily a breach of discipline. Elementary matters like keeping in step when on parade incited his scorn and he expressed this in such a cocky and clumsy way that company commanders were some-times reduced to near-apoplexy. From the very beginning he

demanded to know – in the proper Socialist tradition – why
there had been no election of officers, why he had not been
consulted before certain decisions were taken, and for what
future role he had been cast. ''E's been like that ever since 'e got
'ere', one fellow cockney commented sourly. 'Better shoot 'im.'

All this was in fact very misleading. When it came to the
point Tommy turned out to be a brave and resourceful young
man, but his determination to preserve his independence
forced him in the end to become a stretcher-bearer. 'As a
stretcher-bearer he was universally reckoned . . . one of the
coolest and bravest', Wintringham later wrote.[1]

The whole question of discipline in a voluntary army dedicated to the highest democratic principles quickly produced
scenes which ranged from slapstick farce to near-tragedy, but
there were occasions when the miraculous happened and the
multiple expression of extreme individuality seemed to work.
There was, for instance, the chivalrous Commander Putz of the
growing 13th Battalion quartered in a one-time convent at
a small village near Albacete called Mahora. This battalion,
drawn in large part from French recruits, was a cheerful,
happy-go-lucky battalion mainly because of the personality
of its Commander, a man of 'lean almost frail appearance'.
Putz came from a long line of cultured 'French gentlemen'
and had been a regular French Army officer. His socialism was
a highly idealistic combination of love for his fellows and a
belief in chivalrous behaviour, and he himself might have been
a figure out of medieval history. He shared everything demo-
cratically with his men, from eating the same rations to sleeping
on a straw mattress on the stone floor of yet another convent.
He listened to their complaints like a father figure, he sorted
out their quarrels, he made extravagant concessions to the
pressing needs of the very young, but behaviour which would
have reduced any normal military machine to chaos in a few
weeks produced in the 13th Battalion a remarkable degree of
co-operation. Whenever he addressed the assembled battalion
Putz did so very simply, but his words were full of a gracious
irony. On one occasion he told his men that he had sent three
of their number to the guard-room for being drunk and then
suddenly decided to see for himself what was the nature of the

[1] Tom Wintringham, *English Captain*, p. 70.

place to which he had consigned them. He found it, he said, very cold, very dismal, very bad for morale, and when his political commissar suggested releasing the prisoners he at once agreed. But – and now followed the moral of the tale made with all the subtlety of a fable by Fontaine – he did not propose abolishing the idea of the guard-room which he wanted to fix firmly in everyone's head.

It was otherwise in other battalions. Early in his work at Albacete, Wintringham encountered a man called Wilfred Macartney, once a staff officer in the First World War, whose personality seemed much better suited to the Café Royal than to the dirt, confusion and gloom of a partially blacked-out, primitive training centre. A man who succeeded in reconciling perfect manners with bursts of overpowering pugnacity, a person who either drank good champagne and smoked cigars or drank tea and gave up smoking, he was a civilized individual who might have been unexpected in the International Brigade but for the presence of other highly original types.

What Wintringham did not mention was that Macartney had served a long prison sentence for passing information to the Russians, that he was well known in the night-club world of Mrs Meyrick and had come out of jail 'fully determined to follow what his vision supposed to be the solitary, clear light burning in a corrupt society, but unable to shake off the habit of overcharging his sanguine self with alcohol.'[1]

This was the man who became Commander of the first English-speaking battalion of the International Brigade, but long before it was an efficient fighting force he had to deal with the special brand of disciplinary difficulties which automatically beset a people's army.

All the expected kinds of petty crime, violence and disturbance had to be controlled in the growing battalion as in any other army, but the beginning of a seriously regular system of payment – ten pesetas a day, roughly 4 shillings then, for every man from the date of his arrival in Spain – led to serious drinking bouts. Macartney made arrangements for patrols to visit the drink shops every night, and they manhandled many a drunken character unwillingly back to bed. Macartney laid it down for the English that anyone found very drunk should be

[1] W. F. R. Macartney, *Zig-Zag*, p. 344.

confined to the guard-room, but when, one night, the patrol came upon their own adjutant, Sergeant MacDade, in a very borderline state, they could not agree among themselves – in the best spirit of a free army – what to do.

An orderly carried the message into Macartney's office. 'If he's drunk put him in the guard-room', Macartney said. The orderly retired and was replaced by one of the guards, who asked nervously whether he could – 'bring him in'. In his very precise English Macartney said 'Bring *whom* in?' 'Why, Sergeant MacDade, Comrade – whether he's drunk or not I mean.'

Macartney remembered MacDade. He had fought with the Irish Guards in the First World War and was known as the smallest sergeant with the biggest voice. They said of him that it was necessary to stand him on a table or platform to make sure he was just visible to the troops he drilled with such awe-inspiring force and efficiency. His record covered many countries and many armies. He had served with the English in India and Burma, with Rory O'Connor in the Irish Republican Army and with half a dozen dubious characters in the French Foreign Legion. Macartney knew that the men of the growing English battalion liked MacDade as adjutant, jester and battalion mascot. It was no light matter putting such a man in the guard-room for drunkenness.

'Bring him in', Macartney said.

A moment later the tiny figure of MacDade came marching through the door with military efficiency, halted with a fierce one-two of his feet at Macartney's table, brought a quivering hand to his head in a salute which would have satisfied Sandhurst, and nudged the slovenly guard who escorted him into the correct position beside him.

'You have been reported drunk, MacDade.'

MacDade quivered to even fiercer attention, but for all the steady glare of his enormous brown eyes and the powerful attempts to conceal a gentle sway, it was clear that large quantities of liquor were battling to get the better of him.

'Me drunk, sir?' he repeated with the air of someone asked to believe the impossible.

'I shall not deal with the matter tonight', Macartney said. 'You will spend the night in the guard-room and come here tomorrow.

Too old a soldier to question such a statement, MacDade gave an even more electrically perfect salute, performed an about-turn of ruthless efficiency and marched smartly out through the door again almost dragging with him the fumbling, inefficient guard who gaped in amazement at his charge. Macartney had a shrewd idea as they went out that MacDade was really on his side. He knew what it meant to try to instil order, and more remotely, discipline, among this contradictory crowd of men drawn from every walk of life.

Macartney had turned back to Wintringham to discuss MacDade when an orderly once more burst through the office door in a most unsoldierly manner. He brought a complicated message. The commander of the guard wished to point out that MacDade was not considered drunk by the guard, but 'only by the patrol who had hauled him in, and that therefore he (the sergeant of the guard) proposed to let him go to his billet.'

Macartney listened to this with no sign of impatience but a moment later snapped:

'Send the sergeant in.'

There followed a scene very difficult for Macartney but otherwise full of comedy, until the sergeant suddenly said: 'Well, as one comrade to another . . .' Macartney received this coldly. It was now a question of orders as well as comrades, he said forcefully. The sergeant bridled and declared that on the matter under discussion his opinion seemed to him as good as anyone else's. Macartney side-stepped this reply. The sergeant went on to repeat that MacDade was 'the most popular man in the battalion' who 'could get more discipline into a crowd of rough-necks than anyone else.' Here the sergeant looked sharply at Macartney, but Macartney said nothing. 'If you want real evidence, he wasn't drunk', the sergeant persisted, 'let me tell you, he tried to persuade me not to make a fuss for him. Do you think a drunken man would have done that?'

It suddenly seemed to Macartney that this had gone too far.

'What right have you to discuss my orders with your prisoner?' he snapped.

'Well – as one comrade to another . . .' the sergeant began again. Macartney tried to turn the discussion away from these doctrinaire rapids, and the sergeant fought to stay within them. Suddenly the sergeant became red, fierce and stubborn. Why wasn't there proper discussion about this matter he demanded aggressively, and why hadn't there been a meeting along the correct Communist lines anyway?

'Look,' Macartney said, 'are you or are you not prepared to obey orders?'

'Well – yes', the sergeant said grudgingly.

Macartney now swiftly turned the line of conversation. 'In any case it's comfortable in the guard-room, isn't it? You've got a fire there? Only place in the battalion where there is a fire!' Macartney looked at the empty stove in his own room which could only be lit at the cost of suffocating clouds of smoke. He then gave one short sharp blast at the sergeant. Next time he wanted to talk politics let him try the proper person – the political commissar.

When the man had gone he turned to Wintringham: 'Harry's Anarchists! That's my name for this battalion! All deputations and opinions and little Soviets discussing each order before they obey it, or don't obey it!'[1, 2]

An American volunteer, Bert Levy, left an even worse picture of the early training days: 'Physically unfit in the most, unwilling to train to harden their bodies, falling out on marches as they pleased when trying to harden their feet. A few spending their days in brothels that sprang up in Madrigueras. Walking into Macartney's office when he was away, ripping military orders from his typewriter despite the protests of his clerk. I arrested them and confined them to Macartney's office. One of them, Esmond Romilly – Churchill's nephew. Laughing at battalion rules, staying up drinking until midnight. . . .'[3]

However, the number of wild-cats and those who rationalized their desire to do just what they pleased as political doctrine slowly diminished. Initial efforts to instil discipline aroused feuds and hatreds, but the general run of recruits recognized their necessity. There are individual accounts of different sections of the International Brigade which represent them as overrun by criminals and drunkards, but these were in a minority. A very high proportion were ordinary working men who might or might not have personal problems which they

[1] Tom Wintringham, *English Captain.*
[2] W. F. R. Macartney, *Walls Have Mouths*, pp. 419–20.
[3] Letter to the author, 31 March 1964.

solved at one remove by joining the Brigades, but many of the
early recruits fiercely believed in the ideal of fighting Fascism,
and were ready, in the long run, to obey orders.

Occasionally the early attempts at discipline seized up and a
man was hopelessly victimized as a result, but these examples
were rare. One such man, who wishes to remain anonymous,
left Liverpool on 2 January 1937 with twelve other volunteers
and went through the routine experiences before he found
himself at Madrigueras, the training village some 40 kilometres
from Albacete. There he expressed a wish to join a group of
Irishmen who were about to become part of the American
Lincoln Battalion and went out to celebrate the occasion with
them, only to be picked up late at night, charged with drunkenness, and clapped into the guard-room. This he described in
very different terms from Macartney's comments on the Albacete guard-room. The room had two large windows without
glass, the beds consisted of straw mattresses thrown on the
flagstones, one corner served as a lavatory where the filth piled
up daily, and whenever it rained the whole room dripped water.
The following morning he was taken before the Commandant
and sentenced to 48 hours' detention. There now began a series
of jailings, misunderstandings, beatings and escapes with the
indomitable Irishman each time coming up for more, which was
vaguely reminiscent of Candide.

He went from one jail to another, from one burst of physical
violence to another, and each time the prison conditions became
worse. Finally, to his horror, they did not release him, but
escorted him to the *Guardia Nacional* where a German warder
carefully searched and questioned him, and then had him
taken to a cell with nightmare characteristics. It was some
twenty-four feet square, had no windows, was alive with
vermin and entirely devoid of furniture. There was nowhere to
wash, no lavatory, and eight men lived, ate and slept on the
floor in permanent semi-darkness. The prisoners included a
German doctor, a Belgian captain, three Frenchmen, a Pole,
a Dutchman and a Swiss. The Belgian claimed that he had
been incarcerated here, without any communication with the
outside world and without any hint of a trial, for 28 days, and
several other prisoners behaved in such a way as to make the
Irishman think 'they were going a bit mental.'

Seven days later he was moved on once more. By now he should have come to the end of the line, but the nightmare quality of his saga refused to relent. The strange sequence of imprisonment, attempted escape, beating, fighting, and the threat of being shot continued right up until the last moment, when he was due, after prolonged efforts, for repatriation and once again attacked a guard, only to have two teeth knocked out and to be once more dragged off to the *Guardia Nacional*. But all this was the experience of one man in a thousand.

Chapter 6

The First Centurias

SALVADOR DE MADARIAGA, in his book *Spain*, described the original beginnings of the International Brigades: 'The Russians' technical idea was a mixed Brigade and through their influence and pressure it was adopted as an essential unit of the revolutionary army, against the opinion of the Spanish technicians. The mixed Brigade was a sort of miniature army formed by a number of small units, generally the size of a company with all the services of an ordinary army grouped round the nucleus formed by four battalions.'

Now, out of the confusion of scattered training centres and the multiple sources of supply, with the French providing uniforms dominated by the beret, the first rifles coming from Mexico, and tanks from Russia, there began to emerge not a full-scale Brigade but the components of half a Brigade. The nucleus of the units under formation were the centurias, groups of foreigners mixed with Spanish militiamen and new recruits. From the Italian centuria known as Gastone-Sozzi emerged the Garibaldi Battalion, from the Polish centuria General Wroblewski came the Dabrowsky Battalion, the Thaelmann Centuria was later converted into the German battalion of that name, and the Paris battalion – which had already fought on the Talavera front – was reorganized in Albacete under the name of Commune de Paris.

Before the great battles for Madrid began, some centurias were involved in preliminary actions. Most famous among them, the Thaelmann Centuria, first saw service on the Huesca front in August of 1936. It went into battle with a strange assortment of men and equipment, and one so-called tank which really consisted of an armoured truck with rubber tyres and no gun of any consequence. The truck was so converted that the driver had to steer it almost blindfold, and where the crew of eight stowed themselves the commander – Franz

Raab – did not quite know. The clumsy machinery controlling 'the tank' had a nasty habit of sticking at the wrong moment, and Raab always believed that a couple of home-made grenades would finish it off during one of these moments of involuntary paralysis. Plastered on the side of the tank was the name Lina Odena, in honour of the famous Spanish Youth Leader who had once waved a welcome to the centuria and was later killed at Huesca.

This weird vehicle played its comic-opera part in an operation against a canal on the Huesca front. It was the centuria's baptism of fire and they were given the job of blowing up the canal in the hope that the water would flood the Fascist lines. The Fascists, in turn, planned to open the lock gates at Tardienta, flood the countryside and threaten to bring all military operations to a standstill. A battle of tides followed with the water ebbing and flowing as now one side, now another, sought to drown its opponents. Under cover of darkness the Thaelmann Centuria worked furiously for several nights to place charges along the canal bank. Spectacularly they fired the charges and part of the bank fell away, but the same night the enemy repaired the breach and once more they were on equal terms. Every night, for the following five nights, the whole centuria slipped stealthily out under cover of what darkness they could find – a large persistent moon did its best to reveal every movement – and went to work once more to mine the canal bank. This time the operation succeeded and a huge breach made certain that if the enemy opened the lock gates, the water would flood through the breach into their own territory.

Many early recruits in the Thaelmann Centuria were refugees from Nazi Germany like 'Hans Kauffman', whose story became all-too-familiar as Hitler tightened his malignant grip on Europe.

'My parents', he said, 'were slaughtered by the Nazis in point of fact without any real logical need. They both tried repeatedly to dissuade me from my political opinions – I belonged to the Left Jewish Club. It was no advantage to the Nazis to kill my parents who were perfectly respectable people without any great skills. I was just in time to flee to France but my relations were not so lucky. I had no news of them because it was far too dangerous to write. I went to Paris and had a thin time, until I went on to Spain. It was still under the reactionary Government of Lerroux and I became so politically active against the Government that they threw me into prison. When the Left won the elections in the spring of 1936 I was released. The Fascists then tried to overthrow the Government. I heard of the formation of the Thaelmann Centuria and decided to fight with them.'[1]

Another Jewish volunteer in the Thaelmann Centuria – Gustav Lorenz – had worked in a factory until Hitler came to power and then tried to establish revolutionary cells in Westphalia only to have them betrayed before they were fully functioning. 'I happened to be abroad at the time, and I lived with a friend who took me to Paris, but this was no good for me. I am a simple working man and cannot speak French. When the war started in Spain they couldn't hold me back. I did not have any possessions, I did not own anything, I had nothing to lose, so I simply set out for Spain one day without a map and with very little money and went down to the Pyrenees. Because I wanted to avoid the border guards I chose the most desolate regions and entered into a sort of desert where there was nothing to eat. Eventually, I left France far behind and did not know that I was in Spain until two uniformed men came up to me. It was impossible to hide and they had guessed what I was up to. They turned out to be quite nice, and took me first to the guardroom where they gave me food and wine. . . .' Within six hours he was free again, and had made his way deeper into Spain to volunteer finally for the Thaelmann Centuria.

There were two other Jews in the centuria, both victims of concentration camps, who had been subjected to the routine treatment, but of the original members, the biggest proportion were Gentiles. Among them, Hans Marchwitza was nearly 60 years old, but his work as a stone carrier in the mountains of Upper Silesia had toughened him and kept him fit beyond his years. He, too, had been forced to flee from Hitler's Germany when his Left-Wing activities became known. Fritz Muenster was another exile from Germany who first went to Holland before volunteering for Spain.

[1] Ludwig Renn, *Der Spanische Krieg*.

As the volunteers increased in number and the Thaelmann Centuria slowly grew into a battalion it embraced men from half the world. Preliminary battles revealed serious flaws in the Thaelmann organization. The French had been amused at the early rule of thumb technique used by the Thaelmann. They fired in stolid discipline according to rote – one, two, three – load, aim, fire – and this had led to unfortunate consequences.

It was one day towards the middle of October 1936, when stout, middle-aged Louis Schuster, who had played an important role in the growth of the Thaelmann Battalion, said to Ludwig Renn, author of the pacifist novel *Krieg*: 'You have to help us – we don't even have a leader . . . and everything is disorganized.'[1]

Ludwig Renn (Arnold Vieth von Golssenau) had been a dedicated pacifist, but when he learnt the exact nature of the war in Spain he had volunteered at once, brushing aside pacifist principles. A second discussion about the Thaelmann Battalion followed between Renn and Hans Beimler, one-time Communist Deputy in the Reichstag, a man who had been sentenced to death by Hitler, strangled his S.S. guard, escaped in his uniform and fled to Spain. Renn has recorded in his book how Beimler asked him what he thought of the techniques of the Thaelmann forces. 'Your troops are all in one line', Renn answered. 'That is disastrous. They are so densely packed, one hand-grenade is certain to wound many. Given artillery fire the line would be penetrated in no time.'

'What should we do about it?' Beimler said.

'You should thin your lines in the front and use the others as reserves behind. If the Fascists break through, they can be taken by reserves on both sides.'

Beimler said: 'You don't belong here. The really important battles are before Madrid. I would like you to go there and accept command. . . .'

Many rumours have been circulated that Willy Brandt, now Mayor of West Berlin, fought in the Thaelmann Battalion. This is not true. As Brandt himself says, 'I would not be ashamed if – like some of my friends on the Aragon front – I had defended with arms the cause of the legal Spanish Republic and European democracy.' However, he went to the Spanish Civil War in

[1] Ludwig Renn, *Der Spanische Krieg*, p. 30.

February 1937 as the war correspondent of a Scandinavian newspaper 'and as a trusted delegate of my political friends in exile.' He had reason to hate the Communists. According to his evidence they shot, or otherwise killed, a friend of his, a German volunteer for the Thaelmann, called Mark Rein. The son of a well-known Russian Socialist, Abramowitsch, Mark Rein had been educated in Berlin and belonged to the Left Wing of the Socialist Party. He volunteered for the Brigades immediately after the outbreak of war.

One night in Barcelona he simply disappeared from his hotel, leaving all his belongings behind intact. Brandt made careful inquiries and discovered that Rein had driven away in a car with some friends, to Madrid, but the story did not make sense to him. He next went to Madrid where he could find no trace of Rein and there he intensified his inquiries, finally forcing his way into the office of a German representative of the Comintern in the Casa Carlos Marx. The man denied all knowledge of Rein, but by now Brandt believed that, for reasons he could not fathom, the Communists had kidnapped him.

Abramowitsch, the father, presently hurried from Paris to Barcelona and made his own inquiries, but again without result. A tough old revolutionary who had survived so much with stoical courage, he now appeared to be a broken man and when he talked to Brandt he kept repeating the same simple question: 'Where is my son? Where is my son?'

Brandt puts the end of the story briefly. 'As we found out later, the son had been kidnapped, imprisoned and tortured. When the case made too great a stir, the Communists decided to liquidate it by liquidating Mark Rein.'[1]

Among the Poles who made up the first General Wroblewski Centuria, a proportion came from Poland itself, some were ex-miners who had fled to France, some were émigrés who had lived in Belgium, France and even Canada. The very first Poles were émigrés in Spain at the time the war broke out, and a number of others came from Barcelona where they had been attending the Workers' International Olympics.

[1] Willy Brandt, *My Road to Berlin*, pp. 80–1.

Later, a steady flow across the Polish border into Czechoslovakia and thence on to Spain was organized by a man called Leon Chajn at the request of the Polish Communist Party. Chajn, an accomplished skier and sportsman, who operated in the border area, cultivated one of the commanders of the border guards, learnt all about their movements and finally took a room in the commander's house. Each recruit was instructed to arrive wearing sportsmen's clothes and on the first two days underwent normal training in ski-ing. Later, still under the pretext of training, Chajn would take them for a longer run to a café owned by a Czech, and only when they were settled drinking coffee did he reveal that they were already across the border. By this means, early in August 1936, nine Poles made their way to the Pyrenees, crossed into Spain, fought for a time beside the Republican militiamen and moved on to San Sebastian.[1]

By the end of August they were joined by another group of twenty-nine Polish émigrés from France, with two Hungarians among them, one destined to become the famous leader Chapiev. They now formed a group of thirty-six men and were momentarily absorbed in the Paris Commune Centuria under their leader Boleslaw Ulanowski.[2] Presently, their numbers grew until they were able to form the General Wroblewski Centuria. Towards the end of October they moved to Albacete where scores of fresh Polish volunteers had arrived for training, their numbers swelled until there were over 800, and they selected a commissar, Stanislaw Matuszczak. By now they had sufficient men to complete three companies of rifles and one of heavy machine-guns.

So it came about that the scattered centurias and half-formed battalions of Germans, French, Poles, English, Italians, Americans and many other peoples developed into the elements of a brigade, and a crisis in the Madrid situation brought the first full-scale battle of any consequence, involving the volunteers in large numbers.

[1] *Polacy w Wojnie Hiszpanskiej*, ed. Michala Brona, p. 75.   [2] Ibid.

Chapter 7

In Defence of Madrid

THE battle for Madrid, which began on 7 November 1936, pitted an ill-armed, unorganized but numerically far superior mass of Madrilenos against an army of Moroccans and legionaries, fully trained, properly equipped and numbering roughly 20,000. The Madrilenos had some Russian tanks and aircraft in support and Franco's troops were supplemented by German and Italian men and equipment.

Largo Caballero had taken the Government off to Valencia on 6 November, because he thought Madrid might fall. The ministers, politicians and leading civil servants all left Madrid, carrying with them Government papers and files. This presented a wonderful opportunity to the Communists and Russian advisers like General Berzin, who remained in Madrid, and some of them rapidly took over the executive functions of the absent civil servants. Against the gloom of Republican commanders, Antonio Mije said that the Communists would defend Madrid house by house, and the Fifth Regiment was unreservedly placed at General Miaja's disposal.

Now, as the grey, uncertain dawn broke on 7 November, the ancient city of Madrid heard the thunderous beginning of an artillery bombardment such as it had never encountered before. Women gathered their frightened children in what they regarded as the safest rooms, others went to ground in improvised shelters, police set in motion hastily prepared security schemes, but to everyone's surprise, as the shells burst, houses collapsed, men, women and children were buried beneath the debris and a great film of dust rose above the city like a ghost presence, there were very few scenes of real panic. The propagandists within the city had done their work well. Flaming speeches, powerfully written pamphlets, moving exhortations on the radio and a number of poems charged with stirring imagery had created an atmosphere in Madrid where heroism came naturally to the least expected person. Incessantly the deep, rich voice of La Pasionaria poured away from the loudspeakers, talking in accents from ancient history, calling on the women of Madrid to resist the invaders with every device at their command, even down to boiling oil poured from their windows. Workers of all kinds answered the radio call for recruits and moved towards the front lines, some completely unarmed but fanatically prepared to take up the arms of the killed and wounded. Women and children toiled all day building barricades, and a group of women presently demanded and began to organize a women's fighting battalion. The sheer mass of the population, fired by the spirit – *No pasaràn* – they shall not pass – performed little miracles of not so much heroism as stoical endurance, and there were many who literally carried out the Government's call not to retreat an inch. As Hugh Thomas wrote in his book *The Spanish Civil War*: 'All the time the Republic commanders sent back appeals for more ammunition or news that half their men had fallen. All the time Miaja replied that reinforcements had been sent.'[1]

Sheer weight of numbers, sheer sacrifice of flesh and blood could not for long stem the ruthless advance of a highly organized and quite cold-blooded military machine, but in the Casa de Campo 'the Nationalist advance planned to reach the Montaña barracks only reached the high ground known as Mount Garabitas.' Things however were going badly and despite the extraordinary response of the people, when Varela's artillery resumed its pounding of buildings in the University City on the following morning, 8 November, everything boded ill. By now, the foreign correspondents quartered in the Gran Via and Florida Hotels were sending dispatches back through Europe, England and America that Madrid would probably fall in the next few days.

And then, on the misty morning of 8 November, a strange new band of fighters, disciplined men they seemed to the Madrilenos, wearing corduroy uniforms and steel helmets, came marching, in good order, along the Gran Via towards the front, followed – even more impressively to the militiamen – by two squadrons of French cavalry. Perhaps the horses looked a little mangy, perhaps the corduroy trousers were baggy and not all the

[1] Hugh Thomas, *The Spanish Civil War*, pp. 322–3.

rifles identical, but Madrid was convinced that these men had been sent by their powerful ally Russia, and if the might of Russia intervened on their side, anything became possible again. So the cry rang out from many a balcony on the Gran Via – Long live the Russians!

There were, in fact, few people about when the first contingents came marching into Madrid that morning, but some shouted almost hysterically 'Salud! Salud!' One old woman, with tears streaming down her face, held up a baby girl who also closed her tiny fist in the clenched salute. Another, a charwoman, stood in the entrance to an hotel, once more in tears. The troops imitated their admirers crying Salud! and thrusting up clenched fists. The barman from Geoffrey Cox's[1] hotel turned to him and said: 'The Russos have come. The Russos have come.'

At last there seemed some reason to believe the tremendous proclamations made on the same day by Madrid Radio: 'Here in Madrid is the universal frontier that separates Liberty and slavery. It is here in Madrid that two incompatible civilizations undertake their great struggle: love against hate, peace against war, the fraternity of Christ against the tyranny of the Church. . . . This is Madrid! It is fighting for Spain, for Humanity, for Justice and with the mantle of its blood it shelters all human beings! Madrid! Madrid!' The words used were extravagant, but this was a time for extravagance, and both sides excelled themselves in claiming that right, peace and justice were exclusively on their side.

The first battalions of the International Brigade which marched so spectacularly down the Gran Via that November day included Germans, French, Belgians, Poles and a handful of English and Americans. The German battalion was now rechristened the Edgar André Battalion in honour of Edgar André, a German Communist recently executed by Hitler. The second battalion, the Commune de Paris, made up in the main from French and Belgians, was under the command of Colonel Dumont, a one-time regular French army officer. Both these battalions had a section of British machine-gunners attached, men who had either mastered their techniques

[1] *News Chronicle* Foreign Correspondent; *Defence of Madrid*, Geoffrey Cox, p. 67.

completely, or knew much more about handling guns than the Spanish militiamen. The third battalion, mainly made up of Polish refugees living in France or Belgium, was called the Dabrowsky and led, appropriately, by a Pole, Colonel Tedeusz Oppman.

The whole Brigade was commanded by the Hungarian known as General Kléber, whose real name was Stern. A big, broad-shouldered man who wore a thick grey roll-top sweater, fawn riding-breeches and polished riding-boots, he had a strong open face and thick grey hair and everyone at this stage thought him wonderful.

So it came about that on the evening of 8 November 1936, the XIth International Brigade went into action in Madrid at the height of the crisis in the battle for the city. Kléber took over command of all Republican forces in the Casa de Campo and the University City, and the haphazard methods of the Spanish commanders were replaced by a military efficiency which left them at first disgruntled, and then full of admiration. The Edgar André and Commune de Paris Battalions took up positions – one brigade to every four Spanish – in the Casa de Campo, and the Dabrowsky Battalion went to join Lister and the Fifth Regiment at Villaverde.

There are various estimates of the precise strength of the XIth International Brigade at this time. The present Franco Government claims that it was no more than half a brigade strong, Geoffrey Cox, the war correspondent in Madrid at the time, put it at 1,900[1] and Colodny at 3,500.[2] A figure of 2,000 men would seem to fit the facts best, yet it is difficult to believe that so small a force turned the tide in the crucial days which followed. True, by 12 November the XIIth International Brigade was also in position, but this, in turn, numbered no more than 1,700 men. Of course numbers may be meaningless in a battle of this kind. The spirit of a band of crusaders coming fresh to the battle with an international inspiration which had carried them half across Europe could, and probably did, inspire the Spanish militiamen in a manner beyond the reach of a conscript army. Hugh Thomas considers that the people of Madrid, the militia and workers had already checked the

[1] Geoffrey Cox, *The Defence of Madrid.*
[2] Robert Colodny, *The Struggle for Madrid.*

advance of Franco's troops under General Varela before the Brigade arrived, and the credit for what amounted to a victory in the eyes of the Republic should go to the population of Madrid. This was also the view of the present Polish War Ministry. Franco's violent attack on 7 November, it states, was brought to a standstill by the Spanish 5th Division.[1]

It remains fairly certain that Varela, when he renewed his attacks on 8 November, would have broken through but for the presence of the XIth Brigade. The XIth Brigade went into position on the 8th and on the following day Varela, held in the Casa de Campo, where the Edgar André and Commune de Paris Battalions were stationed, changed the direction of his attack and concentrated on the Carabanchel sector. That evening, in the misty Casa de Campo, Kléber called together all the battalions he had distributed the previous day and a reunited XIth International Brigade reassembled. This was a spectacular moment. Where, before, the Republicans were heavily on the defensive, now at eight o'clock in the evening, the whole of the first International Brigade launched an attack with a great cry in half a dozen different languages. 'For the Revolution and Liberty – forward!'

A terrible battle developed among the gum and ilex trees. The German battalions ran into withering machine-gun fire and suffered heavy casualties, but such was the impetus of sheer idealism that they pressed on and overran one position after another. Time and again it was hand-to-hand fighting in the old 1914–18 tradition, with bayonet charges of a bloodily brave kind. Time and again the battle ebbed and flowed with the Moors encountering machine-gunning as skilled and accurate as their own. The French and German battalions bore the brunt of the battle and John Cornford, the 21-year-old English poet, who was with a small machine-gun group attached to the French, wrote in a letter to Margot Heinemann:

'We advanced into position at exactly the wrong time, at sunset, taking over some abandoned trenches. The Fascists had the range exact and shelled us accurately. Seven were killed in a few minutes. We had a nasty night.' Presently the lines became terribly confused and some dispute arose about the behaviour of the French in the first 24 hours. Cornford

[1] *Polacy w Wojnie Hiszpanskiej*, ed. Michala Brona.

wrote to his fiancée: 'There was a lorry load of wounded behind us. The lorry driver signalled but wasn't noticed and got no answer. The four lines were so undetermined that he thought we were a Fascist column and accelerated past us. Someone put up a wire to stop the car. The wire was swept aside, caught Fred Jones by the neck, hauled him over the parapet and killed him. . . . That day the French redeemed their bad start by a really good bayonet attack which recaptured the philosophy building.'[1]

By the morning of 10 November only Mount Garabitas in the Casa de Campo was left in the hands of the Nationalists, but by then at least one-third of the whole strength of the XIth International Brigade lay dead or dying on the battlefield. The shock of real battle with destruction on this savage scale came as a horrifying experience to many still-raw recruits.

Varela decided at this point to change the direction of his attack once more, and it seems highly probable that the heroic charge of the International Brigade, in a romantic tradition far removed from tanks and machine-guns, may have forced this change of plan.

Guessing at Varela's next move, the Republican leaders Rojo, Kléber and the Russian General Berzin, decided that an attack against the Madrid–Valencia highway was imminent and debated what force to send there.

By now a remarkable feat of organization and improvisation had pieced together in Albacete the elements of the second, known as the XIIth, International Brigade. As André Marty, the commander at Albacete, wrote a few weeks earlier: 'The first of the volunteers had been at the base for ten days, the last for only twenty-four hours. Only the Garibaldi Battalion (of the XIIth) was formed. It had, however, only twenty-five rifles, one machine-gun and no equipment. Half the other volunteers were still in civilian dress. Not one was armed. The rifles were of four different types and there were three types of machine-gun. The artillery had not even a quarter of the necessary lorries. It had no ammunition. It was impossible to work at night since the danger of an air raid made it necessary to keep the lights switched off. . . .'

Then came an order from the Madrid front that another

---

[1] Pat Sloan, ed. *John Cornford*, p. 241.

brigade must, at any cost, be prepared and sent off within thirty-six hours. The situation was critical. Thirty-six hours! It sounded farcical.

'Nevertheless,' wrote Marty, 'Lukacz, the great Hungarian writer and commander of the XIIth Brigade, agreed without hesitation, because he knew that they could rely not only on the scarcely formed, highly qualified military cadres, but on the anti-fascist consciousness of the brigade. . . . There were not enough rifle slings. They were immediately made from linen. There was a shortage of cartridge pouches. Sacks were cut up. The division leader formed the fighting groups while equipment was being distributed. The artillery officers studied range charts, because of the many languages spoken, dictionary in hand. The horses for which there were no saddles were shod. While doctors and surgeons were finding their instruments and medicines, carpenters were making stretchers. . . .

'And . . . a miracle . . . actually happened. On 7 November, at 8 p.m., the XIIth Brigade, in close formation, equipped and armed with artillery, cavalry, scouts, motor-cyclists, a political department and a medical and supply service, left the base . . . to the strains of the International sung in Spanish, Italian, English, German and French.'

General Lukacz, its leader, who was, in fact, the Hungarian writer Mata Zalka – author of *Doberdo* – had served in the Austrian Army in the First World War, been captured by the Russians, joined the Red Army and finally come to Spain. A vivid, animated personality, as Hugh Thomas says he had 'what the casual traveller supposes to be typical Hungarian gaiety.' The Brigade Commissar was the German writer Gustav Regler, a man who first rivalled Louis Aragon the French poet for control of the Republic's cultural loudspeaker van, and then abandoned it to join the XIIth Brigade. The Garibaldi Italian Battalion, led by the non-Communist Republican Randolfo Pacciardi had, as one of its company leaders, Pietro Nenni, who later became secretary of the Italian Socialist Party. The Thaelmann Battalion had for its leader the novelist Ludwig Renn (Arnold Vieth von Golssenau) and attached to the battalion were eighteen Englishmen with Esmond Romilly still among them.

*   *   *

Twenty kilometres from Madrid Zug No. 2 of the Thaelmann Battalion, which included Esmond Romilly, Bill Scott,
Lorrimer Birch, Harry Addley and the American Jerry, became
involved in an attack on Boadilla del Monte, a lonely pueblo
dominated by a small monastery.

It was a crazy sort of action. Tich stumbling along under
bulging blankets, ammunition, pouches, rifle and bayonet
towards the objective summed up the feeling of the whole zug
that day when he said: 'I hope we don't have much more of this
sort of war.' Ten minutes later the American, Jerry, announced:
'I guess I'd like to know where I can hand in my resignation
from this Army.' After a long and cautious struggle towards
Boadilla with every man warned 'to have a cartridge ready in
the breech', they found the outlying farm buildings empty and
the village inhabited by a mangy dog and a dead cat.

Presently the order to advance was repeated once more.
'Forward in lines, ten yards at a time! Keep down, keep down –
keep your heads down!' The second objective was a small fort
garrisoned by Moors of the Foreign Legion. Now the enemy
opened fire and the bullets came scything across the grass
whistling as they went, and the swish-swish mounted to a shrill
staccato until Romilly found himself flat on his face working
like mad 'scrabbling up the earth in front with my hands'.

Jerry, the American, had disappeared from sight, and when
someone called him he didn't take any chances by putting up his
head to join the conversation. Suddenly someone said: 'Think
I'll have a pot', and there followed a deafening explosion which
alarmed Romilly far more than the bullets whistling over his
head. He decided to fire his first round, took a swift look over
his hastily improvised mound of earth, pointed his rifle at 45
degrees and pulled the trigger. 'The result was a click. Furious,
I emptied the breech; but I had done everything right and
another clip of cartridges produced no result.'[1]

There were several others who discovered that their rifles
simply refused to fire that day, and somehow, lying in their
fragile shelters under withering fire, the whole action became
ridiculous when they had no means of justifying their presence
on the battlefield, much less the long, tortuous journeys which
had brought them from Germany, America and England.

[1] Esmond Romilly, *Boadilla*, p. 101.

Many confusing orders were now issued. The different zugs of the battalion received one message from H.Q. only to have it countermanded a few minutes later. Men went forward in one direction only to be recalled and sent off in another. The English machine-gun team of five tried to operate on pre-arranged lines with one firing, one loading, one bringing up ammunition and the remaining two stationed twenty yards ahead with rifles at the ready to reply to any fire it might draw.

An outburst of argument, cursing and clinking was followed, at last, by the rat-tat-tat of the machine-gun, but it shuddered with the effort, stuttered to a near-standstill and was greeted by one of the team with: 'Christalmighty, we're firing at the sky, not the fort.' The reply was instantaneous. The Moors directed a hail of bullets towards them. By now, Tich had put Romilly's rifle in working order again, and quite unable to see any living sign of the enemy, Romilly let fly with five rounds at 1,000 metres, bitterly reflecting that here he was firing a rifle for the first time in his life and he couldn't even see the target. A cry went up behind him. A German called Karl Ostburg, handling two drums of ammunition, had been hit in the thigh and Romilly went back to help him. Ostburg hopped along on one leg, his lower lip covered with blood where he bit deeply into it trying to stop himself crying out again. The search for a first-aid post took Romilly far back behind the front and by the time he returned again it was dark, but the moon had risen and he thought it would be simple to find the machine-gun post again. A whole hour he floundered around the point where the gun should have been and there was nothing; no sign of a gun, a human being or even the sound of voices. Two hours later he sat down under a tree, cold and exhausted, stared at the landscape made beautiful by the soft flooding moonlight and thought: Oh God – I'm lost.

And then, suddenly and miraculously, he heard the voice of the Englishman Bill Scott, but when they had greeted each other with tremendous relief it didn't help very much because Bill, too, was lost. There followed a nightmare series of attempts to make their way back to base, but each sally led to doubt, uncertainty and finally a brisk about-turn in the opposite direction, until they began to fear that in their confusion they would walk

slap into the enemy's trenches and qualify for immediate cas-
tration by the Moors. In the moonlight and shadow, nothing
was real; every bush and tree had a similarity; landmarks were
without character. When suddenly they heard voices coming
along the road, they slipped down, lay dead-still, and watched.
Four men came into view, black silhouettes in the moonlight,
and Romilly's finger itched to pick them off, but as they came
nearer he suddenly realized that they were speaking French.
They turned out to be French and, inevitably, part of the
brigade, but they, too, confessed to being immutably lost.

By three o'clock in the morning, the five men were still
wandering hopelessly from one nameless point to another, when
they suddenly came upon a party of thirty Germans, French
and Poles, sprawled disconsolately among a mass of gear. A
German officer had been sent out from base to collect the lost
and the stragglers, and this grey, disillusioned little band was
one result. They struggled back towards the rear for what
seemed hours, some falling into ditches to sleep, some carried
on stretchers, some, like Romilly, walking in a general dizzy
numbness of aches, pains and exhaustion. The dawn was
coming up as they at last huddled down on a stone floor in a
village barn to try to sleep in full clothes and equipment. The
first day of action was over for Zug No. 2 of the Thaelmann
Battalion.

This kind of confusion was typical of much of the battles in
and around Madrid. Part of the XIIth Brigade had continued
fighting confusedly in a vain effort to take the strategically
important hill of Cerro de los Angeles, but as the fighting
subsided and the remnants of one company after another
made their way lamely back, the hill remained in Nationalist
hands.

This was the Garibaldi Battalion's first major battle and
like all battalions of the XIIth it went into action ill-equipped.
The 520 men were divided into four companies with two very
conscientious political commissars, Roasio and Azzi, and a
young Hungarian medical student playing the role of doctor.
The commander, Pacciardi, found himself preoccupied with
trying to find transport, ammunition, medical supplies and

food for his men. They had no field telephone, just one lorry, and communication in battle relied upon runners. Pacciardi tells the story of the confused ebb and flow of the battle until, by luck, one of his men picked up the password – changed every night for the Fascist troops – and repeated it to one of Lister's companies: Burgos Berlina. The company then presented itself at the entrance to a fortress defending Cerro de los Angeles, gave the password, marched in and captured the village, only, shortly afterwards, to be overwhelmed again.

On another occasion Pacciardi was marching in the centre of his first company beside his friend Maffi, who had his pockets full of sweets and carried a bottle of cognac. As they marched the company's runner, christened the Small One, jumped about in between the bullets as if he got great joy from dodging them. They had taken up position and were flat on their faces when Maffi offered Pacciardi some water to drink and he said: 'Water – that's to wash your feet with!' Maffi lifted himself up to offer Pacciardi a drink of cognac when a bullet hit him in the head. 'Maffi!' Pacciardi cried, 'are you dead?' He had stiffened already like a corpse, but the corpse replied, 'No! No! I'm not dead yet. Take the cognac. I go to the hospital.'

There were many comic moments for the Garibaldi Battalion, but they were overwhelmed by savage realities. 'I feel ill in my limbs,' Pacciardi wrote of the Cerro de los Angeles fighting, 'and in my spirit. Our first trial has not succeeded. I learn to suspect commands. One doesn't attack a fortress with bayonets. Why don't we lay siege and wait?'[1]

Shortly after the battle for Cerro de los Angeles, the whole of the XIIth Brigade was withdrawn from that front and received instructions to enter Madrid itself.

When the commander of Esmond Romilly's company, in the Thaelmann Battalion, a man called Max, announced that they were leaving for Madrid, the highly developed sense of democracy among the English demanded a group meeting to confirm the order after their own idiosyncratic manner. 'I feel every comrade should think seriously about this question', the Chairman said. 'When Max made the announcement we were leaving

[1] R. Pacciardi, *Il Battaglione Garibaldi*, p. 71.

for Madrid he expressly stated that he favoured discussion of
the change of plans. If we don't discuss this kind of thing . . . we
might as well be Fascists. . . . A lot of comrades probably feel we
were entitled to a proper rest back here as we were promised.'

Lorrimer Birch strongly objected and said the whole discussion was out of place. People's Army or no People's Army, it
could not be run efficiently on this detailed consultative basis,
whatever the fine scruples of Marxist principles, and he, for
one, was a hard, fast and practising Marxist. Tich didn't give
much of a damn where they went so long as Max's promise
that they would be fighting in properly dug and equipped
trenches came true. Jeans said very little and looked exhausted.
For one whole hour the wrangling continued with bitter exchanges between Lorrimer Birch and Bill Scott. Even when they
at last agreed that the group would carry out orders, none the
less deploring the High Command's disregard for regulation
rest periods, that was not the end of it. Birch suddenly said:
'Before we finish I want to say that this meeting certainly
ought never to have been held.' There were those at a higher
level of command who would have applauded his words.

Chapter 8

The Battle for University City

MADRID under siege had the air of many a war-struck city. There were barricades across the roads, there were no private cars and every taxi had been commandeered for military transport. Queues formed at all food shops, militiamen directed the traffic, a great deal of rubbish remained uncollected.in the side streets, and every window carried criss-cross strips of paper to prevent blast splintering the glass. A certain confusion invaded all walks of life. A postman wandered along severely damaged streets trying to disentangle non-existent addresses, and groups of solid bourgeois housewives crowded down the streets clutching parcels of food, followed by a trail of children. Occasionally they would undergo a ferocious transformation as a lorry load of troops went by. Their faces lit up, their arms were raised, and they gave the clenched-fist salute shouting – *No pasaràn!* Little bunches of workmen busied themselves at intervals round giant braziers repairing bomb damage to the roads and gas mains. Everywhere slogans and posters called on the population to resist to the last drop of blood and ambulances lay in wait, like ghosts, in side streets.

The air-raid warning had gone just before the Thaelmann Battalion arrived in Madrid and the streets were deserted as they entered the city. No one turned out to cheer and as they crunched over broken glass and passed a dead horse Romilly watched a dog-fight between Government and Nationalist planes overhead, and found himself deeply stirred as an enemy plane came crashing down in flames somewhere just beyond the city's precincts.

John Sommerfield, another Englishman, who became part of the No. 4 section in the machine-gun company of the André Marty Battalion, has left this description of the Thaelmann Battalion as it advanced through the streets of Madrid at the head of the XIIth Brigade:

'They had good khaki uniforms, marched magnificently, singing one of Eisler's marching songs, their voices, low and deep and beautifully together, the words of the song and the beat of the marching feet all together making one single noise. It was a song that they had sung before on demonstration in Germany, it had sounded in their heads as they lay in the cells of Nazi prisons. . . . It was the voice of free Germany and they were singing it again going up the front and knowing better than any of us what they were fighting against.

'There was a big red flag at the head of the column and each company had a red banner. It was a brave sight. It had all the glamour and excitement that governments can use to make men forsake their homes and die on foreign soil . . . but it was *ours*. It was our army and the glamour was real.'[1]

The bombing of Madrid increased in the next few days and brought fresh changes to its appearance and way of life. New techniques for breaking the will of the city were tried with cold-blooded calculation. As Hugh Thomas wrote: 'The German officers of the new Condor Legion [flying for Franco] were interested to see the reaction of a civilian population to a carefully planned attempt to set fire to the city quarter by quarter. The bombing concentrated as far as possible on hospitals and other buildings such as the Telefonica whose destruction would cause special panic.'

A number of technical military experts from all over the world were watching the Madrid battle as they might a circus, with the single purpose of learning new lessons to be incorporated in old textbooks. It caused some astonishment among technical advisers that the combined effects of bombardment from the air and ground, the attempts to reduce large areas of the city to ashes by fire and the propaganda threats by loudspeaker of a steadily more horrific fate awaiting those who continued to resist, inspired as much anger as fear, and when it became clear that neutral centres like hospitals were special targets, fear finally gave way to a blazing anger, stiffening morale in a powerful way.

Between 16 and 19 November, day and night bombing brought worse havoc to the city. Scores of homes were split open to spill their contents into the streets and gaping holes

[1] John Sommerfield, *Volunteer in Spain*, p. 78.

torn in concrete walls revealed private lives to the public eye. The death roll mounted and the scene became macabre. Hundreds of people died, many buried beneath debris, and the flames licking their way unchecked threw whole areas into the sharp relief of a blood-red glare as if the fires of hell were blazing while the damned population 'repeated syllabically like a beat on a distant drum, *"No pas-ar-àn! No pas-a-ràn!"* '[1]

By 19 November more than 1,000 people were dead, over 18,000 homeless, and men, women and children were camping out on the pavements, making do with several layers of clothing, overcoats and blankets. Under the glare of the fires the lines of people living in the streets, some isolated, some huddled together in families and groups, gave the scene an even more ghoulish air. Every week 14,000 were being evacuated to the Levante, but, as much later with the population of London, citizens who had spent their lives in the ancient highways and by-ways could not easily bring themselves to abandon their roots. War further modified a class structure already in the melting pot from Marxist principles, and many working-class families migrated to middle-class areas which seemed, for reasons explicable to Republican leaders, safer than the working-class districts of Madrid. Louis Delaprée, correspondent of the *Paris Soir* – whose paper was constantly charged with Fascist views – wrote in his diary for 20 November 1936: 'Oh, old Europe, always so occupied with your little games and your grave intrigues, God grant that all this blood does not choke you.'

The XIIth Brigade took up positions in Madrid simultaneously with the arrival of a column of 3,000 Anarchists led by the famous Durruti. Characteristically, he insisted on taking over independently one sector of the front to give full play to that kind of bravery, intelligence and technical skill which sprang from Anarchist beliefs and training. Unwisely, the dangerous Casa de Campo was handed over to him, and when Durruti received instructions to attack on 15 November with full air and artillery support, the deadly fire of the Moors so dismayed his troops that – with characteristic anarchist fervour – they

[1] Hugh Thomas, *The Spanish Civil War*, p. 329.

refused to carry out the order. Before Durruti could rally them the Nationalist General Varela began another attack which eventually carried a number of Moroccans and legionaries to the foot of the heights on which stood the prized objective of Madrid's University City. Astoundingly agile, the Moors swiftly scaled the heights and overran the School of Architecture. Reinforcements poured steadily across the river and began to build up in the University City.

At this point, with the threat of a break imminent, once more the XIth and XIIth Brigades were called on to defend to the death the Hall of Philosophy and Letters. A long, bitter and bloody struggle began, and it was as if the Foreign Legion fought to realize the slogan of its founder – down with intelligence – by reducing the University City to a mass of rubble, but the International Brigade also had its slogans, and two ruthless, dedicated bands of men clashed with equally fanatical determination. Local battles presently reached the savage situation where the ground floor of one building was held by men from the Thaelmann Battalion and other floors by the Moors. Each attempted to commandeer the lifts to send up or down hand-grenades timed to explode on arrival, and dramatic sword-and-cloak battles were fought on stairways with hand-to-hand grapples and twisted hand rails crumbling away under gun fire. In the Hall of Philosophy blood dripped down one stairway and the broken bodies of wounded men lay unattended for hours. An extraordinary confusion of singing, explosions, slogans and orders issued in many languages converted the University buildings into a strange Valhalla where the weird battle mounted to the wild, sad Teutonic strains of German marching songs and the barking of orders – 'Garibaldi avanti!' 'Bataillon André Marty descendez vite!' 'Bataillon Thaelmann fertig machen!'[1, 2]

The roar of artillery bombardment was followed by the roar of planes and bombs, but both sides refused to be driven back by the fiercest barrage the other could muster, and as the smoke rose from shattered trenches and masonry, inert figures buried behind mud and mortar moved again to slink stealthily forward or to grapple afresh with the invader. Extraordinary feats of

[1] Hugh Thomas, *The Spanish Civil War*.
[2] Verbal evidence: Dr Ernst Adam, Chief of Staff to Kléber.

physical courage were commonplace. A handful of Poles from the Dabrowsky Battalion held out against savage bombardment, air attack, machine-gunning and bayoneting, dying man by man without yielding an inch in the Casa de Velázquez, until a score of Moors rushed the last two remaining figures who continued firing as they fell riddled with bullets. In the same tradition, a handful of Moroccans burst through Durruti's Anarchists, fought their way along the Calle de la Princesa, and were shot down man by man, until the remnant made a last crazy dash down the Paseo de Rosales and died as they reached the Plaza de España. This episode let loose the rumour that the Moroccans were in the Plaza de España and the militia repeated the story to one another in dismay, until Miaja thought he must personally appear at the front to stiffen their morale. In the wild, flamboyant manner of the whole battle he drove along the front bellowing into a loudspeaker 'Die with your General Miaja! Cowards – die in your trenches. Die with your General Miaja!'

One room in the Hall of Philosophy changed hands four times in one day, with Thaelmann Zug No. 3 finally digging in among its collapsed walls and smashed furniture, but it was not all hardship for some sections of the XIIth Brigade. John Cornford, the English poet with the French Battalion, a great-grandson of Darwin and son of a Cambridge professor, described the conditions in which he found himself, on one occasion, in a letter to Margot Heinemann. 'This was our best front line period – Comfortable, above all warm and supplies regular. A great gutted building, with broken glass all over, and the fighting consisted of firing from behind barricades of philosophy books at the Fascists in a village below and at the Casa Velázquez opposite. . . . I gathered a small cut in the head. After the night in the rather inefficient but very nice Secours Rouge Hospital, where the amateur nurses wash your wounds like scrubbing the floor, I came back feeling all right, but must have been a bit weak from loss of blood. Then came two heavy days' work trench digging in the frozen clay. The afternoon of the second day I think I killed a Fascist. . . .'

Bernard Knox, a friend of Cornford's, also in the French Battalion, wrote: 'We were as happy as I think men can possibly be in the front line in modern war. We were under cover from the deadly cold that so far had been our worst enemy, we had leisure to talk and smoke in physical comfort and, greatest pleasure of all, it was safe to take our boots off at night. The only drawbacks to this battle paradise were the fact that we were a perfect target for the artillery and the realization that we might be cut off at any moment.'[1]

When the fighting eased off in the Philosophy and Letters building, a handful of intellectuals like Cornford and Knox argued endlessly about life, art and literature and when this palled and something more vigorous seemed necessary, they developed a trio whose singing of *She Was Poor But She Was Honest* seemed to dismay the Moors as much as their machine-guns.

'It was here that John got his . . . wound', Knox wrote. 'We had just discovered the library, intact in the basement, and had staggered upstairs with armfuls of Everyman Library. . . . There was a crash which seemed to rip my head open and I was thrown on to the floor. When I looked up the room was full of filthy black smoke and John was stumbling past me, his face bloody. I ran to the door and the cry, "Stretcher-bearers!" echoed down the four flights of stairs. John and two others were taken off to hospital at dusk; when we cleaned the room up afterwards we found a three-foot hole in the wall and hundreds of shrapnel bullets on the floor and on the walls. The great joke was still to come. The artillery expert who examined the bits identified it as one of our own anti-aircraft shells.'[2]

Destruction in the city from fire, shells, bombs and bullets continued to multiply. Half-gutted blocks of flats were still tenanted by men and women who refused to leave their homes and continued to eat, sleep and live, making some attempt at normal routines. Trees were uprooted and broken, lamp-posts leaned drunkenly, café windows were smashed and great shell-holes in the road had filled with water. A sort of sub-life continued under the scarred battle surface, with women emerging from the rubble heaps of a bomb site, carrying firewood, children living a hunted existence harried by the authorities, parents and café proprietors miserably trying to heat their coffee with substitute fuels.

Sommerfield left this picture of one corner of the battlefield which was Madrid: 'By the barricade stood militiamen, cloaked in soaked blankets. . . . By the open space lay two dead Fascists,

[1] John Cornford, *A Memoir*, p. 190.   [2] Ibid., p. 191.

one in the gutter, his head smashed open against the kerbstone, the brains slopping out. A big, lean dog with a famished look came up to the corpse, sniffed and began to lap at the mess of brains. One of the guards drew his automatic and put three bullets into the dog. It lay coughing over the corpse, not yet dead. The guard ran forward, his head held down and finished the dog off with his rifle butt. He stopped when he passed us, looked apologetic, and said in bad French, "It has to be done. They get the taste for human flesh. It is bad. . . ."[1]

The battle for the University City continued until 23 November. It was fierce, bloody, concentrated, with individual rooms of different buildings fought over and changing hands day after day, until every kind of shell and bullet had shattered their frames and the twisted bodies of Moors lay alongside the dead of the Thaelmann and Commune de Paris Battalions.

By 23 November, despite savage resistance, three-quarters of the University City was in the hands of the Nationalists. General Mola's farthest points of penetration were the Institutes of Hygiene and Cancer and the Clinical and Santa Cristina Hospitals, but his push towards the Plaza de la Moncloa was held, despite repeated and wasteful attacks with everything at his disposal. It was, once again, the XIth and XIIth International Brigades, fighting with a terrible determination, which stopped him. Time and again men of the Thaelmann, Edgar André, Commune de Paris and Garibaldi Battalions not merely stiffened the morale of the Spanish militiamen, but died fighting at their posts, refusing to yield an inch of any possible way into the heart of Madrid. Cold statistics reflected the cost. The XIth Brigade lost in dead and wounded 900 of its 1,900 men within a month, and the XIIth Brigade, originally 1,500 strong, was reduced to 800 in the same period.

Living in London at the moment is a first-hand witness of these events who remains unmentioned in any other account of the International Brigades. Dr Ernst Adam became one of the first Chiefs of Operations under General Kléber and then Chief of Staff. As such he was the intimate of Kléber and in a unique position to observe the Madrid generals at work.

[1] John Sommerfield, *Volunteer in Spain*, p. 155.

Dr Adam had been a lieutenant in the German Army during the 1914–18 war and when unemployment reached catastrophic proportions after the war, he became director of an institute devoted to retraining men for other jobs. Unfortunately there were no other jobs. Worse still, Adam quickly came to hate the Nazi régime and finally fled to Paris. From Paris he went to Brussels and there began a new career as a journalist. When the Spanish Civil War broke out it seemed to him the first occasion when the ordinary individual could do something positive against the growing forces of Fascism, and at the age of 37 he made a decision, very different from the youthful impulse of many another volunteer, to go to Spain.

Within a few months, Kléber picked him out and he became Chief of Operations in the Madrid area. He describes Kléber as a man 'with deep brown eyes and full lips who carried himself very erect and conveyed great strength of character.' One of Kléber's worst troubles, at the outset, was the behaviour of a colonel of the French Foreign Legion who became a member of his staff but did not seem to have his heart in the Republican cause. Adam believes that this man was planted in the International Brigades by the French Secret Service, and within a few months he went on leave and never returned to Madrid.

Temporarily, the Staff used a small royal palace north-west of Madrid as its headquarters, but Adam himself was constantly moving around the front line and frequently lived in the trenches. He came back to his dug-out one night to find it almost overwhelmed by an enormous four-poster bed, and when he asked for an explanation his Polish aide said 'Well, some of our men are sleeping on stolen mattresses in the trenches, and it seemed only fitting that the Chief of Operations should have a four-poster – so we stole one'.

Adam believes that the intricate relationship between the Russian military advisers, the Spanish generals and the commanders of the International Brigades in Madrid did not give any overall power to the advisers.[1] Kléber and the Spanish generals met Berzin every evening, but they mainly discussed

[1] The situation is further complicated by General Rojo's evidence. As Miaja's Chief of Staff he claims that Prime Minister Caballero told General Kléber to take his orders from the Spanish General Staff and not from General Miaja. General Vicente Rojo, *Alerta Los Pueblos!*, pp. 51–2.

and agreed on policy, not individual military tactics. Indeed, there was an occasion when many of the best brigades were ordered to the Jarama front, but one battalion of the XIIth Brigade did not arrive. Adam roared off on a motor-cycle to find out what had happened. When he located the battalion he discovered that a Russian military adviser, an artillery officer, had ordered it to take up another position and Adam immediately countermanded the order. Confronting the Russian he said: 'You had absolutely no right whatever to interfere.' The Russian went pale and at last said: 'You are quite right – I shouldn't have interfered.'

Chapter 9

The Thaelmann Battalion

WHEN Sefton Delmer, foreign correspondent of the *Daily Express*, set out to interview the English group attached to the Thaelmann Battalion of the XIIth Brigade he first encountered a tall, blond German with a strained and bitterly neurotic face, a man called Hoffman now in command of the Edgar André Battalion, who immediately suspected Delmer of belonging to the dreaded Fifth Column within Madrid. Presently the Political Commissar of the Thaelmann arrived on the scene to vouch for Delmer. A rough, thick-set German named Artur, whose gums, when he smiled, showed the scars caused by the Gestapo technique of interrogation by burning cigar, the Political Commissar escorted him through a maze of fortified positions each defended by a different nationality – Poles, Frenchmen, Czechs, Bulgars and Hungarians.

Ludwig Renn, commander of the Thaelmann, was down with a fever. 'I found Ludwig in his command post dug-out stretched full length on a hard camp bed, a heavy khaki greatcoat over his long body, a woollen Balaclava covering most of his head. It was a moment or two before I recognized that lined, ascetic, almost medieval face in the dim light of the dug-out. . . .'[1]

Shortly afterwards Delmer went into the front line and there one of the first people he encountered was once again Esmond Romilly. He now learnt from Romilly more of the extraordinary exploits of the Thaelmann Battalion. Romilly had taken part in a series of skirmishes in and around this section of the battle-front with the Thaelmann. One objective, a fortress near the Casa Velázquez known as the White House, three-quarters of a mile from the University of Madrid, led into the usual confusions which seemed to dog his footsteps from the moment he entered the battle area. Tich, the five-foot-nothing Englishman, had been detailed to take six men, among them Romilly, to

[1] Sefton Delmer, *Trail Sinister*, p. 310.

reconnoitre the ground. They raced through some woods towards the fort and to their astonishment did not come under fire. They reached the fort simultaneously with another detachment of eight Germans and still there was no sign of resistance. The leader of the second detachment then battered down a door with his rifle butt and led the way in, with bayonet fixed. Lying around in grotesque and horrible positions were the bodies of nearly twenty Republican soldiers all shot to pieces with shell and bullet mutilations. There were blood-stained rifles, blood-stained ammunition belts, blood-stained cups and blood seeped slowly along the floor of the fort. Within a few minutes as they moved silently among the carnage, first one bullet, then another came whining over, followed by a series of heavy crashes. Smoke from shell-bursts traced a steadily more accurate path towards the fort and suddenly and blindingly came a direct hit which sent down a tremendous shower of bricks, earth and masonry, momentarily knocking four men off their feet and burying them. The order came to retire, but it was not so easy. As they moved back the machine-gunning intensified and Romilly suddenly realized that it came from their own side. Unexpectedly, the whole battalion had moved up close behind them, and Tich gave the order to lie absolutely still and wait further orders.

A brief battle now began in earnest with the enemy opening up and bullets tearing just above the heads of the patrol in both directions. Slowly Romilly's own battalion closed in on him with their fire becoming more dangerous every second. Suddenly a raucous voice bellowed something. A moment later it was repeated and Romilly made out the words: 'Don't shoot them – that's the advance patrol.' Again an order was passed by the patrol leader down the chain of men cowering close to the earth and reached Romilly. He, the novice, the ex-civilian, the play-boy adventurer, had been chosen to crawl back to their own lines, to explain the situation and return with the whole battalion. Dawn was at last coming up and as he began to move slowly across the sullen earth he knew that both sides could see him, and if the enemy did not pepper him with shots some raw and nervous recruit in his own lines might easily let fly in a moment of panic. For a time he slithered like a snake close to the earth, with sudden bursts of fire whipping into the mud around him, and suddenly came upon the body of a dead German with another Thaelmann man, wounded and writhing in helpless agony. Kneeling over the wounded man was an Englishman called Messer. 'God knows if we'll ever get this chap back or ourselves', he said. 'D'you know those Fascists got into that fort a few minutes after we left?'

Romilly never remembered how long they waited. It was a horrible nightmare of bullets smashing dangerously close, of every attempt to move suddenly pinioned by fresh fire and the wounded man still groaning and writhing in agony. The wang-crash of trench mortars suddenly added fresh noise and trouble and the puffs of smoke once more traced a pattern towards them. And then as suddenly as it had begun, the firing died down and swiftly and ruthlessly they scrabbled their way back into the lines dragging the wounded man with them.

By midday another rebel attack had been beaten back by the Thaelmann Battalion and now the Garibaldi Battalion came up to join them in a double counter-attack on the White House. Simultaneously, away on the right flank, the Fascist troops made a sudden attack from the Fuencarral road which carried them across it. Momentarily they were astride the road, but Republican reserves came into action and pushed them back again. Fourteen Moors were surrounded and surrendered. Two sections of the Garibaldi Battalion now tried to follow up their advantage with a spectacular bayonet charge which carried them, shouting Republican slogans, after the retreating enemy, but the enemy in turn called up reserves, the bayonet charge was brought to a standstill and the ding-dong battle died away.

That night the White House and the surrounding houses were a blazing mass of flames throwing half the countryside into sharp relief and Romilly sat drinking hot soup and rum, watching the spirals of sparks, the sudden leap of a flame as its light flickered wickedly across the countryside.

Romilly left a description of the renewed attack launched by the Thaelmann on the following day. It opened as four tanks moved up the road under Nationalist artillery fire and suddenly the poum-poum-poum of their guns indicated that the infantry were due to go in at any minute. 'The suspense was maddening', Romilly wrote. 'I felt an urgent desire to relieve myself, but decided there would be no time.' The British company commander Jeans shouted 'Fix bayonets. Everyone ready!' The Italians were lying on the ridge to the right, the company commander explained, and would cover their advance with rifle fire. Behind the Fuencarral road four machine-guns had started up.

'Forward! Rush ten yards, drop, wait for next advance. Everyone to fire at the windows', shouted Jeans.

'We reached the wall of the White House. It was a mad scramble. We kept near the road and the bullets skimmed over harmlessly at first. Then there was a space of fifty yards running all out in threes. A few of the Germans dropped on the way – it was just like seeing people killed running in an American film.'[1]

They reached the walls of the White House with few casualties. Dead and dying Moorish soldiers, some groaning, some still screaming, lay about inside and the Republican machine-gunners in the Clinic Hospital of the University building continued to rake the road behind with continuous fire which made escape that way for the retreating Moors impossible.

'We entered a courtyard. . . . A deadly machine-gun fire . . . on our left made us stop; a party . . . was storming the National Guard building on the right. A German pulled a Mills bomb from his pocket, extracted the pin with his teeth; he stood up, bullets whistling past him and hurled it in. We rushed in after its explosion. Four Moors had been firing from behind a dead horse. Now they were finished.'

A shell exploded on one wall and it crumbled away into nothingness. 'A figure had lunged through an opening in the mass of bricks and wood which separated us from the next-door shed. The man was dead . . . his body hung suspended over the debris. . . .'

They pushed on, with bullets still whipping past, through eight more sheds and reached a main farm building once more full of Moorish dead. 'Most were not killed by bullets – their bodies had been torn apart by shells, limbs blown off by hand-grenades . . . two mangy cows wandered aimlessly about. They were wounded, but their hides seemed too tough for the bullets. In the middle of the mud I watched a little blaze crackling away – two dead men were burning steadily.'[2]

[1] Esmond Romilly, *Boadilla*, pp. 145–6.   [2] Ibid., p. 146.

One group ended up firing from behind a farm wall, another overran the National Guard building and set up a machine-gun post on the first floor, and then came rumours of a Fascist counter-attack with tanks. It was at this point that the Englishman Messer said: 'If you ask me we've done enough today', and Jerry, the American, joined in with: 'You'll have done enough when some Moor sticks his bayonet up your arse and then you'll get the V.C. When I came out here, they told me this was a revolution, but it's nothing but a f— war.'

Presently the firing died away. Dusk came down. A steady drizzle of rain began. Hot soup arrived from the kitchens but they had to eat it outside the house in the rain. Suddenly everything seemed cold, bleary, impossibly full of physical misery and pain to Romilly. 'I do not know of any word to describe that peculiar combination of dead men, crackling flames and drizzle.' Romilly was unaware of the full extent of the casualties which the Thaelmann had sustained. When the other zugs at last gathered for a rough and ready roll call one man looked round and said: 'Jesus Christ – is this all there is left of this bunch?'

Another German of No. 1 Company described the battle of the White House in his diary: 'The whole attack was like living in a book. I seemed to have been in the midst of everything I could imagine. Heroes, cowards, but most of all great courage. In addition to the tank and machine-gun fire, the mines dropped from the air caused great trouble. One mine alone cost us twelve men and one lost both legs and was a fearful sight. The eternal rain went on. There was no hot food. We dug ourselves in. Later in the afternoon hot coffee reached us and our morale improved. Julius Laupe and Joze Majek, both machine-gunners, died. . . .

'At night we managed to crawl to corpses and bring them back and bury them. An Austrian, Karl Mager, we also buried but he had been killed two days earlier.

'We left two makeshift crosses where we buried them. They are lying side by side, Czech, Austrian and German. They died for the same cause in a foreign country. I cannot help thinking of the ones I left at home. Shall I ever see my wife and children again?'

Ludwig Renn described the experiences of that week as by far the worst he had encountered. In two hours they lost almost every group leader in two companies and in the days that followed one officer after another was killed or wounded.

A battered and exhausted group, very near to breaking point, was at last relieved by the Edgar André Battalion on the 25th. They retired to Fuencarral and took over a beautiful hunting lodge which once belonged to a noble Spanish family and there they relaxed and enjoyed what limited entertainment a place like Fuencarral, undergoing constant air raids, had to offer. The coffee houses closed at 6 p.m., the cinemas at 7 and late-comers who returned by 8.30 had to drive without lights. After 10 p.m. everyone needed a special pass because enemy spies were said to be everywhere, the chances of sabotage were widespread and no one trusted anyone else. Air-raid alarms wailed with monotonous regularity, but sometimes the queues outside the shops simply stood in line and stared at the bombers as they went over. Slowly what remained of the Thaelmann was given a reasonable respite and the whole battalion once more reorganized with fresh recruits.

Meanwhile the weather became colder, winter slowly set in and by 1 December, when they again replaced the Edgar André Battalion at the White House, the frost was severe, the ground hard, and digging-in a back-breaking process. Tiredness and the frozen state of the ground forced even the hardiest to stop digging when the trenches were only 24 inches deep, and these shallow substitutes for real trenches were to cost many lives. Touring the front line on 5 December, Hans Beimler heard the cries of a wounded man lying somewhere out in no-man's-land and decided to call up a tank to rescue him. Beimler himself went out ten or eleven yards behind the tank and was approaching the man when the enemy opened up, a hail of bullets whipped round the tank and Beimler fell, clutching at his heart. Behind him Louis Fischer and a man called Richard rushed up to help Beimler. He simply gasped three times in quick succession 'Go forward! Go forward! Go forward!' and then he suddenly stiffened and within a few seconds fell back dead.[1]

[1] Lise Lindbaeck, *Bataljon Thaelmann*, p. 128.

This was a terrible blow to the Thaelmann. Beimler had been with them almost from the start and he knew every surviving member from the early days of the centuria as he might have known his own family. They carried his body into Madrid next day, and scores of Spaniards, Germans, Italians, Czechs, English and Americans attended a memorial meeting in what had been the Royalty Cinema, with banners lowered over his coffin. General Miaja made a short, moving speech which concluded with the words: 'Your dead are also our dead. Hans Beimler died fighting as he lived fighting. In him the International Workers' Movement has lost a great comrade.'[1]

[1] *Le Volontaire de la liberté*, December 1936.

Chapter 10

The American Battalion

THE formation of a completely American battalion of the International Brigade took several months. The first large contingent, which followed the earlier and smaller scattered groups of volunteers, left New York on Saturday, 26 December 1936 at three o'clock one crisp, sunny day, travelling handsomely in the new French liner S.S. *Normandie*. The first and tourist class cabins were only half-filled but the third class included 96 Americans, mostly in their twenties, many of them crossing the Atlantic for the first time. These men were volunteers in a different sense from many other nationalities. They were not refugees and they had not been driven out of America by a ruthless dictatorship. None the less, two days out from Le Havre the ship's news bulletin published an item which worried them.

'Chairman McReynolds of the House Foreign Affairs Committee declared he would urge the Department of Justice to apply the section of the criminal code providing a $3,000 dollar fine or a year in prison for enlistment of Americans in a foreign war.'

Nothing came of this threat and when the *Normandie* finally docked at Le Havre the 96 men slipped away into France, survived the hazards of crossing the Pyrenees and arrived at Albacete on 6 January. By four o'clock on 8 January they piled into Russian trucks and roared off to Villanueva de la Jara, near Albacete, now the centre for American volunteers, and training began in earnest. More and more Americans from many parts of the States continued to pour into Villanueva de la Jara over the next few weeks, until the original 96 totalled over 400 men.

Training had now developed from a few makeshift rifles and machine-guns, with a handful of bohemian instructors, into a fully-fledged intensive course which made only one concession to Spanish civilian living – the siesta. Equipment from many parts of the world had flowed into Republican Spain and the days of ancient guns and dud ammunition were done. For the next five weeks, the machine-gun and hand-grenade practice, the technique of tackling tanks with petrol bombs and half a dozen new and cunning ways of containing an aggressive enemy were instilled into raw volunteers, many of whom, once again, had never fired a rifle before.

Five weeks . . . in terms of modern army training it was absurdly short, but if Franco had momentarily abandoned the direct assault on Madrid, he was now launching a series of attacks in an attempt to cut the supply roads and encircle the capital. The state of emergency was no less intense. Robert Hale Merriman, twenty-eight-year-old, six-foot-two son of a lumberjack father and writer-mother, now came into the picture. A one-time graduate of Nevada University he was studying in Europe when the Spanish war broke out and he at once hurried off to Spain, offered his services to the International Brigade and exploited his R.O.T.C. experience to train the growing American battalion. When he first arrived he found the Americans in a turmoil, with a grievance committee already established. 'There wasn't even a semblance of military organization. The military commander arrested the political commissar. The political commissar in turn arrested the military commander.'[1] A former seaman, James Harris, claimed wide military experience and when Merriman was appointed a staff officer he received instructions to build up Harris as Commander. Meanwhile a man called Stamber became political commissar.

Together these three men made such a good job of drilling and training the new battalion that a demonstration of military manœuvres was prepared for none other than the great André Marty. However, 'just before the manœuvre a row developed between the commanders of Companies One and Two and they both threatened to arrest each other.'[2]

Despite personal friction, the manœuvre was a success, and Marty and his generals were so pleased with the Americans that they granted them the privilege of being the first to occupy the new model camp for the International Brigades which had just been completed at Pozo Rubio.

[1] Sandor Voros, *American Commissar*, p. 349.   [2] Ibid., p. 353.

On 15 February, their brief training interlude over, the Lincoln Brigade received orders to proceed to Albacete en route for an unknown battle-front. James Harris and Merriman led the way to the famous bull-ring, and they listened to a rousing speech from André Marty by the light of a single electric-light bulb which swung to and fro in the wind, over their heads, throwing weird shadows across their faces. Immediately afterwards twenty men were detailed to haul huge cases from the bowels of half a dozen lorries, and rifles, still reeking from packing grease, cartridges – a hundred and fifty rounds to each man – steel helmets, belts and bandoliers were distributed. The men laughed and joked as they settled the equipment round shoulders and waist, and once more clambered back on to huge trucks.

Harris had become steadily more unnerved as departure time approached and now he began grabbing rifles out of men's hands, saying wildly that he was a rifle inspector. The men thought he was drunk and Commissar Stamber finally took a strong line and ordered Harris – not to be arrested, or to be taken off to the guard-room – but to be put to bed! Harris went quietly at first, but came back again, fired off his pistol in the Guardia Nacional and disappeared once more.

Finally, those who were near enough to Lucien Vidal, the 'Spanish' Commander of the International Brigade base, saw him walk smartly up to Merriman in the bull-ring, salute, and say: 'Good. You know your orders. Go to.' Those orders quickly carried them to the village of Chinchon, which overlooked the rich, rolling Jarama valley.

By January of 1937 the situation around Madrid had improved for the Republicans. Now under the sole leadership of General Miaja, freed from the political intervention of the War Office, trade unions and political parties, the Army was a much more effective fighting force. Colonel Rojo, Miaja's Chief of Staff, had developed a strong defensive line from a point ten miles south-east to the Escorial, and twenty-five miles northwest of Madrid. Hastily dug entrenchments interlocked with natural mountain defences to form a thirty-five-mile barrier with its weakest point on the eastern sector round Guadalajara where the militia were still ill-trained.

Two alternatives faced General Franco. He could sweep

round Madrid and strike at the weakest point, Guadalajara, 'cutting under the northern mountain barrier and approaching Madrid from the east, or retrieve his original error of November and surround Madrid by an attack south of the city. He had, by the end of January, plenty of troops to carry out both operations at once. . . . If he had made this double offensive it is unlikely that the Republican lines could have held. Madrid would not in all probability have been entered rapidly by Franco's forces, but it would have been surrounded and starved out.'[1]

Instead, a clash of opinion between the German and Italian strategists who were now not merely supplying troops, but taking a close interest in every Nationalist manœuvre, led to a dissipation of strength. Franco knew the tough determination of the Madrilenos and the International Brigades in the Madrid area, and he chose to give the new Italian troops an easy victory on the far-off Malaga front rather than break their spirit against the iron walls of Madrid. It was said, at the time, that the Germans 'who were arming and controlling his attack on Madrid would not tolerate Italian interference'[2] and Franco found easy work for them elsewhere.

At all events, by 6 February the Italians were successfully driving on to Malaga and simultaneously German tanks on the Madrid front struck up the Jarama river towards the key Arganda bridge which carried the Madrid–Valencia road over the river. Five mobile brigades, each battalion including many Moors, began the offensive, and the brigade commanded by García Escamez quickly overran the advance elements of the Republican 18th Brigade. By the following day, General Barron drove down to the junction of the Manzanares and Jarama rivers which brought the Madrid–Valencia highway under fire, and made the threat of encircling Madrid perceptibly more real.

Taken by surprise, the Republican forces were further confused by the presence of a number of new brigades within their ranks organized for attack and now faced with the threat of a full-scale retreat. By 8 February drastic action to check the Nationalist advance became necessary and Miaja first sent the Lister and El Campesino Brigades to support General Pozas,

---

[1] Tom Wintringham, *English Captain*, p. 142.   [2] Ibid., p. 143.

the Republican commander of the Army of the Centre, and
then ordered up the XIth International Brigade, now re-formed
and consisting of the Edgar André and Thaelmann Battalions.

A swift reorganization of Republican positions on 9 February
also brought up the XIIth International Brigade, now mainly
drawn from Italians of the Garibaldi Battalion. The newly
formed XIVth International Brigade, which included the
French André Marty Battalion, had a number of men stationed
as sentries at the Pindoque bridge from which began the dramatic events of the night of 10 February. A handful of Moroccans,
skilled in the arts of stealthy night tactics and sudden murder,
wriggled their way silently towards the Pindoque bridge, came
up behind the French sentries, knifed them and sent back
swift signals to two regiments of Nationalist cavalry. It was a
staggering indictment of the training and efficiency of International Brigade sentries, but worse was to follow. Some
terrible inadequacy in the mines laid to blow up the bridge
resulted, when the plunger was fired, in the bridge buckling a
few feet into the air and descending more or less intact at the
same spot. Whereupon the first regiment of Nationalist cavalry
made a spectacular ride into the heart of the Republicans'
lines.

Simultaneously another attack was launched at the Arganda
bridge, and combined bombing and machine-gunning could not
stop the Nationalists' capturing the bridge and beginning a
steady build-up, until by the early afternoon a whole brigade
was across. A head-on clash with the André Marty Battalion
followed. The French fought desperately, outnumbered and
outgunned, but six hours later they dug in and refused to retreat
any further. Such was the ferocity of their resistance that Barron
slackened the head-on attack, pushed round either flank and
surrounded the remainder of the battalion. A terrible slaughter
followed, with the surviving Frenchmen steadily firing on and
on among piles of dead and wounded until their ammunition
gave out and they were completely at the mercy of the Moors.
Barron ordered the Moorish cavalry in to finish them off, and
one by one the Frenchmen were cut to pieces with a mere handful of twenty men successfully surrendering to become prisoners.

Undismayed by the fate of the André Marty Battalion, the
Slav Dabrowsky Battalion now held the line before Arganda

and fought with equal ferocity. Meanwhile the Garibaldi Battalion went into action and brought the Pindoque bridgehead under such fierce fire that the advance first slowed, and then, with vicious casualties mounting, came to a standstill. The attack on yet another bridge at San Maria de la Vega was held by a hail of machine-gun fire, but late the same night a Moroccan Tabor once more slid silently through the night to knife the Spanish sentries with astonishing ease, and again the spectacle of the Pindoque bridge repeated itself.

In the struggle which followed the new XVth International Brigade came into action for the first time, commanded by Colonel Gal, a man of Hungarian birth who had become a naturalized Russian. Everyone seemed to hate Gal. Thomas describes him as incompetent and bad-tempered. Bert Levy wanted to lynch him.[1] No less than 25 nations contributed volunteers to this most polyglot XVth Brigade, but the first battalion was made up largely of Englishmen with some Americans, an Abyssinian, sixty London Cypriots and an Australian. There were three other battalions in the brigade, the Dimitrov Battalion with 750 men from Balkan countries, the Franco-Belgian Battalion with 800 French and Belgians and the new Abraham Lincoln Battalion with 500 Americans and a number of Negroes of several nationalities.

It was this Abraham Lincoln Battalion which came down the Chinchon road on 12 February after its farcical five weeks' training period, led by Major Merriman who had taken Harris's place. Very aware of its inadequacies, almost at once Merriman asked permission to carry out a manœuvre which would have seemed absurd to any other commander or any other army. He wanted the battalion to pause on its way to the front in order to fire off five rounds into the hills for the very simple reason that this was the only shooting practice at least half the battalion had experienced. The tiny exercise was duly carried out. Major Merriman then informed his 427 men that they were moving off the following afternoon and proceeding northwestwards towards Morata de Tajuña along a road under machine-gun, artillery and rifle fire, where they might, at any

[1] Letter to author.

moment, encounter the real, live, vicious enemy in the shape of a set of particularly bloodthirsty Moors.

The convoy of forty-five trucks set off down the winding, narrow road between the hills, moving very slowly because the road was crowded with troops and equipment and every so often a stalled or broken lorry, a wrecked gun, made detours necessary. There were great water splashes to be negotiated which threatened to drench everyone, the result of an implacably indifferent peasantry who continued to irrigate and tend the land in the face of bombing and machine-gunning. Crops were more vital to life and death than bullets, and if some peasants occasionally stood in the fields gaping at the mad foreigners traversing their land for some ideal beyond their comprehension, as many shrugged their shoulders and turned back to work as raised gnarled fists in the clenched Republican salute. Fundamentally the peasants hated troop movements because they brought bombing and machine-gunning and now, as the afternoon gave place to evening, the Lincolns underwent their first real baptism of fire.

On the outskirts of Morata, in the middle of a meal, the rebel planes came over, the battalion scattered, and each man went down flat against the earth as a hail of bullets tore up the soil in all directions, with the occasional roar of a bomb. The sheer noise of the explosions, the enormous size of the aeroplanes' machine-gun bullets and the white-hot flying shrapnel dismayed many a raw volunteer. Against explicit instructions one youngster turned over on his back and could not resist taking a flying and hopeless shot at the planes. A few minutes later Republican fighters were cheered as they came sweeping across the sky to tackle the enemy. Spectacularly, two of the Nationalists were brought screaming earthwards in flames and in the end this first encounter with 'live war' was reassuring. As Edwin Rolfe remarked: 'They would have been even more heartened had they known that the pilot of one of the . . . chasers was an American named Ben Leider.'[1]

Back in their trucks once more, the battalion moved off again and at the next cross-roads Merriman entered a hut which represented Brigade H.Q. to report to a staff officer. Suddenly he discovered behind the muddy, dishevelled person confronting

[1] Edwin Rolfe, *The Lincoln Battalion*, p. 33.

him a man he had last seen, in the tradition of the romantic
Hollywood film, playing Chopin and wearing a dandified
uniform in a café at Albacete. Trauslitz was an Austrian by
birth and now held the rank of captain on the XVth Brigade's
staff. The reunion proved effusive but brief. More important
matters needed attention.

As the swift darkness came down, the American convoy
turned off across a railroad track, and began climbing a hill
with strict instructions from Trauslitz to keep all lights out, to
move with the utmost caution and not even to risk whistling. It
seemed idiotic because convoys moving in both directions
created a tremendous roar. Republican tanks were pouring
back in the opposite direction towards their base near Morata,
and the young Spanish and Russian faces in the open turrets,
cheerful, dirty and smeared with oil, gave a new lift to the
Americans. The tanks were travelling at speed and the mechani-
cal cavalcade rolling by with such assurance conveyed a great
sense of power and confidence.

It suffered a setback in the next few hours. An enemy machine-
gun found the range of the H.Q. hut and began firing one
burst after another. In between one hail of bullets and the next,
the Lincolns dashed across the road, and slowly closed in on
what was to become known as Suicide Hill.

When they at last arrived on the scene at Jarama, a savage
battle had been in progress for several days. On the night of
11 February the enemy had concentrated ten thousand men
east of the Jarama river and launched an attack with heavy
artillery support which carried them towards San Martin de
la Vega and overran Hill 694. Throughout 12 February,
fierce fighting raged around Hill 694 and the Pindoque bridge,
until the Nationalists, by sheer weight of numbers and superiority of artillery, took the ford of San Martin de la Vega and
pushed on towards Pingarrón Hill. Once more the advance
was stopped at Arganda and Hill 620 by Republican forces
which included the British, Thaelmann, Franco-Belge and
Dimitrov Battalions.

Fighting on 14 February reached a new pitch of intensity.
Twenty-six thousand men with thirty tanks and an elaborate
artillery barrage attempted to dislodge the XVth International
Brigade from Hill 620, by concentrating enormous pressure on a

front of four miles. The rebels threw in everything they had with the one idea of creating a break-through which would weaken resistance in the many surviving strong-points, and with casualties mounting at a very high rate they succeeded in penetrating in the direction of Morata and forced the Republicans to withdraw three kilometres to the east.

It was now the Republicans' turn to counter-attack and the XVth International Brigade once more went in with great bravery, bringing the advance to a momentary standstill. Observers claimed at this point that the Republicans had destroyed 21 enemy planes and wreaked such havoc among Franco's Moroccan troops that forty per cent were out of action, but still they came on, and the final attempt to reach Morata began on the 15th. Once they reached the Jarama river to the south of Morata, the Nationalists' right flank would be safe, but each wave of the new attack was first smothered and then stemmed until the situation reached an uneasy stalemate.

Two sequels were now possible: an interlude for rest and recuperation before the attack began yet again, or a powerful Republican counter-attack which would finally break the impetus of the advance. On 23 February the Lincoln Brigade took up position near Morata, to replace the XXIVth Spanish Brigade and on the same day went into the attack. Their first rush carried them down the slope of their own hill and up again, until they reached a ridge immediately below the Fascist troops. Paul Burns was one of those in the front line of the attack and he has described how No. 1 Company advanced 'over a field dotted by occasional olive trees with only the scant shelter of vineyards. . . . Given a withered grapevine, a mound of earth, or the more pretentious shelter of an olive tree, and the boys dug in and opened fire on the Fascist lines. . . .

'A few yards away in a little hollow of earth was Captain John Scott and with him Frank Flaherty, one of the three Flaherty brothers of Boston, who distinguished themselves by their heroic service and leadership under fire. . . .

'The infantry continued the advance. Explosive bullets split the air and the machine-gun bursts raked the field. From behind a row of trees the Fascists increased their fire.

'Captain Scott, rising, had only time to shout, "Continue the advance!" when he fell with three bullets in his body.'[1]

Darkness came down on a scene of confusion and bloody carnage. No. 1 Company had advanced 500 metres under withering fire, but No. 2 Company was checked and temporarily pinned down. A direct hit set one of the Lincoln tanks ablaze and as the eerie flicker of flames grew, it lit the surrounding area and made the silhouettes of crouched figures a perfect target for snipers. As the order came for No. 2 Company to move away from that area, a call went out for volunteers to carry spades up to the far-advanced No. 1 Company.

A man named Joe Gordon has left a record of what followed. It was a fiercely cold night but sweat dripped from Gordon's body as he alternately ran a few yards carrying two shovels, crouched low, dropped close to the earth, scrabbled at it as bullets whipped dangerously close and then rose again to run on once more. As he came to his feet for the third time he suddenly discovered that he no longer knew, in the darkness, where the Fascist lines lay. Blundering on, he presently bumped into one man after another until he dimly recognized the voice of someone in No. 1 Company. He delivered his shovels and dropped to earth again panting, and then he heard a hoarse whisper that John Scott the commander was lying just ahead badly wounded. He crawled slowly forward, sweat still pouring down inside his uniform, and came upon Scott and Bill Henry who was now acting-commander of No. 1 Company. Scott lay flat on his stomach with his right arm under him, his head twisted sideways. Bill Henry was pushing dirt in front of Scott's head to give him some protection. At every move he drew fire. . . .

'I moved over to Scott. "How do you feel?" I asked him. With his left hand he took hold of one of mine. No pressure. I could feel his strength ebbing slowly away. "I'm all right", he answered. He continued to hold my hand. I then told him I would go back and bring aid; he squeezed my hand hard for a few minutes and said: "Don't do it, it's a waste of time."

' "What the hell do you mean, waste of time?" I answered. "You're a human being, ain't you, and besides you're Captain

<hr />

[1] Edwin Rolfe, *The Lincoln Battalion*, p. 41.

Scott, see, and besides Joe Strysand will never talk to you again if you died." [1]

Strysand was Scott's runner and they were devoted to one another.

Joe Gordon did not go straight back but crawled sideways under terrible bursts of fire, until a series of short sprints carried him to the first-aid station. 'Captain Scott's wounded and dying', he yelled. 'Where's a stretcher!' The first-aid men simply gaped at him. Suddenly he realized that these men were French and Dutch and did not understand a word he was saying. It took him several minutes to find someone who spoke English and then he set out with two stretcher-bearers and a dead-white canvas stretcher to bring in Scott. The stretcher proved a menace. Machine-gun fire followed its white ghost until they were forced to leave the road and begin crawling through the dirt. The fire increased. Terrified, one stretcher-bearer suddenly refused to go any further, but the other drew a gun and forced him on.

They reached Scott, hauled him groaning on to the stretcher, and began to move back again. They were close to the road once more when a terrific burst of fire wounded everyone except Gordon. He set off alone to get help muttering to himself, 'What a hell of a situation. You go after one wounded man – and look at this mess.' The fire increased to a brutal hail of destruction and momentarily he fell flat on his face, rooted to the spot. He hoped the fire would subside but it did not, and then he knew what he had learnt from hard experience – if he stayed in the same spot he would get it, some time soon, anyway. Pushing himself along with hands and feet, not daring to raise his body, he crawled a few yards and suddenly began to vomit from fear as a slash of bullets ran close to his face. Then he found a dead soldier, dripping blood, wrapped his own body in a curve alongside the corpse and used the human flesh as bulwark against the bullets. 'Soaked with his blood, which continued running, I don't know how long I lay. I'm sure he saved my life. I was almost afraid to breathe lest I sniff in a bullet.'[1]

In the end, after what seemed a lifetime, they brought Scott back to the first-aid station, but by then he was groaning terribly and there didn't seem much they could do.

*   *   *

[1] *The Book of the XV Brigade*, p. 78.   [1] Ibid., p. 80.

The American attack had failed. That became clear in a very few hours. Many reasons were given, from the difficulties of launching such an action in semi-darkness to the lack of flank support, but few mentioned the appalling fire-power of the enemy, his readiness to suffer heavy casualties, and for that matter, his bravery under attack. Nor did they talk very much about another episode with their crazy ex-commander James Harris. Merriman had been summoned to the presence of Colonel Klaus, Chief of Staff of the Brigade, when Harris suddenly reappeared from nowhere, at the front, and announced, in Merriman's absence that he had been ordered to take over command once more. According to Sandor Voros he proceeded to take No. 2 Company out into no-man's-land, and wander round in great confusion under heavy machine-gun fire. 'As the night progressed Harris became delirious, and he told the men he saw 50,000 Fascists ready to attack.' Merriman, warned by a runner of the reappearance of Harris, came back to the front post-haste and had Harris taken away in an ambulance. This happened on 22 February.

By 27 February the British Battalion had moved up to take over the Franco-Belgian trenches now representing the front line, and the Lincoln Battalion, already with many savage gaps in its ranks, was placed in reserve. The Americans found themselves settled in a number of shallow new trenches to the right of the English, and subject to sniping which, within a few hours, killed the first American Negro volunteer, a painter called Alonzo Watson.

On the morning of the 27th a swift briefing of company commanders and commissars revealed the overall plan for a new attack which was intended, this time, to overwhelm the enemy trenches and drive the rebels back not only towards, but finally across, the Jarama river. The Spanish XXIVth Brigade was dug in to the right of, but some distance behind, the Americans, and the first part of the plan aimed to straighten the line.

Zero hour was 7 a.m. In a misty morning, with uncertain light, the Americans opened fire and heard the crackle of the Spanish XXIVth Brigade's guns. Five minutes later the Spaniards went over the top, but a hail of fire quickly brought their advance to a standstill. Another attempt by the Spaniards at 9.30 also failed to advance more than a few score yards. Brigade H.Q. now telephoned Captain Merriman ordering the Lincoln Battalion into the attack. Merriman could clearly see from his field H.Q. why the Spaniards had been brought to a standstill. There was no question of lack of courage. They had simply entered a murderous hail of lead with insufficient covering fire and it proved paralysing to the boldest spirits. Merriman protested to H.Q. that if the Lincolns went into the attack now, while the still-unstraightened line made it impossible for the XXIVth Brigade to draw the enemy's fire or provide cover, the result would be disastrous. H.Q. said it had to be done. Merriman said the enemy fire would become impassable. H.Q. replied that there was no alternative. Merriman said it would cause a terrible and useless slaughter. H.Q. replied that the order remained an order and argument must stop. Merriman crashed down the telephone and turned to his second-in-command, Douglas Seacord.

'It's murder,' he said 'but it's got to be done.'

At twelve o'clock he gave the order to attack and five hundred men, sixty of them raw recruits who had only arrived the night before, went over the top. Merriman led his men with a great cry 'Forward and smash 'em!' and almost at once a bullet hit him in the left shoulder, spinning him round. Direct enemy fire from straight ahead was crossed by fierce fire from a fortified hill to the right, and in this forest of criss-crossing lead man after man went down.

A young rifleman involved in the action wrote: 'Group after group hopped the trenches, charging the Fascists who were only 250 metres away. . . . Bullets strayed in our direction . . . crossfire from many machine-guns created an impenetrable steel wall against our advance. More groups and sections went over. Soon the calls for first aid came, first singly, then louder and insistently. Many were wounded just as they climbed the parapet to go over. Many wounded men crawled back to the trenches safely, but many others were killed in the attempt.'[1]

Douglas Seacord, following Merriman over the top, was shot dead almost at once, and casualties continued to multiply at an appalling rate. John McCrotty, an Irish-Catholic minister, Robert Walk, Clyde Lenway, Dan Haskell, Maurice Jelin,

[1] Edwin Rolfe, *The Lincoln Battalion*, p. 55.

Joseph Campbell, and many other young men still in their twenties, went down and died in the first wave of the attack. Slowly it became evident that Merriman's words were only too true. This was murder. Men with the kind of courage which made the Light Brigade an immortal part of history had dashed into a forest of death, and as their first impetus wavered and broke, there were those who died trying to drag back the wounded, those bewildered because it had seemed such an overwhelming certainty that they must prevail, others exhausted, bitter, wounded, crawling back to their trenches as the rain began. From noon, far into the afternoon groups of men rallied, fought on, dug in, rallied again, tried to go forward and were beaten back. Towards evening, with the rain increasing, many men had returned to their original trenches, exhausted, cold, cynical because the whole attack had been turned into a fiasco. Others lying out in shell-holes, dug in behind tiny piles of earth, heard the soft silken rain steadily increase until it was beating into the earth, and prayed that the obliterating darkness would come down quickly and give them a chance to crawl back to the muddy walls of a trench which spoke of warmth and comfort, in comparative safety. Away in an adjacent position another newly formed battalion, also alive with raw recruits, had similarly left their trenches and gone into battle only to fall back with dead and wounded multiplying – the British Battalion. That night both battalions realized that the rainy season had begun as the icy winds came across the Guadarrama and blew down their trenches like the cold breath of death.

Chapter 11

The British Battalion

THE call had long before gone out in Britain for a complete British battalion to replace the two small volunteer groups which had performed such heroic feats with the French and Germans, and during November and December 1936 nearly four hundred British volunteers arrived at the training centre in Madrigueras. They underwent the usual short, sharp instruction and then an odd mixture of Madrid veterans and raw recruits, of case-hardened types like George Nathan and gangling boys like John Croston, 145 selected men, came together to form the first small British company. Among them were Jock Cunningham, Joe Hinks, John Cornford, and Sam Lesser, names destined to become well known in Brigade history.

On that cold, star-lit Christmas Eve of 1936 they set out for the Madrigueras railway station with the immaculate George Nathan swinging his swagger stick ahead of them, and put up a fine show of disciplined marching. Merging at the station with the 12th (French) Battalion of the XIVth Brigade, they entrained for Andújar and the Córdoba front.

Almost at once they went into action. 'On the evening of their arrival,' William Rust, editor of the *Daily Worker* wrote, 'the Battalion deployed to occupy firing positions, and fighting started, but on the familiar lines of physical courage against modern weapons. No. 1 Company's machine-guns were twenty-year-old Chauchots, the majority of which jammed at the first shot. The rifles were even older, Austrian Steyrs, which, for the lack of the special ammunition clips which should accompany them, had to be used as single-shot guns. Even then many blew up in the firers' hands.'[1]

Hopelessly equipped as they were, No. 1 Company went into the attack and actually succeeded in occupying a crest on

[1] William Rust, *Britons in Spain*, p. 26.

the outskirts of Lopera, only to be thrown back in a few hours among the surrounding olive groves. On 29 December, this time with artillery support, the whole 12th French Battalion once more went over to the offensive in a vain attempt to encircle Lopera. The British No. 1 Company was bombed, shelled and machine-gunned with everything the enemy had, and after six hours of bloody fighting, mounting casualties made it clear to Captain Nathan that there was only one thing left to do – 'Retreat by sections', he shouted, 'and keep firing.' There was some confusion as No. 1 Company tried to carry out this order and then Nathan's voice rang out again, 'Dress your files! Retire in proper formation!'

It was the classic situation for endangering morale, and many men in more than reasonable fear were hurrying back faster than their fellows. Nathan's words pulled them up, they recovered their section formations and retired in the good order prescribed by the military textbook. It was, above all, a wonderful exhibition of cool leadership by George Nathan.

The story of George Nathan was destined to grow into a legend sometimes embellished far beyond the truth, but never exaggerating the sheer colour and variety of his life. As a soldier in the First World War, he had risen to the rank of company sergeant-major, and in 1918 he became the only Jewish officer in the Brigade of Guards. There, by sheer hard work and careful listening, he gradually acquired an English upper-class accent which was indistinguishable from the real thing, but if he showed a reasonable pride in his accent he never, when challenged, concealed his origins. He resigned his commission following a fierce argument in the officers' mess about the inadequacy of privates' pay, and for long periods in the 1920s he joined the ranks of unemployed outside London Labour Exchanges. One interlude saw him dressed in a commissionaire's uniform, playing the role of doorman at the big store, Peter Jones. Tom Wintringham has developed the picture of him:

'Rather gaunt, long-nosed, carrying his thin head and good shoulders well, he looked a soldier: but his mixture of military and civilian clothes, his sweater and cheap shoes, made him also look like a hard-luck story from a queue of unemployed. And that is what he had been not long before he came to Spain.

Since the Great War he had worked at many jobs and been unlucky at most. . . . He had been a hobo in Canada, and he had been a butcher in one of the flaring South London streets where the trams clatter and yelp. He was disillusioned and hard-bitten. . . . He had always kept clear of politics. . . . It was not so much his political views which had brought him to Spain as a certain alertness and aliveness that could not be crushed out by the Labour Exchange and the hopeless monotony of odd jobs. An adventurer? No: he was not "on the make". He was remaking himself, climbing out of the pit of worklessness so that he could be proud again of being George Nathan. He was sometimes conceited: "That's not George Nathan's way, my lad!" he would say.'[1]

Also in No. 1 Company were two distinguished intellectuals, Ralph Fox, the Political Commissar, a thin, ascetic young man who wore a deerstalker cap, and John Cornford, who had taken part in the early Madrid battles. Cornford had written to Margot Heinemann on the preceding 21 November:

'There's little enough else to say. Everyone here is very tired by the cold nights, often sleepless, a bit shaken and upset by our losses, depressed. And it's affected me a bit though I'm getting a thick skin. If I'd written a few hours ago you'd have got a different kind of letter. For five weeks I scarcely missed you, everything was so new and different and I couldn't write but formal letters. Now I am beginning to wake up a bit and I'm glad as I could be that the last few days I had with you were as good as they could be. I re-read your letter to me yester-day and I was proud as hell. . . . I don't know what's going to happen but I do know we're in for a tough time. And I am glad that you are behind me, glad and proud. The losses here are heavy, but there's still a big chance of getting back alive, a big majority chance. And if I didn't we can't help that. Be happy darling. . . .'[2]

And then on 8 December came a letter which neither he nor Margot Heinemann knew would be the last:

'Well, one day the war will end – I'd give it till June or July and then if I'm alive I'm coming back to you. I think about you often, but there's nothing I can do but say again,

[1] Tom Wintringham, *English Captain*, p. 66.
[2] *John Cornford*, ed. Pat Sloan, p. 238.

be happy darling. And I'll see you again one day. Bless you. John.'

The No. 1 British Company went up to face the biggest offensive launched against the Escorial road on 29 December. They took up position in a barn with their guns carefully trained to meet any counter-attack, and all day watched the ebb and flow of battle as the XIVth Brigade infantry attacked, retreated and counter-attacked in quick succession, with the enemy fire becoming more powerful as their forces were concentrated. When the Brigaders made their last retreat at sundown, Jock Cunningham, an ex-army sergeant, handsome, tough, energetic and destined to play a steadily more important role in the British Battalion, remarked sourly: 'Now we're for it – they'll attack tomorrow at dawn.'

Bernard Knox has written this description of what followed: 'The storm burst as John [Cornford] was taking us up to relieve a Spanish machine-gun post. We found ourselves under fire from the heights which we were meant to relieve, and a few minutes later, as we squeezed and strained ourselves into the earth, the remains of our front line came crawling back pointing up and shouting excitedly "Los fascistas, los fascistas". As if we didn't know. There was nothing for it but to go back and hold a line in front of the village. So back we went and how we covered that four hundred yards I shall never know. One of us . . . was repeating slowly to himself "Even when you have to retreat, do not run." And so we walked, dragging the guns over the ploughed land, that crumbled as the bullets hit it.'[1]

And then it was that two bullets singled out first John Cornford and then Ralph Fox, and they both died.

No. 1 Company of the British Battalion retired from the front line after nearly a month of fighting, but the bearded, exhausted little group which marched back into Madrigueras was sadly depleted. The bands played, a guard of honour lined the streets, men, women and children cheered and Nathan, always the brilliant opportunist, embraced a little girl who came up to greet him, and hand-in-hand with her, he led the dirty, bedraggled company down the main street. Impossibly, among all the

[1] *John Cornford*, ed. Pat Sloan, p. 193.

dirt and confusion, Nathan's boots were once more polished, his swagger stick swinging, his step alert, and but for the beard, a straggling, bristling beard, and haggard cheeks, he did not look so very different from the day, one month before, when he led No. 1 Company out to war. There was one other all-important difference. Of the 145 men who had marched away only 67 now remained. Not that death had overtaken 78 men. A high proportion were wounded.

By now, 600 Englishmen were undergoing intensive training at Madrigueras and the 1st English Battalion had begun to be something more than a vague blueprint in the mind of a Comintern bureaucrat. A number of men who had rebelled against life in the British Navy and been discharged distinguished themselves in the growing battalion. Men born to be leaders at a lower level of command, there was some evidence that the Royal Navy had not given them – whether for reasons of snobbery, obtuseness or tradition – the right opportunities, but now, in the raffish atmosphere of a people's army, they came into their own. Alternatively, men who were misfits in conventional society successfully solved their personal problems in a more bohemian organization with the avowed purpose of challenging what they regarded as the Fascists who had rejected them in civilian life. Sam Wild, who once worked on the lower deck of the Navy, became Battalion Armourer in the Brigade and one year later took over command. Fred Copeman, an ex-able seaman who had led the Invergordon mutiny, quickly rose to high rank. Yet another mutineer – Jock Cunningham – who had started 'trouble' in the Argyll and Sutherland Highlanders in Jamaica and been sentenced to several years in the glasshouse – became, in time, a battalion commander. Tom Johnson also began life as a Royal Naval Marine. Extraordinarily, Johnson, Copeman and Wild each made their separate ways to Spain, but all had served in the same ship, H.M.S. *Resolution*. They went on to serve together in the Jarama battles, and as Sam Wild eventually remarked, 'We woke up together in the same hospital at Alicante.'

By the end of January the British Battalion, now composed of four companies and auxiliary units, was at last roughly ready – after the hasty tradition of the Brigades – for action.

Tom Wintringham summoned its six hundred members to the dreary theatre billet in Madrigueras, which always had 'the sour smell of a badly kept stable', to deliver a final speech in January 1937. 'In a very short time we shall be going to the front. I cannot tell you ... whereabouts we shall be sent because I don't know. Wherever our first action takes place it will almost certainly seem to us a bit of a muddle ... wars always do. ... Let me sum up the job that the International Brigade can do and is doing in this war. It can help in the holding of Madrid. So long as Franco fails to take Madrid he is losing the war. Secondly it can hold other parts of the line as the third of our brigades is doing now while the new Spanish Army is trained and equipped and got really ready behind our trenches. I have put these two holding jobs first because this war is, for us, still mainly defensive, still the sort of job that the French did at Verdun in the Great War – holding and going on holding until the enemy are worn out. The third job we have is to carry out "pushes" at places where Franco does not expect us ... the aim being not so much to capture this position or that, as to keep his reserves busy and frighten him from stringing out his army too thinly. That is what our Second Brigade did south of Madrid and what our Fourth Brigade has just been doing a long way from Madrid near Cordova in the south. .... But the important thing, over all, is not our success in doing these jobs but our example.'[1]

The day before the English Battalion was due to leave for the front, unexpected trouble blew up. André Marty had now revealed a pathological preoccupation with spies and a readiness to shoot people which ill accorded with the ideals of a people's army. He called a conference of the whole battalion, now including a rumbustious Irish section under the leadership of Frank Ryan, and made an endless, detailed speech, which quickly bored the Irish. Towards the end Ryan came to his feet to complain bitterly of the political treatment meted out to the Irish section. Marty tried to call him to order but Ryan ploughed solidly on. Someone bawled at Ryan to sit down and a number of Irish responded with cheers for Ryan. Marty shouted louder

[1] Tom Wintringham, *English Captain*, pp. 138–9.

than anyone else in a last attempt to silence him, and when this failed, he literally screamed an order at Ryan: 'Sit down or be arrested.' Never gifted with very good hearing, Ryan 'continued in better spirit than before with the lusty help of some of the Irish, American, Canadian and British delegates'.

Marty gave a swift order to one of his aides and four guards detached themselves from the platform, hurried through the crowd and put Ryan under arrest. The meeting, which included some of the most famous figures in the Brigade, continued in an atmosphere charged with tension. Later that night bands of Irishmen, armed to the teeth, went to the guard-room demanding Ryan's release only to find that he had been freed two hours before.

Fresh trouble developed over Wilfred Macartney, commander of the British Battalion. According to Fred Copeman, the Party leadership could not quite countenance a non-Communist leading the battalion in its first action, and a conflict between efficiency and political beliefs reached a point where it was privately indicated to Macartney that he might perhaps stand down in favour of a Party member, but he refused to consider the idea. On the very morning the battalion was due to leave, the commissars summoned a meeting of brigade leaders and Macartney was brought post-haste to headquarters by official car. The Political Commissar of the British Battalion, accompanied him, and somehow on the brief journey a gun went off accidentally and Macartney was wounded. According to George Aitken, they were unaccustomed to handling guns and when Macartney turned over his Colt as an insignia of relinquished office the accident occurred. It led to the result desired by the Party hierarchy, since Macartney had to go to hospital and Tom Wintringham, a card-carrying Communist, took command. The Scot, Jock Cunningham, became his deputy and Kit Conway, an Irishman, commander of No. 1 Company.

According to Mrs Wintringham – Tom Wintringham's widow – the story ran very differently. Her husband, the Political Commissar and Macartney were all sitting in a room at H.Q. when the Commissar began fiddling with a gun, saying playfully – 'It isn't loaded.' Next minute, the gun went off accidentally and Macartney was wounded in the elbow. The following morning he sought out Mrs Wintringham and she tried to persuade three new nurses to treat what had become a very painful wound. Since they were entirely fresh to Spain and had not yet established a first-aid post, much to Mrs Wintringham's fury, they were reluctant to do this. When, a few days later, Macartney returned to England, he did so not because the Party wanted to get rid of him but because his six months' parole after his prison sentence required him to report back to London.[1]

Nor was this the end of the battalion's troubles. André Marty suddenly drove up to Battalion H.Q. on the morning of the day they were due to leave, and informed the new commander, Tom Wintringham, that all his Lewis guns – now organized as an anti-aircraft unit – should have been transferred to the French Battalion. Why had this not been done? The answer was simple, but Wintringham did not give it. The order for the transfer had arrived by messenger the previous morning, but the men were so furious at the idea of losing guns which they had so lovingly learnt to handle that they swiftly and effectively 'lost' them and reported the strange incident to Wintringham. Some hitch in transport, they elaborated, had probably delivered them to the wrong site. It was a furious André Marty who arrived to inquire into what was plainly a piece of subterfuge, and he now gave some explanation of the necessity for the transfer which satisfied Wintringham who at once demanded that the missing guns be found.

In the event, the apparent idiocy of this decision turned out to be No. 1 Company's salvation, but that was later. The anti-aircraft section, now led by Fred Copeman, received in exchange for six Lewis guns double the number of heavy German Maxims with a very long range. The only immediate snag seemed to be that No. 1 Company had no experience whatever with this type of gun.

And then, at last, one January night, the battalion set out down the winding road into the Morata valley on the Jarama front, and almost at once a series of fires, burning almost aimlessly on the hillsides, gave the impression of action and war. 'Early in the morning we reached a farmhouse and bivouacked in the orange grove opposite. The wind was cold but dry. We could see lines of troops wending their way in single file along

[1] Verbal evidence from Mrs Wintringham.

the edge of the road and up through the foothills.'[1] From the distance came the sound of gunfire.

Colonel Gal had stubbed with a sausage-thick finger at three thick blue lines pencilled on an ancient map where the mountains were shown like brown furry caterpillars and the scale seemed subject to odd caprice. The left-hand line represented the English, he said to Wintringham, the right-hand the French and the centre line the Dimitrov, a battalion of Italians, Czechs, Austrians and Balkans, 'to be held', Colonel Gal grunted, 'in reserve'. Wintringham asked whether there was a map of the area for his own use and received no more than a grunt in reply.[2]

Wintringham hurried down from Brigade H.Q. on the back of a motor-cycle, repeated his orders to Cunningham, Wild and Copeman, and the different British companies moved off. Presently the battalion was 'spread out as its Commander desired', but alas, not for long. Wintringham had watched his men moving into positions in perfect order for some time, when suddenly he heard the roar of a car coming up the track, and there, stepping out of it, was the immaculate figure of George Nathan. Romantic centre of the English Battalion, Captain George Nathan had recently been promoted to major and was now Chief of Staff to the whole XVth Brigade. A man who seemed the living incarnation of the old myth about charmed lives, he appeared, disappeared and reappeared at various parts of the front in his perfectly polished riding-boots, his uniform as near immaculate as he could get it, his hat set at the right angle, his swagger stick swinging, and wherever he went eyes followed the extraordinary figure in such contrast to the rest, a man walking upright under fire and by some miracle escaping what seemed certain death. Brave as a lion and yet a mercenary soldier, non-Communist but prepared to fight to the death with working men, born of lowly parents yet behaving like a Guards' officer, Nathan was already the pride and joy of the British Battalion who never ceased spinning stories of his heroism, luck, audacity. Now as he stepped out of the car,

[1] Fred Copeman, *Reason in Revolt*, p. 86.
[2] Tom Wintringham, *English Captain*, p. 148.

his swagger stick under his arm, he sucked at an empty pipe.

'Your battalion's a bit late, Tom', he said, as if they were part of a dress parade. . . . 'I've told Conway to hurry on and swing left a bit. And I've sent a message through him to O. Get them over to the left, but be ready to turn the whole battalion half-right. The battle seems to be mainly up north from us, over there.' He waved his swagger stick, nodded and walked off, erect and very calm, back towards his car.

It was all done as if the powers that be knew exactly what confronted them and were capable of redisposing forces to meet any emergency. The immediate result, in practice, was to leave the British Battalion without a reserve company. Kit Conway, leader of No. 1 Company, simply brought his men up into line with the others, and the first violation of textbook technique occurred.

Presently, as the three companies moved into new positions on what became known as Suicide Hill, Wintringham, following in their wake, tried to study the ground ahead through his field glasses. Beside him, an excited Russian engineer unwound from his drum a length of telephone cable which ran back through the olive trees, towards Brigade headquarters. While the telephone still refused to work, two other Brigade engineers began yelling into it, and one of them, a Russian, suddenly saw groups of Nationalist infantry advancing towards them. He poured out floods of Russian to Wintringham, indicating with brave gestures that they, the English, must go into the attack. A moment later he literally gave alarmed orders to the English, but Wintringham continued to study the terrain through his field glasses, ignoring the interruption.

Suddenly the telephone line began working. The Russian engineer at once bellowed into it. Colonel Gal's voice answered. Wintringham had a smattering of Russian and he picked out enough words to know that the engineer was excitedly complaining that the English were doing nothing in face of a full-scale Fascist attack.

Colonel Gal sent back his orders. Attack! There was no mistaking the blunt command. Bullets began singing around Wintringham and the engineer officer vanished from sight. A French telephonist took over, and Wintringham now reported back to H.Q. that a line of British riflemen had already gone into the attack.

Wintringham moved along the hillside to get a better view as the telephone rang again, and he hurried back to be told it might be better to stay near the instrument. Presently his riflemen were under terrific fire and slowly went back on the defensive. The telephone rang again fifteen minutes later. A French staff officer spoke to him and now, instead of arrogant talk about 'attack', he was asking whether he could continue to hold his position. 'Yes,' Wintringham answered, 'if there is support on my flank, but what's happened to the Franco-Belge?' There was a swiftly muttered conversation at the other end of the line and then vague talk about support from the French cavalry coming soon.

Ten minutes later the fire became much hotter, the telephone rang again and there was the imperturbable Nathan saying in his assured upper-class accent, 'Watch yourself, Tom. The Franco-Belges are having quite a time. You've got to hold on. Sorry I can't talk any longer now. . . . See you –'

One hour later it became clear to Wintringham that his battalion was stuck way out alone like a dangerous promontory without the support of either side which should have been forthcoming from the French and Dimitrov Battalions. The situation worried him.

Chapter 12

The Battle of Jarama

HERBERT MATTHEWS, correspondent of the *New York Times*, described what followed: 'The rebels struck again on the Jarama River Front, this time up the line of the Taguna valley towards Morata. Once again they broke through and plunged ahead and once again the mixed brigades held them in a battle which up till then ranked as the greatest and most sanguinary ever fought on Spanish soil. . . . It was the most critical point the war had reached. For days it was touch and go. . . .'[1]

Wintringham himself recalled the night of 13 February vividly: 'Pitch dark and bitter cold, half my battalion gone, an unpleasantly chancy battle to be fought – I woke at 2.45 hours with the feeling that yesterday had been sleep-walking, today we must really fight and hold.'[2]

That day, in fact, opened well for the British Battalion. The quick Spanish dawn ran across the countryside, the Moors came pouring into the attack and the Maxim guns under the command of a man called Fry caught them and scythed gaps in their ranks for twenty minutes or more until 'the guns were throbbing with steam and the belts empty.'

Away to the right, the Nationalists' attack was more successful. Two brigades reinforced by new units from the Nationalist 2nd Division concentrated their fire on the Edgar André, Dimitrov and Thaelmann Battalions. All three had suffered heavily the previous day and every machine-gun of the Edgar André was out of action, with the Colts of the Thaelmann – exchanged for the Maxims – hopelessly jammed. As H. Galli of the Franco-Belge wrote in his diary for 11 February at the front: 'A rain of steel is falling along the whole of the front occupied by our Brigade. . . . The Fascists are increasing the intensity of their fire. We are giving way – it is necessary to

---

[1] Herbert Matthews, *Two Wars and More to Come*, p. 252.
[2] Tom Wintringham, *English Captain*, p. 306.

retire. Slowly we move backwards. All are sweating and the perspiration is pouring down their faces, which are smeared with mud and blood. The machine-gunners are struggling along with their useless guns. . . .'

And Laza Wovicky, a Pole of the Dimitrov Battalion, wrote in his diary for 12 February: 'Five times the enemy attacked us with tanks, five times we retired and five times we took up our positions again. It was indeed a critical day. We lost very many comrades . . . among them . . . our commander, comrade Grebenareff. . . .' Now, in quick succession, the Thaelmann commander and Political Commissar were hit and carried away on stretchers; the Edgar André Battalion commander went down with a machine-gun bullet in his thigh; the Dumont Battalion of the French obeyed an order to counter-attack and suffered terrible casualties; one company of the Thaelmann Battalion – crack men who had come through hell many a time without breaking – now lost so many men that the remainder retired in utter confusion. The whole of the XIth International Brigade was in heavy, continuous, damaging action. Weaving in and out between the battalions, George Nathan rode on a chestnut horse, the same incredible figure, waving the same absurd stick, the perfect target with the charmed life. Colonel Gal in his different, more blunt way, Čopic and Springhall, Brigade Commissars, also carried inspiration from one company to another, moving among them with the same courage. Sometimes they spoke the wrong language, sometimes they could not find the right curse in the right language, sometimes a torrent of words obviously meant nothing to the men they addressed, but they rallied the fugitives of many a broken unit, and many men, paralysed with fear, recovered the will to fight, and the line stiffened again and held.

It was Springhall who came to Wintringham with a new H.Q. order – be ready to make a big new counter-attack. Wearily Wintringham laid his plans, but before he gave the order he waited for the tank support he had been told to expect and the air bombardment of Suicide Hill. The air bombardment came in the form of a lame attempt by three planes to unload three bombs each and 'make a couple of dabs at the hill with their machine-guns'. It made no difference to the enemy gunfire. As for the tanks – there were none.

So Wintringham waited. Against orders, he lay in wait because he believed it would be criminal to try to cross 600 yards of open valley against forty – he had reported to head-quarters eighty – machine-guns. When the Fascists began to bring artillery to bear on Fry's Maxim section, Wintringham decided to launch an attack very different from that required by H.Q. He made up a party of 35 men and tried to manœuvre round to threaten the flank of the enemy machine-gunners who were facing Fry on Suicide Hill.

'Two men – big Manoel and Phil the boxer . . . went forward up to the fringe of the trees. Meanwhile the remaining 33 men opened fire with the aid of spotters and field glasses.'

It was a small bluff in gigantic stakes but it succeeded – for a time. The enemy turned its artillery to meet the new attack, and Wintringham himself moved back to the protection of a sunken road.

14.00 hours and he made a new reappraisal of the battalion's situation. 15.00 hours, and a runner brought a message from the field telephone to say – 'advance at once or you will be placed under arrest!' 'Necessarily,' Wintringham said, 'I disregarded this order!'

Now this is a very remarkable statement. In the 1914–18 war when H.Q. ordered an advance, no lesser officer dared to question it however much slaughter must inevitably follow. Obviously, Wintringham did not want his men wiped out, but local obliteration in one section of the line might mean the success or failure of overall strategy and H.Q. knew quite well at what cost any advance would be made.

In the confusion which followed it is not surprising to find Wintringham ordering not an advance but a retreat in direct contradiction to H.Q.'s instructions. Certainly something had to be done. The Dimitrovs had been forced back and the gap between the British and the Dimitrovs had increased to the point where Moors were filtering in between the two.

An American known as Yank Levy [Bert Levy], with Harry Fry's Maxim Company, described what happened next. 'Then . . . about 3 p.m. the enemy drops 2 shells on the plateau on our right; looking that way I am amazed to see 4 Company running hell-bent for leather to the rear with O leading by about 25 yards. . . .'

O, commander of No. 4 British Company, had lost his nerve completely. As it turned out later, he had twice made false reports to Wintringham claiming that he still had some of his men alongside Fry, when this was quite untrue.

Levy's account continued: 'Now . . . here's the whole damn thing that happened in the next two minutes. I am aiming at a tree waiting for a Fascist to stick his head out in the open . . . when to my amazement, directly in line with my sights, about 20 yards in front of me, stands from the knees up a Fascist soldier. Goldberg is on my left, shouts "Blimey, who's that?" Someone else shouts "Who are you?"

'I shouted . . . "Fascists!" and dropped the one in front of me. Then they are in front of us and the boys are doing a good job. . . . Doran's pressing the gun trigger when I see him crumple in front of me. I shout at Plumb, his number 2, to take the gun, when I see him dead on his knees in the same position he was in while feeding the gun. . . . How the hell did they get killed? They were both protected by the gun shield and Plumb was sitting in the trench.

'Looking to my right I see 5 Fascists only 20 feet from us running towards us . . . shouting . . . they came from the same side of the little stone wall we were on.'

If O had not fled with his riflemen the enemy would never have been able to take No. 1 Company in the rear. As a result scores were killed and wounded, Fry, Levy and twenty others captured, and then, according to Wintringham's own account, as he was running down the sunken road towards Fry's men a bullet smashed into his leg just above the knee and brought him down. According to Copeman, Wintringham said to him: 'I shall never command this battalion again.'

How did the battle now stand? The enemy had first tried to break along the western bank of the Jarama river towards Arganda bridge, bringing the main Madrid road under machine-gun fire, only to be checked by a counter-attack from the two International Brigades. Swiftly turning the full force of their attack, the Nationalists widened their foothold across the Jarama river some miles downstream from the bridge, and threatened and took a second bridge connecting San Martin and Morata. Troops then poured across, spreading through the uneven countryside below Suicide Hill, but an attempt to take the hill failed. A second enemy division came streaming across the bridge and could have been deployed in three ways. The Nationalists could throw it into the battle north of the road, or against the English on Suicide Hill, or hurry round Suicide Hill to the south where a weak spot occurred, masked by the determined defence of Suicide Hill. No troops of any consequence lay to the south of the English, and an enemy attack in force, with a new second division, would undoubtedly have broken through. But the defence of Suicide Hill convinced the Nationalists that the weak spot did not exist, and by the time they did probe deeply in that direction, three days later, Republican troops had moved up and strengthened the line.

There were now involved in the battle four International Brigades – Hans Kahle led the XIth Brigade, Lukacz the XIIth, Gomez – the German Zeisser – the XIIIth, the Alsatian Colonel Putz the XIVth, and Čopic the XVth. From their point of view things were not going too badly.

Fred Copeman, as Maxim Section Leader of Britain's No. 1 Company, had a different view of the battle and from his vantage point way out ahead on Suicide Hill he realized that unless the French arrived soon the Moors would reach the higher ground in the olive groves behind his position and outflank them. Once the Moors reached the road itself, fire would begin from the right and the rear of the English positions.

'At that moment,' Copeman wrote, 'I saw my first real casualty – Davidovich, a young Jewish lad. He was very saucy and a great friend of Cunningham. He had received one in the stomach and it wasn't a nice sight. He staggered around trying to hold it in without much success. I myself bent down instinctively as if I had something to hold in front of me. . . .'[1]

As the casualties mounted, Kit Conway, leader of the first company, continued to stride through the scrub with a walking stick for a weapon, as if in imitation of George Nathan. Copeman held a swift parley with Conway, warning him about the danger from the Moors in their rear. His answer was to repeat the message from Nathan, who had arrived ten minutes before, once more on his chestnut horse, still swinging his swagger cane:

[1] Fred Copeman, *Reason in Revolt*, p. 89.

'Get your chaps up to the high ground on the other side of the valley and those buggers behind you will be in a mess', he had said.[1] Conway now attempted to carry out this manœuvre with Copeman's help. Ten minutes later Copeman suddenly encountered an old friend of his, a carpenter called George Bright who was at least sixty years old. Copeman stared in amazement at the old man who had volunteered for the British Battalion but should not have been anywhere near the front line. Copeman said, 'What the hell are you doing here, George?' and as he said it, George opened his mouth to reply, there was a small plop and a hole appeared in George's forehead, spilling blood gently down his face. He staggered a moment, fell flat on his face and died almost at once. 'His union card fluttered out as he fell – A.S.W. I thought what an awful thing it was that he, at his age, should be here, and yet I am certain he would not have wished for any other end.'

And then the sturdy, purposeful figure of Kit Conway, still ploughing ahead against enemy fire, suddenly jerked to a stop as though some hidden hand had pushed him back. He stumbled, clutched at his stomach, and fell. Copeman ran to him, knelt over him, swiftly came to the conclusion that he hadn't long to live, and felt a sudden urgent and vengeful need to locate the machine-gun which had not only felled Conway but was threatening to slaughter Companies 1 and 2. As he turned away a fierce flame burned suddenly into his left hand and he glanced down to see that a bullet had gouged out the inside of his watch and embedded itself with half its length still protruding. Copeman grasped the bullet and tried to drag it out without success. Already the burning had reached an intolerable pitch of pain, but there was no blood and Copeman quickly wrapped a field-dressing round it and pressed on to locate the machine-gun.

To his astonishment the fire seemed to be coming from the foot of an embankment where the tanks and lorries of his own brigade were stationed. Either the Dimitrov Battalion was busy murdering its own people, including the British, or their tanks and lorries had been overrun by the enemy. Where, anyway, were the British machine-guns? One alone, in full operation, would have cleared up this mess. It was then that he came

[1] *Volunteer for Liberty*, February 1937.

upon Fry, the company commander, with his guns placed behind a wall but completely useless for the simple reason that he had no ammunition. 'Why the hell don't you get up and look for some bloody ammunition?' Copeman roared. 'That's what I have done', Fry roared back. The heavy machine-gun company with the eight Maxims exchanged by Marty had hauled their guns, at great cost, up to this commanding plateau, turned to fill the belts with ammunition – and there was no ammunition. Harry Fry, speechless with rage, had sent ten men post-haste back to where the ammunition lorry should have been, but the lorry had vanished.

As he turned away again, Copeman felt a jolt, 'everything went warm and sleepy' and he realized that a bullet had hit him in the head. It felt as if half his head had been shot away, but when he reached the dressing station the wound turned out to be 'not too bad'.

Moving back towards the front again, Copeman came upon an overturned lorry with .303 ammunition spilling from its broken shell. This lorry was the key to Harry Fry's little disaster.

Wintringham had given careful instructions to Sergeant H, the lorry driver, never to leave this lorry, and he had even insisted that he should sleep in it, but no one knew that Sergeant H was terrorized by the thought of going into action again, or that he had filled himself up with large quantities of brandy on the morning of the attack. When a message came through from Brigade H.Q. saying that further supplies of ammunition were now waiting back at Morata, without unloading the Maxim ammunition he drove the lorry at high speed towards the town. Half-drunk, he took a corner too fast, the lorry over-turned, his co-driver was killed and Sergeant H vanished from the scene.

So there were the Maxims empty and useless, there were Fry's men searching for the missing lorry, and there, miles away, spilled all over the road, was the precious ammunition . . . until Copeman by accident stumbled on it. Instantly, he organized a handful of men to get the boxes moving towards the front. He did not then know that in the meantime Fry's power-less unit had been overrun by the Moors, Fry himself captured and only six of the guns salvaged. Heading towards battalion H.Q., now located in a partly protected sunken road, Copeman came upon four of the six salvaged Maxims. Simultaneously George Aitken, one of the Political Commissars, appeared like an apparition out of nowhere, and between them they organized half a dozen men to drag the Maxims into a position commanding any new advance the Moors might make.

Automatically, without any discussion, Copeman took over command of the guns. Already anti-tank guns across the valley had become interested in the 'busyness' around the Maxims, and shells began to fall close. Copeman could see some of the crews getting jittery and kept them hard at work filling the ammunition belts. The artillery fire he said would 'ease up at sundown' and dusk by now was creeping over the whole landscape. As the sun went down the shelling ceased, but another, far more urgent menace appeared over the summit of the hills. Numbers of Moors slipped across the crest, formed into lines and marched down, openly, as if on parade, their crimson-lined cloaks flowing in the wind, their red turbans staining the hillside. It was a beautiful and sinister sight. A mass of men silently pouring down the hills as if borne on the wings of their cloaks.

Copeman knew exactly what it meant, and explained the situation to the Maxim crews. The Nationalists were about to launch a mass infantry attack intended to overrun the Republican positions before night really came down in all its black reality. 'So long as you stick to the guns and fire – anyone coming across that valley is done for – and remember – they don't know we're here. They don't know we've got this little lot' – he indicated the Maxims – 'waiting for them. Now this is the drill. . . .'

The guns were fully loaded, but no one was to fire a shot until he gave the word. Since the reputation of the Moors for the most brutal behaviour had created a legend of horrible proportions, none of the Maxim crews wanted to be overrun by men who were liable to stab, decapitate and castrate without discrimination. Nerves became very jittery as they crouched there, silent, waiting, and the twilight deepened. The double line of Moors had reached the valley and was beginning to charge up the slope.

'Not a shot until I give the word,' Copeman called. 'All guns to sweep the line together from left to right.'

'To hell with you, I've got to fire', a young Irish voice muttered. The man lay beside a gun on the left. When he repeated the threat Copeman strode over to him, 'sailed into him and laid him out . . . we needed a new No. 1 on that gun.'

They could hear the high-pitched battle-cries of the Moors now as the red turbans separated out from the distant mass, the mounted officers became distinctive figures, the murmur of feet, hooves and cries merged into a roar and Copeman quickly reminded everyone that this was part of the technique – to reinforce the legend with as much carnival, noise and apparent barbarism as could be concentrated in a double line of men.

'Wait for it – wait for it! When you see the havoc we're going to make you'll understand better. Wait for it – wait for it.'

His men were now openly pleading – even bawling – to be allowed to fire, and the battle of nerves reached a pitch where even Copeman found his whole body tingling with a mixture of fear, excitement, exultation. 'All sorts of suppositions passed through my mind, producing a million and one doubts – had I trained these crews properly – supposing the guns didn't go off. . . .'

The Moors were now plainly visible, the roar of sound deafening and some of the Maxim crews literally writhing round their guns in a sort of agony, cursing and blinding.

'Fire!' Copeman shouted and the burst of curses from the crews, the maniacal relief on twisted faces, the venom with which men took the judder of the guns, was overwhelmed by the concentrated blast of the Maxims all firing at once.

Highly trained, some of the Moors fell to the ground immediately they heard the sound of gunfire, but great gaps were torn in their lines, the shock stopped the rest dead in their tracks, and straggled groups of what looked like writhing cloaks fell dead and wounded. It was a slaughter. Nothing in the valley offered any sort of shelter. Three or four hundred men had come charging up the hill. Half that number now tried to make a miserable, crawling retreat, but still the Maxims fired on, taking a dreadful toll, and the men who fired them sang and laughed, and would have danced but for the necessity of continuing the fire. Copeman suddenly thanked the day when Marty had arrived and insisted on exchanging the light

British Lewis guns for the heavy Maxims. Their range made these tactics so much more successful.

The bravery of these men was not characteristic of the whole battalion. There were many exceptions. Casualties had been heavy in other sections; there were many dead and wounded; some had 'withdrawn themselves and were hiding in the hills'; others had become 'stragglers' following the injunction – every man for himself.

Copeman now went back behind the front line and began rounding up the stragglers, but word of his activities reached them and many went underground. Their final place of refuge was only revealed by the astuteness of an Egyptian volunteer, André Diamond, who reasoned that the obvious hide-out was the wine vaults of a farmhouse where a long tunnel ran into the hillside with enormous empty vats offering sleeping accommodation for scores of men. Diamond and Copeman descended into the vaults to be met by the kind of complete silence which made them suspicious. Copeman turned to André and said in a voice which echoed through the tunnel: 'Give me those ruddy hand-grenades, André. If there are Fascists in here we'll soon clean them out.'

The silence broke at once. 'For Christ's sake don't throw anything – it's us!'

A motley assembly of nearly 100 men now stumbled and cursed their way down the tunnel into the light, some too drunk on wine to worry, some afraid of the consequences of martial law, some just waiting their chance to break out again. They were given no chance. Formed into two straggling lines, they collected arms and ammunition and with Copeman at the head and Diamond at the rear, the column of tired, rebellious, uneasy men moved back through the semi-darkness towards the front again. Copeman was afraid some of them would try to break away as they neared the front, but none did.

A decisive piece of duplicity on the part of the Moors now threw what remained of the British Battalion into fresh confusion. Somehow in the roar and crash of battle, with men wounded and dying everywhere, Copeman was 'discussing' with Jock Cunningham – who had taken over command from Wintringham – the possibility of withdrawing the remaining Maxim guns to safer positions, when they heard voices coming towards them singing the Internationale. What did it mean? Unexpected relief troops? An attempt by some inspired corporal to boost their low morale? A moment later, marching towards them out of the carnage of 'Battle Valley' came a line of forty or so men, cheerful, waving rifles in greeting, singing lustily and all correctly dressed in the uniforms of the International Brigade. They came steadily forward as a few Britishers raised a cheer and some even joined in the singing. Within a few minutes the ghost company had infiltrated into the Maxim positions, their guns and rifles were levelled, they threatened to shoot, and without a struggle of any kind they took over the Maxims and made the crews prisoner. These, of course, were enemy troops dressed in uniforms taken from the Republican dead.

Copeman saw the whole episode unfold before his eyes from a piece of high ground where he had stationed one of the Maxims and there he crouched in an agony of frustration with the impostors right in front of his gun sights, but completely protected by the men of No. 2 Company who were being marched away with hands above their heads. Simultaneously, an enemy tank began to move down the road and as its gun opened up a score of men ran for it. There followed the amazing sight of Jock Cunningham 'actually walking round the tank trying to tell the lads what to do'.[1] In the midst of a holocaust of fire and noise he remained quiet, purposeful, trying to make certain that what was now a full-scale retreat did not develop into a rout.

At last Cunningham shouted grimly to Copeman: 'Don't see many of our buggers left around here!' and moved off down the line, for some reason beyond analysis quite unscathed by tank, rifle and machine-gun bullets. As the two men withdrew they gathered together scores of stragglers again, but the torn, weary and often bleeding band which presently gathered back at the cook-house, clamouring for hot soup, numbered only 180 out of the original 600.

Even now, with the battalion divided, broken and hopelessly

[1] Fred Copeman, *Reason in Revolt*, p. 96.

beaten back, the Commissars still did not give up. Rallying speeches were made by Frank Ryan and Copeman. Colonel Gal suddenly drove up in person to deliver a powerful appeal to the men: The Madrid–Valencia road was absolutely vital for the continued defence of Madrid, he said; without it Madrid itself – the very heart and symbol of Republican resistance – might collapse: the battalion had revealed a courage and endurance rarely seen in years of warfare; but the retreat had left a gap in the line for which there were absolutely no other men available; he wanted them to gather together the remnants of their courage, to remember the cause they were fighting for and to ask themselves this question – could they leave that gap undefended?

Jock Cunningham saluted in the best tradition of the British Army and said quietly:. 'We'll go up and fill that gap.'

Meanwhile Copeman had organized his own last stand with a number of stragglers and André Diamond, who still led about ten men of No. 1 Company. They tried to build a defence line with heavy stones across a road and two French crews with their 75-mm guns came along to take up position beside them. While they were still holding on to a ridiculously inadequate defence system Copeman once more heard voices singing the Internationale and was instantly on the alert against another piece of treachery, but this time the voices came up behind him and there he saw the heartening sight of some two hundred British, French and Slav troops, all singing at the top of their voices, and marching steadily forward, inspired by the words of Colonel Gal.

There was an hour to go before dark and the men continued to advance on the flank of the Moors who had penetrated the gap in the line. A terrific struggle followed until the English fought their way back to within a hundred yards of the sunken road which had been Tom Wintringham's original headquarters. The Nationalists now threw in everything at their disposal but they, in turn, were in some confusion because of this totally unexpected sally.

What began with 180 men rallying to burst through the advancing Nationalist troops was quickly reduced to a little over 100 men who formed something resembling an island defended by hand-grenades, rifles and one or two machine-guns.

And then, suddenly and unexpectedly, the whole situation underwent a dramatic change. Lister's Spanish Brigade, reinforced by reserves, came up on their left flank, and the Moors were suddenly confronted with a new fighting force. Half an hour later, the Moors were in retreat and Jock Cunningham suddenly let out an exultant shout as he realized that with Lister's aid they stood every chance of closing the gap.

Further north, the Nationalist assault towards the Arganda–Colmenar road was halted and driven back to the Jarama by Germans in the XIth International Brigade, a small unit of Russian tanks and the Dimitrov Battalion. The disposition of Republican forces now meant that four International Brigades held the front line from Arganda to Morata.

A period of horrible uncertainty followed. The battle went forward, swung back and went forward again, until on 16 February the 100 remaining men of the British Battalion were driven back fifty yards and there they decided to stick. Lister's Brigade also, at this point, decided to dig in, and stalemate ensued.

Both sides claimed the battle of Jarama as a victory. Certainly Franco had pushed his line forward 15 kilometres along a front of some 20 kilometres, but the Madrid–Valencia road was still in Republican hands, and Madrid had been saved from possible encirclement. Casualties in the end totalled 20,000 Nationalists and 25,000 Republicans, and among these proportionately, the four International Brigades were the hardest hit. The British Battalion lost one of its most distinguished intellectuals, the Communist writer Christopher Cauldwell.

Chapter 13

The Thaelmann and Garibaldi

At this stage of the Civil War, among the higher echelons of the Republican Army, considerable jealousy developed which led to a radical change in the leadership of the XIth International Brigade including the Thaelmann and Edgar André Battalions. Largo Caballero, who had taken the Government off to Valencia, was jealous of the prestige of those leaders like La Pasionaria, Miaja and Kléber, who had remained behind in Madrid. Caballero suspected that General Kléber wanted to use the International Brigade to realize a Communist *coup d'état* and Miaja found it hard to face the increasing reputation of a 'foreigner' like Kléber who was whispered in some quarters to have played a bigger role in saving Madrid than Miaja himself. Kléber pressed strongly for launching an attack on the Madrid front, but Miaja was flatly against it, and found support from the Anarchists who thus indirectly came into alignment with Caballero for the first time. There was a great deal of friction and argument and at least one stormy scene.

Once before – in January 1937 – Kléber had expressed fears of a fall from grace to his Chief of Staff, Ernst Adam.[1] He knew what drastic consequences sometimes followed. Shortly afterwards he was summoned to Moscow but he had returned safely from that reappraisal and taken command again, only, in May, to confront this second and far worse crisis. Feuds and jealousies mounted to the point where Kléber dramatically resigned under heavy pressure from the German Communists who made out that he was a weakling, a man with doubts in a situation where doubt had no place. They wanted to hear no more of him and gradually forced him out. He retired to a small hotel in Valencia and left the Germans and the Spanish to sort out the fate of the International Brigades and particularly that of the Thaelmann Battalion.

[1] Verbal evidence from Dr Adam.

Hans Kahle, one-time leader of the Edgar André Battalion, now came to the fore. Kahle, a tall, dark, energetic man – said to be a womanizer – was the son of 'a good German family', and had automatically been trained in the German cadet corps before World War I. He became an officer, fought heroically in the war but came to hate nationalism and afterwards threw up his military career to start life afresh as a radical journalist. When Hitler came to power, Kahle wrote vigorously against him and in the end had to fly from Germany. Before Beimler died, Kahle went one day to consult him about the future of the XIth Brigade, and afterwards called on Ludwig Renn: 'I've just been with Beimler', he said. 'He thinks we should command the XIth Brigade together. I should be Commander and you Chief of Staff. . . .' Renn immediately agreed but asked who would take his place as commander of the Thaelmann. On 4 December 'Hans and I took over command of the XIth International Brigade from General Kléber', Renn wrote, but he made no reference to the new commander of the Thaelmann, a man called Richard who was known as 'a man of iron'.

After Christmas the Nationalists launched a new attack on the Madrid–Corunna road, and on 6 January the Thaelmann Battalion was summoned from reserve and sent to Las Rozas to hold it at any cost.

According to Renn this battle became, for the first time, a battle of modern warfare deploying infantry, artillery, tanks and aeroplanes in a life-and-death struggle, but the three battalions of the XIth International Brigade were sadly weakened battalions and the Thaelmann in 'very bad shape'.

At the height of the battle a Russian called Loti, from the Spanish General Staff H.Q., arrived at field H.Q. and asked Commander Richard: 'Can you hold your position for three days?'

Richard shrugged his shoulders. 'If the Fascists encircle us in the Park of El Pardo I don't know what happens. . . . If they make a frontal attack – there is some hope we can hold our positions – not very much.'[1]

Shortly afterwards two messages reached Renn at H.Q. One, from the Thaelmann, said that the Fascists had launched a new attack, and then at dusk came word from the Edgar André

[1] Ludwig Renn, *Der Spanische Krieg*, p. 113.

commander that he had only 120 men left. An order to retreat was now sent, but it did not reach the Thaelmann for the simple reason that they were surrounded and more or less cut off. During the remainder of the day the battalion grimly held its ground and the Nationalist General Barron was forced to throw in planes, tanks and wave after wave of infantry. Still the diminished Thaelmann held on. No order to retreat had reached them, and the old cry rang out – *No pasaràn!*

Meanwhile another remnant of another battalion, the Edgar André Battalion, surrounded by dead and wounded and equally in danger of obliteration, tried to sing the Internationale to raise their spirits, but it was no good; the mingled roar of guns, rifles, bombs, tanks and the cries of the wounded and dying drowned out the words. Still the Thaelmann and Edgar André fought on among incredible slaughter. Slowly, man after man in the Thaelmann collapsed, wounded or dying. Once the Moors broke into the last trench and bayoneted the wounded, dead and living without distinction, only to be shot to pieces, knifed and bayoneted out of the trench again.

It was late in the afternoon when a runner at last managed to carry back to Renn's H.Q. the grim message that there were only 100 Thaelmann men left alive. Towards dusk came the final scene. A solitary man staggered into Renn's H.Q., his face smeared with blood and oil, his wet coat hanging loosely from his shoulders. Before he said anything he sank down, buried his face in his filthy hands and sobbed. Then he pulled himself together and managed to make a halting, slightly incoherent report, which Ludwig Renn recorded: 'Towards dusk the Fascist tanks came once more. We stood in the trench – you know the one near to the castle. One tank suddenly comes from the right side and moves behind the trench, another one comes from the left side. Now they have us from both sides and shoot with their machine-guns. We ran and huddled towards the middle of the trench and the tanks simply shot into the heaps of humanity.' As he reached this part of his story, Renn said, the man collapsed once more into sobbing. 'They were all dead!' he went on at last. 'The leader of our company and all the Englishmen and that very brave man Arnold Jeans. When the tanks stopped shooting, the Moors came and poured more bullets into the heaps of dead and wounded.'

Finally Hans Kahle asked him: 'How many are left?' and the man answered: 'Perhaps 20 – ill, hungry – exhausted. They are no use for anything.'

There was 'a sort of silence' as they heard these words. They had never seen a man so broken as this one, but they were affected by something much more disturbing than the sight of a single broken man. His clumsy, incoherent account had somehow vividly evoked the death of yet another form of the Thaelmann Battalion.

The telephone rang at that moment. Hans took up the receiver and spoke in Spanish. Someone said to him from H.Q.: 'Before dawn the Thaelmann Battalion will be relieved', and Hans replied: 'It can't be relieved – it's no longer there – it's dead, wounded, dispersed.'

As he put the receiver back he turned to Renn and said, his voice charged with emotion: 'It's not very difficult to relieve twenty men, is it?'

The final state of the battered remnants of the Thaelmann, Edgar André and Commune de Paris Battalions is best conveyed by an entry in the diary of Alfred Kantorowicz:

8 Jan. 1937

This evening Hans, brigade chief; Richard, commander of the Thaelmann Battalion; Wilhelm, commander of the Edgar André ... came over to see Nicoletto. There came, too, the Political Commissars of the battalions: Artur from the Thaelmann, Paul from the André, and Ribière from the Commune de Paris. But what a condition they came in! Richard, the man of iron, the foremost battalion commander. ... I could almost cry to think of it, and wouldn't be ashamed if I did – Richard was pale as wax with quivering hands, his face sunken, his features moving convulsively. I had to turn away. Hans, always serene and cheerful, who keeps his nerve and his good humour under the most trying circumstances, had dark rings under his eyes and looked worried and all done in. Ribière the playboy always gay, always up to tricks, as brave as they come ... threw himself into a chair, dropped his head in his hands and cried as if his heart would break. ... Nobody spoke. ... Nobody dared ask where is this fellow or that one. ...

Then Hans spoke up: even though the battle had meant the sacrifice of their best men, the Fascist drive had been stopped. Once more Madrid was saved.

One other episode in the Thaelmann story at this stage must be recorded. Walter, leader of No. 1 Company of the battalion, was one of the handful of men who survived to tell the strange story of how he re-encountered an old friend on the battlefield. Walter had served in the German (Nazi-organized) Army until Easter 1936 but by then he could stand it no longer, and ran away to become one of the best officers in the International Brigade. Among his school friends was a man named Kurt Kneiding who later joined the same flying school as Walter. At the height of the Corunna road battle a Fascist plane was shot down and Walter helped to haul the pilot away from the burning machine only to be confronted, 'like a terrible apparition', with the charred and already dead Kurt Kneiding. It was a strange moment of confrontation which brought the struggle in Nazi Germany directly into the Spanish Civil War with a Nazi pilot dropped dramatically dead at the feet of a German anti-Nazi. Franco's German fighter planes completely dominated the air in this battle and it seemed poetic justice to Walter that one pilot at least should be ritually sacrificed at the feet of his friend, but it wasn't entirely hate that moved him. He knew Kneiding's parents, and he remembered them as pleasant people. One day when the heat and horror of battle had subsided he decided to write a letter to them. It was dated 12 January 1937, Madrid:

Highly respected family of Kneiding. We consider it our duty to inform you of the death of your son Kurt Kneiding who was an officer of the Immelmann Fighter Squadron. He was shot down together with five other German planes by our aircraft on the afternoon of 5 Jan. . . . German volunteers of the Thaelmann Battalion lifted his body from the wreck and buried it with full military honours at the cemetery of Fuencarral, a working-class suburb of Madrid. You may rest assured that we understand your grief at the loss of your son. We, too, have fathers and mothers, wives and children in Germany who are anxious for us. Let us add this – we neither can nor will believe that you would willingly have let your son go to Spain if you had known that his duties here would consist in protecting frightful air-raids by heavy bombers against defenceless women and children. We enclose a letter found on your son's body.

Of course, this was false in one sense. The ferocity of the Civil War had by now produced appalling barbarities on both sides and it ill became either to claim exemption.

It remains to record that Russian tank tactics in this battle were unsuccessful. Led in person by the Russian General Pavlov, they carried on a guerrilla warfare of their own, ploughing in among the enemy and destroying one unit after another, but they were unable to make any co-ordinated advance.

Between 14 January and 7 February 1937, like a phoenix from the ashes, the indestructible Thaelmann Battalion was once more re-formed but now, such were the appalling casualties, that it became more Spanish than German. Ludwig Renn remarked to Hans Kahle one day in January: 'You talk of International Battalions – but now there's a Spanish troop in every company and the XIth Brigade as a whole – with four battalions – is more than half Spanish.'[1] By April of the same year Giacomo Calandrone said that the proportion of Spaniards had increased until there were 35 per cent in the Garibaldi, 35 per cent in the Dabrowsky, 45 per cent in the Rakosi, and 85 per cent in the Thaelmann.[2]

Renn estimated that there were 10,000 international volunteers in the Republican Forces in January 1937, but Franco, once more according to Renn, had at least 30,000 Italians fighting for him. These figures, of course, are roughly reversed by Spanish Nationalist historians.

Early in March 1937 the re-formed XIth Brigade, numbering 1,300 men, travelled to Morata, and now in some groups there was only one German, French or Austrian with nine Spaniards. Between 8 and 21 March they were at the Guadalajara front and here began the tremendous clash with thousands of Il Duce's crack Italian troops sent to win the war for General Franco.

[1] Ludwig Renn, *Der Spanische Krieg*, pp. 156–7.
[2] Giacomo Calandrone, *La Spagna Brucia*, p. 114.

Normally a stagnant provincial capital, Guadalajara commands a gorge through which pours the Henares river hurrying down from the Guadarrama. Cheek by jowl, lies the airport of Barajas, then the headquarters of the Russian air squadron fighting for the Republicans. On 8 March, suddenly and unexpectedly, Coppi, the Italian commander, launched his Black Flames Division, consisting entirely of armoured cars and trucks, against the two Spanish Divisions then holding the Republican front and for perhaps the first time the watching military hawks of many European countries observed the great success of what later became known as blitzkrieg tactics. Coppi's Black Flames Division broke through at the first assault. Simultaneously Moscardo swept through the Republican lines towards Soria.

From the outset the Republican planes had the advantage of operating from a conventional aerodrome instead of the improvised air-strips of the Nationalists, and they harried the advance continuously. Heavy rain began to fall, followed by sleet, ice and fog, until the Nationalist aircraft were grounded. The Republican planes continued flying from their better-equipped base. Despite bad weather, tiredness and superior air strength, Coppi's Black Flames drove on again the following day, reaching Almadrones at 10.30 in the morning, and swinging to the left flank in an attempt to widen a gap in the Republican lines. Moscardo pressed on to capture Cogulludo, and the Black Arrows took over in the centre.

By the evening of 6 March the Republican Command, responding swiftly to what had become a critical situation, concentrated a 4th Army Corps, led by Colonel Jurado, at various danger points. The XIth International Brigade was included in the 11th Division led by Lister, and found itself deployed with three other brigades in the woods along the road from Trijueque to Torija. Another International Brigade, Lukacz's XIIth, headed by the Garibaldi Battalion, was part of a Second Division concentrated along the Brihuega–Torija road.

In the dawn of 10 March the sleepy, ancient, half-walled town of Brihuega suddenly awoke to shattering gunfire and the roar of motorized troops as the Italian Black Flames and Black Arrows once more swept into it with blitzkrieg speed.

By now the Republicans had re-formed their line, and at noon the Garibaldi Division went over to the attack. A comedy of tragic errors began, because the advancing Republicans had no idea that Brihuega was already overwhelmed by the Nationalists. A glittering array of Italian names, later to become world-famous, were involved in the Garibaldi attack with 'Vidali (Carlos Contreras) as Inspector General of the whole front, Luigi Longo (Gallo) holding the same position for the International Brigades, and Nenni, who commanded a company in the battalion',[1] moving down the road towards Brihuega.

What followed is best described in the words of Hugh Thomas. Within five kilometres of Brihuega the first Republican patrols 'encountered a motor-cyclist from Coppi's Black Flames who, hearing the Italian voices of the Garibaldi Battalion, asked if he was right in supposing he was on the Torija road. The Garibaldi motor-cyclists said that he was. Both groups now went back to their headquarters. Coppi assumed that the Garibaldi scouts were part of Nuvolari's division. He therefore continued to advance. Ilse Barontini, the Commissar and acting commander of the Garibaldi Battalion, continued also. He established his men in woods on the left of the road, where they made contact with the similarly far-advanced XIth International Brigade. Coppi's tanks now appeared. They were attacked by the machine-guns of the Garibaldi Battalion. The Black Flame Infantry was sent in to attack. Two patrols of the opposing Italian forces met. The Black Flame commander asked why the other Italians had fired on him. "Noi siamo Italiani di Garibaldi" came the answer.'[2]

A civil war within a civil war now sprang to life and a battle began between all-Italian units around a big country house called the Ibarra Palace. As Pacciardi remarks, there is an old Italian saying – who takes first takes twice – and, now, momentarily the Garibaldi, having fired first, had a short-lived advantage.

It was on the day following the 'civil war' that the now re-formed Thaelmann Battalion came into fierce action again as the Black Arrows broke into Lister's 11th Division, capturing Trijueque and pouring on towards Torija. The Black Arrows attacked the Thaelmann and Edgar André Battalions with at

[1] Hugh Thomas, *The Spanish Civil War*, p. 385.   [2] Ibid.

least twenty-five tanks and flamethrowers, when – according to Renn, now Chief of Staff – 'we were only a thin line'. Under a tremendous artillery, tank and infantry attack the Edgar André Battalion cracked and the Thaelmann retreated as the weather grew steadily worse. Snow came down blindingly. Presently the only 'still reliable' battalion was the Thaelmann, and the Fascists already threatened to outflank them. Casualties multiplied and the Thaelmann again withdrew. As darkness blotted out the landscape the enemy spent the night within four kilometres of the XIth Brigade's staff H.Q. They had penetrated the brigade's defence lines on a front of five kilometres and there was now a gap of at least six kilometres. 'If they aren't mad', Renn wrote in his diary that night, 'they will move into this gap – although we can't see it because of too much snow.'

All that night Renn tried desperately to get some news about the Edgar André Battalion. The field telephone had gone dead, but some single messenger should, by all the statistical chances of war, have come through to report the number of survivors. Instead there was absolute silence. In the morning Hans Kahle decided to set out personally for the last-known Edgar André position, while Renn tried to make contact with Lister's divisions in the hope of 'borrowing' some reinforcements.

Presently Renn stumbled on a small company of men huddled together in a hollow and when he spoke to their officer he suddenly realized that they belonged to the XVth Brigade.

'Are those the remainder of the XVth Brigade?' he said.

'Yes,' the man answered.

Renn gestured and said: 'Ah – well – in our situation a few soldiers can be of great help.'

'We haven't eaten for two days.'

'I'll get you some food,' Renn said. 'Are you a professional soldier?'

'No,' came the reply. 'I've never done any service.'

They were raw Spanish recruits, famished recruits, the remnant of a disintegrated brigade, waiting dismally for some sort of lead. Renn realized that somehow he had to bolster up their morale and bring them back to help fill the appalling gap beyond the XIth Brigade's lines. He explained the nature of the gap to the officer, who seemed very alarmed. 'You don't have to be afraid of those Italian troops,' Renn said. 'They have good arms but are badly led.'

He then devised a remarkable piece of strategy whereby the re-formed company of Spaniards did not so much advance on the enemy as threaten them by moving towards their lines. The distinction was a nice one which must have been difficult to appreciate in the snow, fog and confusion but its effect seemed surprisingly successful. First a movement ran among the Italian troops and Renn picked out what he took to be a messenger racing back to H.Q. Then the shooting began and Renn felt the Spaniards behind and round him waver as bullets skimmed over their heads. This was the really difficult moment. 'Look,' he shouted, 'they are nervous and shoot too soon.' Like any other man Renn knew fear under fire but now he rallied his men and boldly walked ahead of them into the most erratic shooting he had ever encountered. A light machine-gun rattled away but the strange movement of the 'advancing' troops must have unsettled its crew as it did the riflemen, and the bullets went wide of their mark. Renn saw a group of Italians barely a hundred yards away suddenly leap up, race back and throw themselves down again. Once more they fired in even more erratic fashion and the bullets shot harmlessly overhead. As coolly as possible, Renn continued to walk on and now it seemed a miracle that he was not hit. Over to his right he saw another group of Italians pick up their light machine-gun and disappear into a hollow.

'There, you see,' he shouted to his own men, 'you don't need to be afraid of these heroes.'

Reassured, the Spaniards pressed on and now began a cat-and-mouse game with the enemy retreating fifty metres as this solitary paw which had not yet shown much sign of claws reached out after them again and again.

Amazingly, the remnants of the XVth Brigade advanced several hundred metres without any serious opposition and found itself emerging on a small plateau which commanded the surrounding countryside. Here Renn ordered a pause while they consolidated their position, and a runner went back to bring up some hot soup from the now far-distant field kitchens.

The whole episode had a slightly unreal quality. The swift breaking of the original Republican line was not unexpected but according to Borkenau the Republican claim that six Italian divisions carried out the attack was false. 'Two divisions were actually in battle while a third one stood in reserve and was involved in the final catastrophe. These so-called divisions were very small, something like 3,000 men each. Both wings were protected each by one Spanish division. Nine thousand Italians then and 6,000 Spaniards altogether on the Fascist side. At the beginning of the fight the whole attacked sector was defended by one Republican brigade of 2–3,000 men.'[1]

But by now the Republican command had thrown in five brigades within twelve hours. Some were broken, some suffered serious casualties and the XVth was practically wiped out, but the remainder rallied and pushed back the Italians. Renn had played his own remarkable part at this stage of the battle, and now he wrote: 'I myself went back and stood on a high crest of the mountain in order to jot down the exact times in the war diary of the Brigade. . . . When I had made my notes I went back to the Observation Post.'[2]

He found Hans Kahle waiting for him at the post, a much happier Kahle, who roared with laughter as Renn came up and said, 'You are leading a private war – what have you been doing on this plateau?'

Kahle had watched Renn's spectacular advance through his field glasses and finally had seen him standing on the mountain crest, silhouetted against the sky, busily writing in what seemed to be the middle of the shooting. 'If Egon Kisch had seen you,' he said, referring to a German journalist who frequently reported their battles, 'he would have said: "He stood there writing a poem in the middle of a battle!" '

Kahle brought more good news. The Spanish Apoyo Battalion was on its way up to reinforce the remnants of the XVth Brigade. The Apoyo shortly afterwards appeared out of a grey, foggy day worthy of London at its worst, and Renn was relieved to find that it consisted of three full companies.

He now learnt from Kahle what had happened to the Edgar André Battalion. At 10 o'clock the previous morning the Nationalists had moved into the gap between the Edgar André and Thaelmann Battalions, penetrated the André's flank and

---

[1] Franz Borkenau, *The Spanish Cockpit*, p. 267.
[2] Ludwig Renn, *Der Spanische Krieg*, pp. 218–19.

quickly overwhelmed them. They used tanks, artillery, flame-throwers and infantry, and like the Thaelmann, the Edgar André Battalion had been virtually wiped out, but not without serving an important purpose, partly as the result of which the Italians were now themselves in full retreat.

A few hours later, General Ivanov drove up in his car to hold quick consultation with Renn. 'Look, Comrade General,' Renn said, handing him his field glasses, 'look over there – the Fascists are running for it.'

Ivanov made one quick survey and burst into laughter. 'Attack!' he said. 'And I'll send you the tanks immediately.'

As the fresh Apoyo Spanish Battalion moved swiftly after the retreating Italians, another Italian battalion launched a new attack from the Republican side on what was known as the Ibarra Palace.

This was the re-formed Garibaldi Battalion which played a spectacular part in the battle that followed.

Not unexpectedly, in what had now become the very mixed battalions of the International Brigades, a refugee novelist from Nazi Germany – Gustav Regler – acted as Political Commissar to the Garibaldi Italians. Preparing the attack he went to work in the classic tradition with his loudspeaker vans and leaflets intending to soften up enemy morale, and it is worth seeing him at work with a technique which played a bigger part than the military mind admitted.

It was an extraordinary scene. Heavy snow had fallen, blanketing the trees, the hills and the craggy outline of the Ibarra Palace in white, making a hush over the battlefield as a number of Poles in the Garibaldi Battalion wriggled forward in short, rapid advances, and machine-guns were installed among the bushes, but no shot was fired. The loudspeakers under Gustav Regler had to speak before the battle began.

'I looked up at the black, gaping mouths in the white-clad trees. The first was already speaking. I stood directly beneath it a hundred yards from Ibarra Palace, listening to the men of Garibaldi calling to the men of Il Duce: "Italian brothers! Marshal Graziani, whom you call the Libyan hyena, and whom the Ethiopians christened 'General Yperite', has been overtaken by their revenge. He was seriously wounded in an attempt to assassinate him. You, too, if you stay where you are will be in danger. The hatred of Spain will sweep over you! Italian brothers, the Spanish people are fighting for freedom. Desert the ranks of their enemies! Come over to us! We will welcome you as comrades-in-arms, we, the men of the Garibaldi Battalion." [1]

Instantly a bullet spattered against the wall where Regler was standing, and Boursier, the youthful commander of the Garibaldi Battalion, turned to him and said: 'And what are we supposed to do next – send them love letters?'

Instead, Boursier gave the word for the attack to begin and Captain Augusto, commander of No. 1 Company, a popular Spanish officer, waved his men forward as he led the way in a spectacular twenty-yard dash towards the Ibarra Palace. By the time the enemy machine-guns opened up, they were flat on the ground again. Another dash and another, with the bullets getting uncomfortably close, and then Regler went into action again with his loudspeakers. Softly, gently, from a somewhat battered record, the loudspeakers poured out over the enemy the famous Italian song, 'Fratelli nostri'.

Augusto made a last crab-crawl rush and was within ten yards of the palace when the bullet hit him; he clutched at his heart and fell on his face in the snow.

It was a difficult and expensive operation to recover his body, and such was Augusto's popularity that the men who brought him in were weeping. 'I bent down, uncovered his face and kissed his forehead on which the melting snow lay', Gustav Regler said.

'Murdered by an Italian', one of the stretcher-bearers cried.

'*Cado*', Regler corrected him, 'fallen in battle.'

The palace now poured out fire against the attackers and the brutal reality of bullets seemed to make Regler's propaganda slightly ridiculous, but if his loudspeakers fell silent he continued distributing pamphlets. He worked his way along into the Polish lines, and as he wriggled through the rocky ridges the scene had comic-opera elements. The leaflets said that Mussolini's Italians were ready to desert, and as he lay flat against a rock one of the Garibaldi soldiers said: 'Then why the hell

[1] Robert Payne, *The Civil War in Spain, 1936–1939*, p. 203.

don't they shoot their officers and do so?' The leaflets said, 'in the mud of the trenches the ideal of peace smiles upon us', and one of the Poles said, 'Christ – we aren't the Salvation Army!'

That night Regler had the leaflets wrapped around innumerable stones and flung among the Nationalists, as they lay sleeping, and many a man came awake in horror and grabbed at his gun as he felt the soft pebble explode its message.

On the third day, one troop of the Garibaldi were in open rebellion against propaganda warfare. 'We have not come here for this sort of thing – we want to be revenged for the shame of exiles – we want to be revenged for the life Mussolini has taken from us . . . blow them to bits with mortar fire. . . . Let's have more guns to teach them what we really mean. Leaflets? You must be mad! . . . Only a highbrow would think of that. . . . Why don't we attack Brihuega with knives between our teeth! They captured Luigi today, the light-hearted Luigi. . . . God knows what they'll do with him in Brihuega. . . .'[1]

It is some measure of the sheer expediency of Communist tactics that they could now announce 'the enemy is on the verge of surrendering' simultaneously with putting more emotion into the voices broadcast over the loudspeaker system and increasing the volume of 'Fratelli nostri . . .'

But that evening the propaganda balloon was pricked once more. A patrol came upon the body of Luigi lying in a shallow trench hastily abandoned by the enemy. 'His wrists bore the marks of torture, and all the teeth had been battered out of his head. He was scarcely recognizable, but the Garibaldi men knew him.'

They did not weep, they did not – for Italians – say very much, but Regler knew that he must temporarily shut up shop and fade into the background. Under the walls of the Ibarra Palace, in the foxholes approaching Brihuega, in the enlarged field furrows which were trenches, the news sped from point to point – Luigi is dead – dead from torture – and Regler knew that if he dared to drop one more yellow leaflet that night they might shoot him.

So he bided his time.

* * *

[1] Gustav Regler, *The Owl of Minerva.*

He did not have to wait long. The following day a red flag waved from a window of the Ibarra Palace and a group of Black Shirts came pouring out waving their arms in welcome. The propaganda machine had succeeded after all, it seemed. Presently they surrounded a tank and Republican Spaniards manning the tank sprang out to greet them and swarmed round the deserters exchanging greetings in ebullient Italian. And then the firing began, the Spaniards were picked off, the tank abandoned and a small pool of panic momentarily paralysed that part of the Republican line. It was once again a carefully planned trick, but even now Regler was not quite disillusioned. One or two at least among the deserters, he felt, were genuine, and as the moment for another big attack drew near he redoubled his propaganda assault.

'More loudspeakers were brought into action. Our Italians drafted fresh texts. Loudspeaker vans were brought from Madrid as close as possible to the front. Actors spoke to the soldiers, appealing to their pride, invoking their home-sickness, and as though talking to children, reminding them of the danger in which they stood.

'Ritornate alle vostre case, non dovete morire – go home, you must not die.'

At zero hour the following day, Regler brought up all his vans to release, in consort, a great rolling wave of music in the inevitable form of the Internationale.

As the melody swelled out over the countryside the French and Italians were visibly moved and the Poles, joining in the song, fixed their bayonets with a fresh enthusiasm. Then the Nationalist artillery went to work and shells crashed and exploded in the Italian lines.

Barontini, the Italian Commissar, heard someone leap down into the trench beside him, and ducked as the earth quivered to a tremendous explosion. The notes of the Internationale rose again above the bombardment and he turned to Regler standing beside him and said: 'Theatre! Mass murder of volunteers with musical accompaniment.' He snorted with indignation. 'Another idea from headquarters.' 'What do you mean by headquarters?' Regler said. 'I'm here beside you.'

A moment later Italians, French and Poles swarmed out of the trenches into the attack and momentarily carried everything before them. Among the Italians the 4th and 5th Companies of the Garibaldi Battalion had been chosen for this operation and they were led by Brignoli, the Communist carpenter from Lombardy, who had just recovered from a neck wound.[1] They attacked at 11 a.m. on the 14th, proceeding, at first, behind armoured cars. This technique seemed to distress the Nationalists who abandoned their covering positions in a nearby wood and took shelter in the courtyard of Ibarra Palace. As the attack developed, the Nationalists made another mistake. They abandoned their positions on and around the outer walls of the palace and retired into the main buildings which seemed to offer better protection.

Brignoli's men moved in swift, short spurts towards the outer wall, reached it, and found fresh shelter crouching beneath it. They were now able to shoot straight up, without offering much of a target themselves because the Nationalists dared not lean out of the windows. Slowly, Italian, French and Polish troops tried to encircle the whole palace, and the Nationalist commander called up an artillery unit to preserve gaps in the line, but the Garibaldini managed to silence the gunners by concentrating their fire for twenty minutes. Next, a number of Nationalist troops tried to escape from the rear of the palace, and another episode of mistaken identity followed.

One patrol of the Garibaldini, skirmishing in the rear of the palace, encountered another group of Italians dressed almost identically. The Nationalist troop leader hesitated and shouted in Italian 'Who are you?' Suddenly, Brignoli realized that these men were 'Fascists', and ordered his troops to open fire. The Nationalists suffered heavy casualties before they ran for it. Brignoli now awaited the support of two more companies from the Franco-Belge Battalion, and when at last they arrived about three o'clock in the afternoon, he completely surrounded and cut off the palace. A circle of fire poured into it from all sides, and suddenly and spectacularly a few shells from the small cannon of the armoured cars hit the main tower and it crumbled and fell, sending up choking clouds of dust. Everywhere the masonry,

[1] The following account is based on Luigi Longo's narrative in *Le Brigate Internationali in Spagna* and the Italian edition of *The Volunteer for Liberty*.

windows, walls began to crumble under the hail of lead and the enemy's answering fire slackened.

Brignoli ordered a cease-fire at this point, and through a megaphone from the surrounding wall called on the Nationalists to surrender, guaranteeing them safe conduct. 'We already have 34 happy prisoners with us', he shouted and a number of men threw pamphlets wrapped around stones into the ruined windows. The pamphlets carried a photograph of the 34 prisoners gathered about their commanding officer, all happily smiling. While Brignoli spoke, a number of Garibaldini stealthily slipped over the surrounding wall and slithered along towards the inner wall of the palace itself.

By five o'clock there was still no response to the appeal to surrender, and Brignoli ordered the advance scouts to set fire to the palace. As the smoke and flames poured up, a wail of fear and rage came out of the palace, and then followed a fearful and inexplicable crash. Simultaneously, Brignoli ordered a new general attack which carried everything before it until they entered the inner courtyard and found the remnants of the garrison gathered in one corner, half-defiant, half-afraid. 'Don't shoot', Brignoli cried and immediately invited the Italians to throw down their arms and surrender. Both sides now stood in uneasy hesitation, and Brignoli called on the Nationalist captain to give them a lead by throwing away his revolver. The captain laughed mockingly at the invitation, but Brignoli shouted that they were trapped – there was nothing left to do but surrender or perish. The Nationalists asked for a truce period to discuss the question of surrender. Brignoli agreed, and set up machine-gun posts to command any avenue of escape. A moment later the Fascist captain threw a hand-grenade, killing two Garibaldini, and as he ran for the gate was himself shot down by an armoured car. Rage, excitement, fear ran through the courtyard and as the Garibaldini were about to open fire again, Brignoli intervened once more and made a last effort to reason with the enemy, shouting to the Nationalists: 'This is your last chance – surrender now – or die.' At last the Nationalists decided to give way, and for the time being the prized Ibarra Palace was in the hands of the Garibaldini.[1]

Scenes of remarkable sensitivity followed on what had been a

[1] *Le Volontaire de la liberté.*

brutal battle. Regler described the Italians of the Garibaldi as looking almost shyly at prisoners of their own kind. It was as if they were ashamed of holding such men prisoner, he said. When an Abyssinian volunteer of the Garibaldi Battalion pushed his way forward with two prisoners roped together, he saluted with a broad smile, and even the prisoners smiled back. Regler embraced the Abyssinian, congratulated him, and then said, 'And now take the rope off.' It was a travesty of the horrible business of war.

Not only tanks, guns, ammunition and prisoners fell into Republican hands during this battle but letters, some of them moving letters, addressed by young wives, mothers and sweethearts to their serving menfolk.

One wife wrote to her Italian husband:

'What a beautiful honeymoon mine has been! Two days of marriage and twenty-five months of interminable waiting. First comes the country I know, and afterwards love, but I am an egoist and with reason, for you were one of the first volunteers. . . . I pray God that one day He will make it possible for you both to serve the country and also provide bread for your family.'[1]

The Nationalist General Roatta now launched two counterattacks with his remaining divisions, Rossi's Black Shirts and Bergonzoli's Littorio Division. Both were beaten back. In the battle some confusion momentarily overtook the Garibaldi H.Q. Following a burst of artillery fire, three tanks made a concerted dash for their field H.Q. and one, an older tank, came within range of hand-grenades and was blown up. Another succeeded in penetrating into the H.Q. area, and proceeded to play hide-and-seek with the Staff, compelling them to 'run round the house', before it was driven off again.[2]

A three-day lull followed, and on the third morning, 18 March, unfortunately for Roatta he slipped away to Salamanca to seek fresh aid from Franco. At half-past one on the afternoon of the 18th, nearly a hundred Republican planes bombed the defences surrounding Brihuega, artillery followed up with a heavy bombardment, and at two o'clock two divisions, the Lister and Cipriano Mera, went into the attack supported by seventy tanks. They had almost succeeded in encircling the town when

[1] League of Nations Document No. 267.
[2] R. Pacciardi, *Il Battaglione Garibaldi*, p. 168.

General Kléber, whose real name was Stern, Commander of the XIth International Brigade at the time of the Siege of Madrid.

Above A group of American volunteers arriving at the Gare St. Lazare in Paris, February, 1937.

Wide World Photos

Below Captain Malcolm Dunbar, Chief of Staff to the XVth Brigade, Lt-Colonel Čopic, Commander of the XVth, and John Gates, American political commissar.

John Cornford in 1936.

Major Robert Merriman, Chief of Staff of the Abraham Lincoln Brigade and highest ranking American officer in Spain. He was formerly instructor of economics at the University of California.

Spanish Loyalist stretcher bearers bring a wounded comrade to an American hospital set up behind the firing line.

Tom Wintringham in hospital in Valencia. The silver-headed cane which was his only 'weapon' on the Jarama is in the corner.

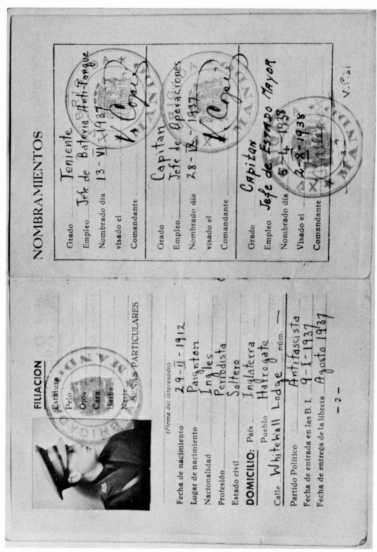

The identity card of Malcolm Dunbar, who was educated at Cambridge and rose from the ranks to become Chief of Staff to the XVth Brigade.

Commanders of the different battalions in the XVth International Brigade. Left to right: the coloured commander of the Washington Battalion, Oliver Law; Captain Saul of the French April 16 Battalion; Fred Copeman of the British Battalion; an American from Brigade H.Q.; the Commander of the Dabrowsky Battalion; two Spanish Battalion commanders.

The Croat Communist Commander of the XVth Brigade, Vladimir Čopic.

Members of the British Battalion at a machine-gun post and preparing food on the Aragon front.

Keystone Press Agency

the Italian garrison received orders to carry out a full-scale retreat. Quickly the speed of the retreat increased to the point where it became a rout. Here was part of the explanation of Renn's recent success. When he rallied his small band from the XVth Brigade, the Italians were already at the point of collapse.

This was a tremendous moment in the long, savage struggle for the Republican forces, and particularly for the International Brigades which had played such a vital part. After eight months of retreats and confusions, of defensive withdrawal and the steady loss of ground, they believed that they had won a decisive victory, and for the first time literally routed the enemy. The battle of the Guadalajara road was over and Madrid once more saved.

In retrospect, the picture seems less glowing. Politically, the Republican success had profound repercussions, but the military situation was not markedly changed. Franco's attempt to complete the encirclement of Madrid had once again been thwarted, but the Nationalists did retain some twenty kilometres of the ground they had gained in their initial thrust, and in terms of sheer territory the Republicans had lost rather than gained. But a retreat was a retreat and nothing could have boosted their morale higher.

As an object lesson for those European generals who were watching from afar, the battle seemed to undermine the idea that motorized troops could bring about a swift and decisive victory, but different schools drew different conclusions. The French ceased to believe in the possibilities of blitzkrieg – with what disastrous consequences in the Second World War we know too well – and the Germans, cynical and nationalistic to the last, argued that you could not possibly base any sound theory on the behaviour of troops so contemptible as the Italians. This, in turn, was grossly unfair to the Italians.

Most of their troops had set out from Italy expecting a spell of Abyssinian garrison duty, only to find themselves involved in a savage European war of which they knew little. As an officer of the XIth International Brigade said: 'The Italians advanced in columns of four along the road to our defences. They did not seem to expect any resistance and when we opened fire they appeared to be completely confused. . . . Once the surprise was over, the Italians fought well during the first two days, but when they were faced with the very stubborn resistance of the Spanish troops with plenty of ground-strafing and bombing by Government planes, their morale broke. . . .'[1]

Whatever the mood of Franco's Italians there was no doubting the jubilation of the Republicans. There were tremendous celebrations around recklessly blazing camp-fires, speeches were made, songs sung, and endless toasts drunk in anticipation of the day when they finally flung the enemy back and broke, once and for all, the stranglehold on Madrid.

The Garibaldini drank special toasts to Pacciardi, and many a lesser leader like Brignoli, Bocchi, Nicoletti, Negroni and Cremonini, whose names have now been forgotten. Like most of the pioneer battalions in the International Brigade, the Garibaldi had come through terrible slaughter – in one day, an appalling Christmas Day, 600 men had been reduced to 200 in a single battle – and now, here was something to compensate, and they sang, drank and celebrated with all the verve which sprang from their Latin blood.

[1] *Fact*, 'The Spanish War', July 1938, pp. 9–10.

Chapter 14

The French

LIKE all other elements of the International Brigades the French underwent many changes from the original handful of men who formed the Commune de Paris Battalion to the disasters and re-formulation of later days. They fought bravely in defence of Madrid, they were moved, like many another international battalion, from one danger spot to another and time and again they received the full fury of the enemy's attack. The individual stories of the men in the Commune de Paris Battalion would, once again, need another book to do them justice. They were at Jarama, Brunete, Saragossa and many other battles.

Inevitably the French were more individualistic than many other battalions, first because it was in their Latin blood and second because they did not risk the imprisonment and death which would have been the fate of many Germans and Italians who dared to return to their homelands. Restlessness showed itself easily among the French, and when they did not like the way things were organized they openly rebelled. This could lead to a typically French exchange where words and gestures reached fever-pitch and rank was no protection against savage invective, or it could end in physical violence, and if anyone dared the final idiocy of challenging André Marty – to death from the all-too-ready firing squads.

It was André Marty, the French commander at the Albacete base, who now found himself forced to justify what were said to be brutal and pointless executions. Henri Storc, a veteran Brigader, attacked Marty in too wholesale a way to be taken seriously, but his was one of the less hysterical attacks. Storc wrote in *Jeunesse de France*:[1]

'I accuse André Marty of having installed in the Brigades spies and denouncers . . . of having unjustly punished Comrade

[1] 23 July 1938.

Pierrecourt on Feb. 1st. . . . I have been described by Marty as a Fascist and he affirmed that he would smash me. Knowing that a single word from Marty meant arrest and then a little walk at dawn which would be the last, I preferred to risk more dignified death, . . . and having asked to come out of hospital I joined the Brigade again in front of Teruel. . . . I formally accuse André Marty of being the assassin of 40,000 [sic] young Frenchmen.'

The figure was absurd – far more than the total number in the French battalion – but there remains the evidence of other men like Oloff de Wet who wrote: 'Discipline was very strict and penalties varied according to nationality. Capital punishment was sometimes meted out for mere drunkenness and in particular cases the execution squad became the only form of punishment for the most insignificant offences. It was a hellish existence – yes, hellish – I use the word not merely as an explanation but as a description. It is the only one adequate for the life of those volunteers which was something beyond imagination.'

Gustav Regler also gave his view of Marty: '. . . it is not so easy to turn a mutinous N.C.O. into the commander of an army, a fact of which the last war furnished notable examples. Marty covered his forgivable inadequacy with an unforgivable passionate spy-hunt; he was genuinely convinced that many of the volunteers who came to his headquarters were Fascist spies. He put all his energies at the service of his mistrust and did not shrink from conducting day-long, soul-destroying interrogations or even from sacrificing the tranquillity of his nights and his peace of mind by promptly liquidating doubtful cases rather than harm the Republic by what he called "petty bourgeois indecision".'[1]

When he himself first volunteered for the I.B., Regler was subjected to Marty's cat-and-mouse tactics, and asked to answer a dozen staccato questions in quick succession until he finally had flung at him: 'Show me your membership card of the POUM.'

Regler had no idea, at that time, what the initials POUM meant, and he was suddenly overwhelmed with the desire to jump up and knock the suspicion out of his interrogator. He

[1] Gustav Regler, *The Owl of Minerva*, pp. 277–8.

would probably have paid for the blow with his life – such was Marty's absolute power – but instead, he produced a letter stating that he was the Spanish correspondent of the Moscow-published *Deutsche Zeitung*. Marty remained dissatisfied. Regler thereupon left his office.

Later that afternoon he was summoned back, to be received by a new and more affable Marty who quickly led him upstairs to his wife's bedroom. There Marty made some excuse to leave them and an extraordinary interlude occurred. The wife, a very attractive woman, proceeded to spread out on the unmade bed an array of pistols, and invited Regler to make his choice. 'I did so with a deliberate coolness, bowed to the very good-looking woman and withdrew scenting a suspicious mixture of politics and sex.'

By the summer of 1937 rumours had spread, secret reports were made, and a whole network of intelligence went to work until at last Marty was called upon to explain the mounting number of executions. On 15 November he duly delivered a report to the Central Committee of the Communist Party in an attempt to justify himself:

'In Spain, mixed with good militants, Communists, Social-ists, Italian anti-Fascists, German émigrés, and anarchists of all countries and races, came several hundred international criminal elements, and while one section limited themselves to living comfortably without doing anything, and without fighting, many others took advantage of the confusion of the first days and a number of abominable crimes, violations, violence, robbery and killing for the sheer wickedness of killing were committed. Not content with this they organized bloody rebellions against the authorities of Valencia and some devoted themselves to spying for Franco. . . . While one section of the above-mentioned elements managed to clear themselves by fighting valiantly and falling in the hardest battles fought by the Brigades in defence of Madrid, others proved to be incorrigible and some tried to continue their criminal enterprises . . . in other towns. When placed in concentration camps they sometimes escaped by attacking and killing their guards. In these circum-stances I did not hesitate and ordered the necessary executions. The executions ordered did not go beyond 500.'

A mixture of special pleading, half-lies and half-truths, the report did not take account of a considerable number of summary executions casually carried out on men who were drunk and disorderly, men no more than suspected of spying and a few who failed to satisfy Marty about their origins. Nor were the executions exclusively limited to other ranks.

When the Republic launched its abortive attack on the Córdoba front – the attack which produced the famous communiqué, 'During the day the advance continued without the loss of any territory' – André Marty suddenly appeared at field headquarters. General Walter commanded the XIVth International Brigade which included the French Marseillaise Battalion led by the dandified Major Lasalle, who always wore polished, black-leather leggings. Angered by the failure of the attack on the village of Lopera, Marty placed the blame on Lasalle and accused him of spying for the Nationalists. At the critical moment of the attack on Lopera, Lasalle had, according to one witness, withdrawn half a mile behind the lines, but field commanders could more than justify such a manoeuvre and in any case it had nothing to do with spying. A brief military trial followed during which Lasalle passionately defended himself against charges of cowardice and spying. It was useless. The tribunal found him guilty and condemned him to death. Before the firing squad he shouted imprecations at Marty and pleaded for the intervention of Colonel Putz, the still-much-loved Frenchman who was now President of the Council of War. Lasalle died still protesting his innocence. According to Hugh Thomas, Lasalle was not so much a spy as a coward and once more Marty's pathological obsession with espionage had brutally destroyed a man. There is some evidence to show that Marty went in fear of being shot down himself by hired assassins and each man he destroyed represented the removal of yet another danger to his own person.

The story of Lasalle's trial and death is not complete without the evidence of two other men – Tom Wintringham and Piet Jansen. According to Wintringham: 'Commandant Lasalle moved further back during the day because of the air bombing. He was arrested and a court martial called to try him. *It was a very fair court martial, deliberate and meticulous. It gave L. a hearing and he was shot.*'[1] Wintringham added the final comment. 'A

[1] Tom Wintringham, *English Captain*, pp. 88–9.

strange army in which they did not shoot privates, but did shoot a cowardly major.' This, again, was untrue. They did shoot privates. Piet Jansen, the Dutch translator at the trial, said that Lasalle 'was missing during the night and that he went up through the front into Lopera itself.'[1] There 'he had a rendezvous with the Fascist commander of the village' and according to some of the evidence which Jansen translated, he deserved to be shot.

Ilya Ehrenburg, many years later, gave this verdict on Marty: 'I met André Marty, who was imperious, very short-tempered and always suspecting everyone of treason. We talked for some two hours and this conversation left me with a sense of bitterness: he spoke (and occasionally acted) like a mentally sick man.'[2]

Colonel Putz remained one of the most popular figures in the whole long story of the French contribution to the International Brigades. Putz from the very early days was commander of the 13th Battalion which Wintringham described as 'the most cheerful fighting body I have ever been attached to . . . its cheerfulness derived mainly from the humanity and enthusiasm of its Commander.'

A lean, frail person, Putz combined the roles of cultured French gentleman and regular army officer, Socialist and sophisticate with a grace and charm which won the hearts of all his men. He also had a gift for dealing with delinquents. 'Punishments were given quickly when need be; but every man felt that he had been dealt with by a human being.'[3]

However, the small group of Englishmen temporarily involved with the French Battalion found the French methods of justice unsatisfactory. It was one thing to lock a drunken man in the guard-room; it was quite another for the commandant to decide on the sentence – usually the full stretch of five days – without giving the man a hearing. From the days of Magna Carta and King John, an Englishman had to have a hearing. 'A hearing?' the French said laughing. 'But a drunken man can't talk sense when he's tight and can't remember much the next day – what's the use of giving him a hearing?' Occasionally

---

[1] *Reynolds News*, 23 July 1961.
[2] Ilya Ehrenburg, *Eve of War 1933–41*, p. 167.
[3] Tom Wintringham, *English Captain*, p. 83.

the demand for a hearing was given a mock satisfaction and exchanges of this kind took place:

Officer: You are charged with being drunk last night.
Culprit: Not really drunk, sir – just –
Officer: You were drunk – five days' detention.

The hearing had been granted. Occasionally there were far more serious scenes. A drunken man ran berserk with his gun and had to be shot down by the guards: another man planned and carried out brutal robberies and was summarily executed: a razor boy tried to set up a gang: once a prostitute or camp woman was found murdered on the streets and no one took too much trouble to investigate her death.

The seamy side of the French Battalion – which was somewhat worse than that of some other battalions – can be seen through the eyes of Nick Gillain, one of the earliest recruits, who survived any number of skirmishes and battles. Gillain claims that almost from the start, when they were quartered at Torrelodones, a small village north of Madrid, equality of treatment for officers and men was abandoned. Officers received beautiful new uniforms and other ranks held protest meetings, almost mutinied and were threatened with 'concentration camps'. That there were 'concentration camps' of a kind seems possible, but they did not resemble Dachau or the horrors produced by Nazi Germany. There was no torture, no deliberate starvation, no attempt to kill men by overwork, but living conditions were harsh, men were very occasionally shot out of hand and Gillain spoke of flogging. 'When one man complained that he had received a flogging which left him with marks across his face an officer replied: "So much the worse for you. You will have to avenge yourself in the same way at the first chance."'

An unnamed volunteer who underwent a nightmare alternation of brawls and imprisonment, arrests and interrogation, release and re-imprisonment, finally claimed to have ended up in a 'concentration camp', but he no sooner used the term than he added, 'this place, however, was much better than the prison we had just left, for it was spotlessly clean and the supper we were given of bread, a pint of soup, stewed corned beef and black beans was not so bad.'

The prisoners in the camp received a square meal of this

kind twice a day, and anyone who later experienced Dachau would have considered it paradise. 'The place was run on the Soviet system, at least, that is what we were told. . . . Although armed sentries were [present], a good-conduct prisoner was in charge of each working party who reported the work done and the conduct of each prisoner. Every night a certain number of names were read out as having been selected for good work that day. . . . When a prisoner's name appeared on this board for seven days in succession it was placed on what was known as the Stakhanovite list. If a prisoner was lucky enough to have his name on the list for ten days in succession *he was then released no matter how long* his sentence might be.'[1]

This particular recruit continued his extraordinary sequence of release, trouble, fighting and rearrest until he reached an altogether different type of establishment where the Guardia Nacional ordered him to give up all his property which he simply refused to do. 'About half a dozen of the guard . . . set about me and beat me up. . . . I was laid out and when I came to I found that I was strapped in a strait-jacket lying in a small room on the floor. I could not lift up my head and I ached all over while the place seemed to be turning round. My mouth was swollen and I could scarcely open it – I lay there all that night.'[2]

Gillain described the different battalions of the XIIIth and XIVth Brigades as virtually partisan bands who made their own laws, and it was General Walter who coined the phrase about the French-Belgian Battalion – 'dear bandits' – a term which signified to Gillain 'much affection and compassionate contempt'.

Drink and gambling remained a preoccupation with some of Colonel Putz's men, and there were occasions when the food situation got out of hand. According to Gillain, while his battalion was stationed in Andalusia the Spanish Commissary Corps provided 25,000 rations for 4,000 men, and at the Jarama front 12,000 rations arrived for 1,700 combatants. Food was allowed to rot on the ground and in one day alone 140 cavalrymen received 'half a steer, five hams, eight smoked sausages, two small cases of sardines, 170 eggs, 70 kilos of potatoes, 60

[1] *In Spain with the International Brigade – A Personal Narrative*, p. 21.
[2] Ibid., p. 51.

kilos of chick peas, 50 of rice, 50 of beans, five of lard, two of butter, 20 kilos of jam, two cases of nougats and chocolate, coffee, sugar, salt, wine, etc.' In fact, subdivided between 140 men, such supplies may not be so extravagant as they sound, since no indication was given of how long they were expected to last. Certainly there were days when the civilian population had too little to eat and this particular battalion had too much.

As for clothing, Gillain claims that the French and Belgians regularly replaced uniforms and kit before they were anywhere near worn out. Over-provided with clothing and food, they were under-provided with guns and ammunition. Many a night small bands of French soldiers made their way into the lines of Spanish companies, while they slept, to steal guns and ammunition, but the best time to 'acquire' equipment was when the Nationalist planes bombed the Republican lines and everyone went under cover. These expeditions were by no means exclusive to the French. Copeman recalls some spectacular feats by the British along similar lines. Nothing remained sacred. Cars, horses, pistols, cigarettes, all were fair game on a starless night with an enemy bombardment in progress.

Among the French, the personality of Putz continued to hold the men together, against the worst that drink, gambling and midnight raids could do. In battle, too, he remained their inspiration. When the French fell back before repeated enemy onslaughts at Jarama, it was Putz who rode up on his horse in positively medieval fashion, and rallied the fleeing men with a few phrases in the most expressive French vernacular. The men hesitated, checked their flight, re-formed and prepared for a counter-attack. 'It wasn't for love of the proletariat,' Gillain wrote, 'the great cause of the unfortunate, or the political ideals of the Internationale that they took up the fight again after a moment of hesitation. No, it was for Putz's sake – in order not to leave him out there alone.'[1]

Gillain believed that as the composition of the Brigades changed their character, jealousy between them grew. 'For propaganda reasons the high command diminished the effectiveness of the French to increase that of the Italians. *Espagne* announced to all the world that the battle of Guadalajara had been won by the anti-Fascist Italians but the real truth was

[1] Nick Gillain, *Le Mercenaire*, pp. 107–8.

that most of the success was due to the intervention of the Commune de Paris Battalion. At the Arganda bridge the French stopped the Nationalist offensive but the honours were awarded to the Garibaldi Battalion.'[1] Such rival claims were common among different nationalities.

The French also played a considerable part in the battle of the Ebro. One group of volunteers from the Commune de Paris Battalion, led by André Gautier and Sergeant Marraches, stripped naked, armed themselves with daggers and hand-grenades, and prepared, on the morning of 24 July 1938, to swim across the fierce current. Their aim was to demolish a nest of machine-guns commanding the very point at which they wanted to construct a pontoon bridge. When they were about to dive into the river, orders came postponing the operation until the next day.

During the night, rafts were brought up to be concealed in the reeds and preparations with cables and canoes went on steadily.[2] At 12.25, a dozen volunteers slid silently into the water once more. Their comrades watched helplessly as four of the twelve found themselves in difficulties before they were half-way across. The current seemed even fiercer than usual, and swirls and eddies presently took hold of man after man and swept him away from the objective. Only five finally reached the other side and the cries of the others, as they found themselves in trouble, gave the enemy forewarning of the attack. They opened fire and the five survivors took what cover they could, pin-pointing the exact position of the machine-gun posts. The first boat then nosed in-shore carrying the cables for the pontoon bridge, and the five volunteers went in with hand-grenades to silence the machine-guns.

Mortar fire now spattered the growing beach-head as new boats, filled with fresh troops, began to disembark at high speed. There were many casualties. One unit was completely wiped out. The remainder, with their numbers still increasing under heavier fire, advanced in the direction of Santa Barbara, but a few hundred metres from the Ebro encountered a heavily defended canal. The first wave which went across the canal was wiped out. Fire redoubled as mortars went into action again

[1] Nick Gillain, *Le Mercenaire*, p. 121.
[2] *L'Épopée de l'Espagne*, 'Brigades Internationales', pp. 162–3.

along the whole length of the canal. Enemy machine-gun and infantry units then moved into position and brought the canal under cross-fire. Frantically the French tried to dig in, but there was no time for anything beyond scooping shallow depressions, and when one of their leaders, Captain Bohec of the 3rd Company, received a bullet in the mouth and died a horrible death, there seemed nothing for it but retreat.

The Commune de Paris fought on heroically, but as dawn broke enemy artillery fire became much more accurate. Units of the Republican Air Force went into action but could not silence the guns. Lieutenant Leymarie, who was directing the construction of the pontoon bridge, suddenly fell into the water with a bullet in his stomach and shortly afterwards his adjutant, who took over, also collapsed seriously wounded. The rafts and boats forming the skeleton of the footbridge were now so severely damaged that it could not be completed. The Commune de Paris found themselves defending a tight arc three hundred metres across at the base, under heavy and continuous fire. Once more they dug shallow trenches and repelled several counter-attacks, holding on in the desperate knowledge that if they remained in position until nightfall, reinforcements might then be smuggled across the river. Their guns fired so continuously that time and again they overheated and jammed and the few armourers who had reached the beach-head found themselves hard put to it to get them restarted. Presently, the beach-head shrank a little more, as they were once more forced to retreat, and the fight in the redoubt now became murderous. One message was constantly repeated: they simply had to hold until evening.[1]

The enemy now brought up armoured cars in an attempt finally to smash the bridgehead, and the huge figure of a Frenchman called Pluquin, supported by Commissar Paul Houppert, led a group who counter-attacked with hand-grenades. Commander Cazalar remained in the thick of the fighting directing the French with the sang-froid of someone conducting an orchestra.

Hour after hour went by. The bridgehead shrank a little more, and then at last came darkness, and with it the immense relief of fresh reinforcements making their way across.

[1] *L'Épopée de l'Espagne*, 'Brigades Internationales', p. 163.

Soon they were in a position to attack once more, and now, slowly but certainly, they pushed the enemy back again towards Gandesa where the main attack had meantime succeeded. Such was part of their contribution to the great battle of the Ebro.

Like all the battalions, the French knew long periods of stalemate when weather conditions, or the caprice of the High Command, left them solidly sitting opposite the enemy doing nothing, and the time-worn tradition of fraternization came into its own.

During the summer of 1937 the Commune de Paris Battalion was stationed at Las Navas, on a promontory which looked out over a scene of dream-like beauty, with a wooded ravine below, the river Rio flowing steadily through the ravine and a far prospect of plain and hill, rich in gold and purple. An average day for ten consecutive and idle days began in the hushed expectancy of dawn as the first birds sang and the swift sunrise pushed back the darkness. Down from their posts into the ravine climbed man after man, anxious to reach the river before the sun became too hot, and now began a wonderful early morning bathe followed by a picnic breakfast. There were times, in the silence of the dawn, with the cool fresh waters of the river washing past their bodies, and the smell of brewing coffee on the air, when the scene became idyllic and might easily have belonged to a peace-time holiday.

By eleven o'clock the sun was hot enough to make the metal parts of horses' harness burning to the touch, and the air quivered with ever-increasing heat. At eleven-fifteen came the only active moment of the day, when the regimental postmaster arrived and letters were distributed. Not that the wives, relatives, mistresses and friends of the Brigaders were good correspondents. There were few letters and fewer parcels, and the big brown containers which brought hundreds of copies of L'Humanité were sometimes received with undisguised groans.

After lunch, a rich, full, wine-laden lunch, the heat became so stifling that the nearly vertical rays of the sun seemed to bite into the very rocks themselves, the air became difficult to breathe and as one man after another fell into profound siesta, the absolute silence was only broken by the soft and distant voice of the Rio murmuring far down below.

Towards five o'clock, men stirred from sleep, some surly, some full of life, some desperate to find a means of overcoming boring idleness. They would play cards, argue, quarrel and drink. Sometimes a fight broke out, sometimes they climbed down into the ravine once more and went fishing. Frequently they deliberately waited for the one big diversion of the day when two women – one the Brigade dentist, the other a doctor – came down to bathe. One was plain and unattractive, the other as Gillain put it 'enough to inflame the best of men'. When the women first appeared there would be muttered ribaldries interspersed with obscenities, but as they came closer these would die away, and then came a moment of high-tension silence when one lovely young woman calmly took off her dress and disclosed, to the gaping and almost gasping men, a long, firm body hardly disguised at all by close-fitting tights. Both women then walked slowly and calmly past the men down towards the river, for all the world as if they were unaware of the excitement which their passage caused.

When night came down on the Las Navas front the best sharp-shooters would set out to forage the countryside and usually came back with some partridges or wood-pigeons. These were cooked over open fires and then began an evening feast with much drinking of wine. After dinner a number of men made token gestures in the direction of duty, hauling on all their kit and returning to the line for a quick look at the enemy, but for weeks it was a meaningless piece of routine. Scouts were sent out regularly after dark, but once again it was a formula with a few shots exchanged which died away on the night air and did no damage to anyone.

Night brought a welcome coolness and silence, with the mysterious background murmurs of the wild and beautiful countryside multiplying. Once the guards had been posted, many men fell to playing cards and then, as they lolled around in groups, a voice would come rolling over from no-man's-land. 'Reds! Reds!' it said. 'Do you hear me?' The voice echoed mysteriously from wall to wall of the ravine.

Sometimes the men ignored the voice, sometimes a guard shouted – 'Shit' – in reply but occasionally they dropped their

cards and came to the trench-front to look and listen. Then
began a verbal duel between a Spanish priest in the enemy's
lines who spoke perfect French, and the French Political
Commissar of the Commune de Paris.

'Reds – Reds – do you hear me?' the priest would say. 'Why
do you continue this disastrous fight? What have you to gain if
you win? Why don't you see it's a terrible waste of time and lives
and give up your weapons and come out of your trenches . . .'

A long silence. Then the voice again: 'There must be some of
you tired of it all. . . . Some who are tired of sleeping in trenches.
. . . When it is dark, very dark, later – in the middle of the
night – come across to us – we will welcome you!'

And then the French Political Commissar spoke back through
his megaphone. 'You're wasting your time – priest – we don't
like priests – no one is going to desert from our side. But what
about yours? Do you hear me – you who have been hired for
money to die – you Moors and mercenaries – why not give it up
and go back home to your own country? You won't die so soon
there. For be assured if you stay where you are, you will die!'

The priest suddenly drowned out the commissar's voice with
a burst of Spanish music and the effect was miraculous. Rising
above the ravine, the French could see the beautiful, black,
rugged heights held by the enemy from which the flood of
crystalline music came; above that again was an indigo sky
with great glittering stars; and behind the French, the heights
soared up, topped by sombre masses of pine. There, in the still,
hot silence of the night, the lilting rhythms of the bolero pouring
across no-man's-land seemed to Gillain 'like a hymn to a pagan
god'.

It held everyone enthralled until the music slowly died away,
and then came a long silence, a silence charged with emotion
as the small murmurs of the countryside reasserted themselves
and men spoke and moved uneasily again. And then, out into
the glimmering night from the Republican side went the great
echoing chords of the Internationale played like a military
march. Some found them raucous and disastrous. Others were
no less moved than when they listened to the bolero.

Now the enemy answered with a rain of shrapnel shells
'tearing up the soil in geysers of fire', and it seemed grotesque
after the exchange of music. Artillery bombardment represented

the ultimate contradiction of what had gone before. Ugliness, brutality, sheer noise for noise's sake, reigned over the ravine and the night once again.

The most sensational moment in the long story of the French battalions – which cannot be told in detail here – came in the battle of Brunete during July 1937. The XIIIth Brigade – made up of French, Belgians, Poles and Slavs – had been continuously involved in battle for several days, and when, at the height of the offensive, they were ordered back into the line again without the usual rest period, their officers rebelled. At least three contradictory accounts are given of what followed. According to Gillain, the brigade commander, Kriegger – a former Communist Deputy from Trieste – had issued the order to return to the line and he was quickly surrounded by a score of officers all strongly protesting that this was madness. A violent argument broke out and suddenly Kriegger demanded: 'Where do you think you are – back in an office or kitchen? Do you think this is a place where you can resign?'

Another burst of argument followed and then Kriegger announced: 'I shall examine your case after the battle. Now I order you to go immediately and put yourself at the head of your battalion!'

One officer in particular seems to have conducted much of the argument and he said: 'I refuse to move.'

'What do you mean?' Kriegger shouted, and shook his fist in his face. A moment later he said: 'You are under arrest. Disarm this man.'

But none of the officers or men would undertake either to arrest or disarm him. Kriegger realized that something much more drastic was required to restore discipline and he walked up to the officer, levelled his revolver and said, 'Obey my orders or be shot!' Kriegger was now in a highly nervous state and as his nerves broke through, his manner became more brutal. He repeated his words and when there was still no response calmly levelled his revolver and shot the officer dead. The scene that followed came close enough to mutiny to be indistinguishable from it.

The account given by the Spanish historian Lizón Gadéa is

different. 'One of his [Colonel Kriegger's] convincing arguments . . . was to assassinate with a pistol a few who wouldn't be convinced. In reprisal the soldiers of the 13th put their machine-guns into position and would not let their commander pass. Kriegger thereupon killed one or two soldiers, and then one Spaniard . . . threw himself on him with a hand-grenade forcing him to run away, slightly hurt. Without permission the soldiers abandoned their positions and marched up to Torrelodones where some companies of shock troops disarmed them under the orders of [General] Miaja. . . .'[1]

Whichever version one accepts it led to the same conclusion. Within a very short time the XIIIth Brigade was disarmed, reorganized and later underwent the mysterious process known as re-education.

[1] Adolfo Lizón Gadéa, *Brigadas Internacionales en España*, p. 36.

Chapter 15

The XVth Brigade Rests

FROM 11 to 21 April Madrid suffered a new, heavy and indiscriminate bombardment which still failed to produce the kind of panic that certain Nationalist leaders expected. Ernest Hemingway visited Madrid in this period and left some vivid accounts of what it was like when rifle, machine-gun and mortar fire continuously broke into the life of the city and no one knew who would be the next victim of the next air-raid. Hemingway lived in the comparative comfort of a Madrid hotel, but for many mornings he woke to the sound of high-explosive shells screaming through the air.

'There is the acrid smell of high-explosive you hoped you'd never smell again, and in a bathrobe and bedroom slippers you hurry down the marble stairs and almost into a middle-aged woman wounded in the abdomen who is being helped into the hotel entrance by two men in blue workmen's smocks. She has her two hands crossed below her big, old-style Spanish bosom and from between her fingers the blood is spurting in a thin stream.'[1]

A policeman explains that the shell went through the sidewalk and burst underneath. Otherwise there would have been fifty casualties instead of two, the wounded woman and a dead man. As he talks he is busy covering up the top of the trunk of the dead man from which the head is missing. A tired-looking charwoman comes with a bucket, soap and brush and begins scrubbing the blood off the marble floor. A man from the gasworks drives up in a truck, jamming the brakes to a screeching standstill. A hundred other people daily pass the very point where the dead man dies. 'Someone makes a joke about missing teeth and someone else says not to make that joke. And everyone has the feeling that characterizes war. It wasn't me, see? It wasn't me.'[2]

The hospital provided by the American Friends of Spanish

[1] *Fact*, No. 16, 15 July 1938, pp. 17–18.   [2] Ibid., p. 18.

Democracy sends a message to Hemingway – 'Raven wants to see you', and he travels out to meet a man he has never encountered before, whose name means nothing to him. The man is three-quarters covered by a mound of shoddy grey blanket and from one end protrudes 'something that had been a face but now was a yellow scabby area with a wide bandage across where the eyes had been.' Raven came from Pittsburgh, Pennsylvania, where the great Gettysburg battles were fought, and his university training led him to take up the life of a social worker before he volunteered for Spain. Now, as he talked to Raven, Hemingway noticed that he had the soft white hands of the non-manual worker.

'How are things in America?' Raven asked. 'What do they think of us over here?'

'Sentiment's changed a lot,' Hemingway said. 'They're beginning to realize the Government's going to win this war.'

'I'm awfully glad,' he said. 'You know I wouldn't mind any of this if I could just watch what was going on – I don't mind the pain, you know. . . .'

When Hemingway went downstairs again the doctors told him that Raven was badly wounded in the legs and feet, but the worst thing of all was his eyes – he had lost them both.

'I wonder if he'll ever know it,' Hemingway said.

'Oh, sure he will,' the doctor said. 'He's going to get well.'

Walking back along the road, Hemingway came upon a strange apparition, a thick-set powerful little Scot with a determined scowl on his face. The man walked with the gamecock walk of the professional British soldier, a difficult feat because one of his arms was splayed out in front of him on an aeroplane splint, the other arm had three bullet wounds, one of them septic, and a fourth bullet was lodged in his body. He told Hemingway about the action in which Raven had been wounded, an action where he himself had carried out a hand-grenade attack down a trench with his 'own boys at one end and the Fascists' at the other, holding the line until reinforcements came up. There was neither exaggeration nor false modesty in his account which came out blunt and straight in a thick Glasgow accent. The man was the commander of the British Battalion, Jock Cunningham.

*   *   *

The incident which cost Raven his sight happened at a time when spring was breaking through to change the life and appearance of Madrid, the Jarama valley and many parts of embattled Spain. The vines in no-man's-land were beginning to sprout delicate green tips, the sun had melted the frozen mud, the water dried out of the trenches and presently the Americans were sweeping away dust instead of bailing water. And then on 14 March a surprise rebel attack, supported by tanks, began, and broke through the Jarama defence line. Two Americans, Robert Raven and Philip Cooperman, had set out to get some tank support for the very hard-pressed Lincolns. At an agreed point, they parted company and Raven waited while Cooperman went on alone. When Cooperman came back to the agreed rendezvous Raven was not there. Many weeks later Cooperman received a letter from Raven explaining what had happened.

'Dear Coop,

'Just writing to let you know what happened to me after you left. I rushed up about 350 metres of empty trenches bringing up all the Spaniards I could rally round. Then I met a Canadian. The trenches had been filling up gradually at our exhortations of No pasaran! Suddenly we ran into four soldiers who we thought were our own at first: but their helmets and clothes proved them to be Fascists . . . we tore away from them, ran back thirty metres and grabbed some grenades. The Canadian opened the lever of his grenade and handed it to me which he should not have done. However, I crawled up towards the Fascists under cover of the fire of the Spaniards . . . and was about to toss the grenade when there was a terrific concussion in front of me and I felt my face torn off. Naturally I just dropped the grenade, my hand having been knocked out. My own grenade exploded at my feet filling my legs with shrapnel.'[1]

It turned out to be one of those minor moments in the war which resulted in a small penetration of the line and gave no one any particular advantage, but like many small skirmishes of its kind it reduced one human being to a blind and battered wreck.

As the sun broke through and the buds became bolder, as the trenches dried out and the rawness in men's bones lost its ache, the Garibaldi and Dabrowsky Battalions, 'fresh from their

[1] *The Book of the XV Brigade*, p. 100.

triumphs over Mussolini's motorized divisions at Guadalajara and Brihuega', prepared for a counter-attack to regain the section of the line so tragically abandoned that March day when Raven lost his sight.

The Lincoln Battalion which took part in the attack that followed was no longer the old battalion. Only 155 of the original 500 men remained and Captain Merriman had been replaced because of his wound by a Pennsylvanian, Martin Hourihan.

The action began on 5 April, when the Americans at first supplied covering fire, and then, under British cover, left their own trenches and went into the attack. The XVth Brigade as a whole – the Franco-Belge, the Dimitrov, the Spanish XXIVth, the English and the Lincoln – finally succeeded in straightening the line, but gained no new ground. Twenty-two more Americans were added to the long list of casualties that day, but the worst among them was Raven.

Most of the International Brigades now experienced a quiet period which extended through the rainy season to become known by the Americans as 'the long vigil'. As the rain diminished the Americans found a sharp dip in the land behind a ridge on their section of the Jarama front and set up ping-pong tables. Occasional bursts of firing and lone snipers' bullets shot overhead, while different teams, stripped to the waist as the sun came out, dashed round the ping-pong tables, animated, laughing, behaving as if any idea that the tragedy of Raven might repeat itself were impossible.

As for the English 'after 27 February the Battalion settled down to a humdrum trench life, which, with only two very brief periods of rest, was to continue until the middle of June. Four months in the trenches! Sometimes the men wondered if they had been forgotten.'[1]

An entry in the diary of Bob Elliot for Sunday, 7 March, read: 'Slept in, first time – for breakfast – cigarette and chocolate – English. Angus brought and distributed American fags. Comrades reading contentedly.'

And Jock Cunningham on Monday, 8 March: 'Lectured Diamint our new Quartermaster on the importance of his job.

[1] William Rust, *Britons in Spain*, p. 23.

Reprimand two drunks. Wrote home. Telegram received from home signed by prominent labour leaders.'

On Wednesday, 10 March, Cunningham wrote: 'Mild morning. Very little shooting. Shells dropping close to our lines. Select four men for Tank Corps. To be transferred later. Visit from Stephen Spender. Get surprise on reading *Daily Worker* of 4.3.37. I am reported killed. Send two telegrams. Five of the enemy surrendered. Reported that enemy was weak but was preparing to attack. . . .'

The attack took a long time to materialize. Meanwhile, the sense of stalemate became overpowering, and for month after month the British and the Americans dug fresh trenches, lived it rough, and tried to get used to the eternal lice.

Both sides were very well dug in with sandbags, machine-gun posts, barbed-wire entanglements and all the clumsy paraphernalia of trench war. The British, like the Americans, found dips in the ground behind the trenches where bullets sped overhead, and they played cards, sunbathed, played ping-pong and football. As the sun grew hotter it was nothing unusual to see a score of men, stark naked except for their boots, playing a tough game of football, rushing madly around with great whoops and cheers, while three hundred yards away a Nationalist and Government tank were fighting it out helped by artillery from both sides. A football skirmish went hand-in-hand with a small-scale military skirmish, neither taking much notice of the other.

Towards the end of this prolonged lull the Glaswegian, Alex McDade, wrote the verses which, set to the tune of 'Red River Valley', became very popular in all international battalions:

> There's a place in Spain called Jarama
> That's a place that we all know so well,
> For 'tis there that we wasted our manhood
> And most of our old age as well.

> From this valley they tell us we're leaving,
> But don't hasten to bid us adieu,
> For before we make our departure,
> We'll be back in an hour or two.

Miles Tomalin, a new volunteer from England, joined the British Battalion about this time. A middle-class intellectual, he quickly made friends with Malcolm Dunbar, commander of the British Anti-Tank Battery, and kept a diary for the next few months: ' *Tuesday, June 8th.* . . . The institution of compulsory political discussions once a day ordered from above is evidence that we are being treated more seriously than usual. In short we are a "special idea", and therefore less likely to be buggered about with!

' *June 11th.* This is an odd army. We did nothing all yesterday afternoon and nothing all this morning. Yet we are likely to move up to the front on Sunday or Monday. . . . I understand from Dunbar that compared with conditions as late as February, our organization is model.

' I notice that far more grumbling is done by the working-class man than the bourgeois Brigaders, especially about food. . . . It gives the lie to the many bourgeois intellectuals who enjoy saying that bourgeois intellectuals are good-for-nothing. In this battery we are six in thirty-six. . . . '

Chapter 16

Dissent and Desertion

THERE had always been trouble among the Brigaders. Highly individualistic types from dockers to miners, writers to petty crooks, poets to sailors, students to Communists, they could hardly be expected to conform to the requirements of an efficient army.

Unrest increased in the lull. Partly it was produced by letters which filtered through more freely from wives, sweethearts and mistresses, some revealing infidelities, some asking for divorces, some sent by sly informers. Many Brigaders now clamoured to be released from service, but the voluntary principle which had brought them into the I.B. conflicted hopelessly with military needs when they wished to get out. Time and again men applied for release and were turned down. Many tense and sometimes violent scenes ensued.

Scores of men claimed that they had volunteered for three months' service and had a moral right to return home. It was argued that the Communist leaders interpreted their role too harshly, favoured Party members when granting leave and generally dispensed privileges to their 'own kind', and some of these charges were true. It would be romantic to expect dedicated men not to satisfy the needs of other dedicated men, although certain non-Party members of the Brigades now referred to their leaders as fanatics. Widespread dissatisfaction led to attempts at desertion and the deserter, if caught, might go to a re-education camp, or, if he fell into the hands of men like Marty, be shot. Discipline became increasingly difficult to maintain. It was easy to grant the very discontented a spell of leave in Madrid, but the pleasures of café and brothel persuaded many to overstay their leave and they had to be rounded up and brought back forcibly. The military police always knew where to find hardened deserters – in the brothel area. Some who were not deserters reached a stage of fatalistic depression where they felt themselves trapped in a war which would go on for ever. Others had long ago lost their sense of inspiration. Some stole lorries and deserted in small groups, but few actually succeeded in slipping through the Republican security net. The news of the terrible Stalinist purges now beginning in Moscow increased the sense of disillusionment with the Communists among the younger and more liberal of the volunteers. For a time all cell meetings of the Communist Party inside the International Brigades ceased.

When Stephen Spender visited Spain in 1937 he encountered a young Englishman on one of the Madrid fronts who had 'run away from school because he identified the Spanish Republic with the cause of Liberalism'. When he discovered that the Brigades were run by Communists, he was bitterly disillusioned. Spender pointed out that Communists or not Communists, the cause of the Republic remained a liberal cause. 'I don't know about that,' the young man said. 'All I see are the Communist bosses of the Brigade.'

'You are under age,' Spender said. 'Shall I try to get you out of here?'

'No,' came the answer. 'My life is to walk up to the ridge here every day until I am killed.' Within two months he was killed.[1]

Among other reasons for visiting Spain, Spender wanted to find and talk to his friend Jimmy Younger, who had joined the Communist Party under Spender's influence and volunteered for the Brigades. Spender had received a letter from Younger which said: 'The battle of Jarama was one of the toughest of the whole Civil War. The Moors and the International Brigade clashed head-on in the hills. At the end of the first day, my battalion, the Saklatvala, 400 strong to start with, was reduced to less than 100. I could hear the wounded moaning and calling us as they lay between the lines. At the end of a week I knew the meaning of war. I can still see the blood and the dead faces; worse still the expression in the eyes of the dying. I felt no anti-Fascist anger but only overwhelming pity.'

A terrible sense of responsibility for introducing Younger to such a fate drove Spender to go to Spain and search him out. When at last they encountered each other, Younger's first

[1] Stephen Spender, *World Within a World*, p. 224.

words were: 'You must get me out of here!' His whole outlook, he said, had changed. Originally he joined the Brigades on a wild impulse, but now he knew that he no longer had any great desire to die for the Republic. War he had come to loathe to the point of embracing a militant pacifism. Above everything else he desired to become 'an ordinary chap' back in the sweet security of England again. 'I said that I might ask for him to be transferred to some non-combatant position in the Brigade, but not for him to leave Spain.'

It was some time before Younger reconciled himself to this possible compromise, and it still remained to convince the hard-headed, ruthless, political commissars of the British Battalion that the change was not merely politic, but necessary. The following day Spender sought out Commissar Peter Kerrigan, a tall, grey-haired man, with an austere face contradicted by a flickering sense of humour. He at once admitted to being troubled about the case of Jimmy Younger. It was all well and good to say that a sick man should be treated accordingly, but if they allowed everyone who claimed to be sick or malad-justed to leave the Brigades they would quickly undermine morale. . . . 'It is difficult to withdraw one man without dis-couraging the rest', Kerrigan said. Spender fully appreciated the point, but insisted that he was not asking for Younger to be withdrawn and sent home; he merely wanted him transferred to non-combatant duties. They talked on for some time and then at last Kerrigan said: 'All right. We'll keep him here but I promise he won't have to fight.'

Sandor Voros, the Hungarian-American who came into the picture fairly late, throws interesting light on similar troubles within the American section of the Brigades. A member of the Communist Party, he had volunteered for Spain in the fall of 1936, but the Central Committee ruled that the Party had too few experienced comrades to spare anyone at his level. Sum-moned to Party headquarters again, in the summer of 1937, he was received by Saul Mills who told him, very confidentially: 'The Party is in trouble, Voros. All that stuff you've read about the heroic Lincoln Brigade in the *Daily Worker* is crap. If the truth comes out and the enemies of the Party pick it up, we're going to have a tremendous scandal. The truth is that the Lincoln Brigade mutinied the first day it went into action and had to be driven at pistol-point into attack. The comrades in Spain are now completely demoralized. They want to come home and many of them are deserting.'[1]

Voros was then asked to go to Spain with twelve other top Communists in an attempt to raise morale. He arrived in June 1937 and quickly ran into trouble. Survivors from a volunteer boat, the *Ciudad de Barcelona*, which had been torpedoed by an Italian submarine, were coming into Valencia Station, and he was so shocked by their stories that he decided to cable the news straight to the American *Daily Worker*. And then he met Bob Minor, the massive, silver-haired, ageing American whose real job was to co-ordinate the propaganda efforts of the American and Spanish Communist Parties and to represent American interests before the Comintern. He seemed to Voros to have grown deaf and arrogant in the process, and now when he heard how Voros intended using the torpedoed ship story he roared out: 'Not a word of this must leak out – do you understand?'

Voros protested that this was marvellous propaganda for the Americans back home: 'Americans torpedoed and drowned on the open seas by Fascists!'

Minor answered even more forcibly. 'You're not to mention a word about this to anyone – that's an order!' It was Voros's first taste of Communist authority in the field.

Appointed to an artillery battery, he found the men in his section demoralized. Quickly transferred into the Political Section of the Brigades, he became part of its Historical Commission, and from thence onwards was in a special position to penetrate wherever he wished to observe and record what he found. He carried out a number of interviews – one with Robert Merriman – and collected and read a number of diaries.

In Albacete itself, he discovered many rebellious, discontented and demoralized men who were spoken of by André Marty and his officers as 'bad elements'. 'It was amazing how eager they were to open up after I convinced them their confidences would be respected. I was shocked by my findings. Instead of international solidarity, dog eats dog seemed to be the rule governing the relationships of the various Communist

[1] Sandor Voros, *American Commissar*, p. 271.

Parties with one another: their leaderships were in cut-throat rivalry for the favour of Moscow.'[1]

The bad elements were the men with amputated limbs, the shell-shocked and the crippled 'who swarmed about the streets of Albacete searching for post-operative care, sleeping accommodation, food, back pay, repatriation – or merely a friendly word.' These were the survivors of Madrid and other death-or-glory battles, once the centre of attention in the American press, but no one wrote now of their crippled state, or their helplessness. Voros found them sitting on the street kerbs, on park benches, in the tattered remnants of uniforms, depressed men who craved only one thing – to get back to their home country.

'It was easy to see why these "bad elements" felt themselves betrayed by the party. They had been made to believe that they were volunteering to join a People's Army where all would share the vicissitudes of war equally. Then came the shock of reality, they found themselves under a military rule, paralleling that of the Soviet Union where caste differentiation and the privileges enjoyed by officers and commissars were incomparably greater than those existing in the armies of capitalist countries.'[2]

Voros went in search of a man named Brodsky, who had been placed in charge of the first ninety-six American volunteers by the Communist Party. According to Voros, when he at last found him he was kept in seclusion by the Party awaiting repatriation.

'I found him a broken old man although barely in his thirties. He wouldn't talk to me at first, he had been pledged to secrecy. When I finally induced him to confide in me, he not only talked, he spilled over.'

He revealed to Voros the terrible political troubles which, he claimed, had disturbed the Lincoln-Washingtons from the very beginning. He talked of the time when the French had become openly hostile to the Americans and had forced them to sleep in barracks the floors of which were literally littered with human excrement. He talked of his vain attempts to reconcile the complaints of the Americans who held him responsible for the French hostility and the French command

[1] Sandor Voros, *American Commissar*, p. 330.   [2] Ibid., p. 331.

which asked him to subdue the rebellious Americans. The Americans expected him to insist on certain conditions being fulfilled, and the I.B. command were 'disgusted and contemptuous of those spoiled city-babies, the arrogant Americans'. Brodsky had found himself crushed between two irreconcilable forces. As a result, Brodsky said, the Americans went into Jarama and many another battle without proper training or equipment.

A few days after Voros's talk with him, Brodsky was whisked away back to the States by the Party, in ignominious secrecy.

Voros had another revealing encounter with a man called Dave Doran, an American commissar who had condemned a number of men to death for cowardice or other reasons. 'He asks me what I think of the way he has conducted those court martials and he's taken aback when I tell him dryly it is quite a ham Shakespearian performance. . . . Throwing all prudence aside I denounce Doran's act to his face as sheer madness, saying it will bring disaster to the Party back home. . . .'

The argument between these two men finally became a shouting match until Colonel Čopic unexpectedly arrived, and to Doran's astonishment turned out to be on Voros's side. Doran was forced to give the condemned men another chance. It has to be remembered in assessing this evidence that Voros, according to men like Alvah Bessie, was not an objective witness.

What remains of the official Republican records are in the hands of the present Government of Spain and it is difficult to get any exact details of trials and sentences. Certainly a number of deserters suffered re-education and very occasionally, when they still failed to respond to the 'call of duty', were shot. Certainly, in the middle of 1937, trials for desertion were a not uncommon occurrence. The papers in the Spanish archives for Trial No. 81 of Menier Anthelme and 23 other members of the brigade deal with desertion in all cases. These men appeared before the Special Court of Inquiry No. 5 on 22 June 1937, and claimed that when they first volunteered they were told that after three months' service they would be given leave to visit their relations. Such leave never materialized and the men thereupon refused to continue serving. They were arrested and charged with desertion. Witnesses insisted that local Communist offices had definitely undertaken to release them after three months, but the concession appeared to be verbal and could not be supported by written evidence. One man, Liévin Lionen, from Ghent, claimed that he had entered the brigades without signing any engagement form whatsoever and could not, therefore, be said to have committed himself to any long-term service.

Similar evidence was given by Antoine San-Celme, Roger Maury and Albert Enrietto. Questioned on 31 March 1937 at the Porlier Prison in Madrid, San-Celme stated that when he enrolled at the Toulon Communist Party office, he was informed that the war would be over in three months, and his return home was certain within that period.

The Nancy and Nice Party offices had made similar statements to Maury and Enrietto. Albert Enrietto had in fact managed to reach the French Consulate in Madrid, and equip himself with a passport, but the military police arrested him as he tried to leave the city. In his evidence, he claimed that he was the sole breadwinner for his French family, who desperately needed him, and on no account whatever would he go back to fight.

Passports were, of course, the main difficulty for the deserter. Without acceptable papers he was liable to be arrested at any border point and whatever the motives of the International Brigades in confiscating original passports it certainly gave them strong disciplinary powers.

Folio 37 of the trial of Albert Enrietto contains a letter written by Inspector of the International Brigades Luigi Gallo [Luigi Longo] saying that the police had no charges against the comrades mentioned and adding: 'I recognize their interest in returning to their Brigades to defend the cause of the Republic.' The official Franco Government comment on this document says: 'This proceeding was the result of the work done on the arrested men by Lieut. Perrey Raoul, attached to the 35th Divisional Headquarters, assisted by 2nd Lieut. Patin, Secretary of the Divisional Battalion, and Comrade Gautrat, Political Delegate of the same Battalion after an attempted hunger strike, in which some Brigaders had refused to take food. . . .'[1]

It is difficult to establish whether there was any planned overall policy to deceive recruits. Some individual cases of deception occurred. As for beating deserters back into obedi-

[1] *The Red Domination in Spain – Notes for the Spanish History, 1936–1939*, p. 350.

ence, forcing delinquent or unwilling members of a volunteer army to fight with any effectiveness must have been a difficult undertaking. The general truth was probably much more simple. Originally calling on volunteers without specifying any length of service, the brigade chiefs now wanted to retain as many as possible simply because the war situation demanded it.

By April 1937 the swelling chorus of complaints from the French volunteers led to action by the French Consulate in Madrid. The Assistant Secretary M. Salustien Dussaildant appeared before the Fifth Military Court on 17 April and made a plea for volunteers who wished to return home. 'The Government of the French Republic held that those volunteers who had come to serve the Spanish Republic, being only volunteers and not having signed any undertaking whatsoever, should be free to return home when they thought it necessary to do so.'[1]

The story of Nick Gillain's final defection is more colourful than typical. Long before he left the XIVth Brigade he spoke of continuous 'quarrelling and altercations' especially with Captain Bastien, a Belgian commander, and Colonel Dumont who had replaced Colonel Putz. Many among the French, he said, longed for the return of Colonel Putz.

The first real outbreak of desertion in the XIVth Brigade occurred after a rumour spread that the Minister of War had given permission for a certain percentage of volunteers to return to their home countries, but when it came to the point and the convoys of trucks arrived to provide transportation, the repatriates were suddenly replaced by prisoners. A number of enraged French and Belgians promptly deserted, but most of them did not get very far before they were arrested. Some, in a state of reckless fury, tried to defect to the enemy, others tried to shoot their way out.

While Gillain was stationed at the Escorial, a man he described as the Officer of Information took a dozen men and went over to join Franco's troops. Another device for escaping further service was the age-old one of self-inflicted wounds. Gillain describes an occasion when ten men were sentenced to death for injuring themselves and were subsequently shot at dawn. This attempt to instil fresh discipline led to further trouble and a new

[1] *The Red Domination in Spain – Notes for the Spanish History, 1936–1939*, pp. 351–2.

political commissar was appointed to the XIVth Brigade to cope with the situation. The new commissar at once fastened on Gillain as a possible agent provocateur and watched him day after day with a 'gimlet eye'. If he did not openly accuse Gillain of being a Fascist he certainly suspected one of Gillain's friends, the Commissariat Officer, who was later arrested and charged with embezzlement.

The Commissariat Officer had entrusted Gillain with his gold cigarette case and when the court sentenced him to life imprisonment Gillain decided to hand over the case, whereupon he, too, was arrested, as an accomplice of the condemned man. Later they released him, but when he returned to his unit he discovered that detailed inquiries had been made about him, even to the point of approaching his dancer girl-friend in Madrid. Bursting with anger, he demanded an audience with Colonel Dumont. When this was granted, without any ceremony he at once exploded: 'We're not in Spain to plot. We're here to fight!' Colonel Dumont remained calm, but his face went red as he asked Gillain to explain himself. According to Gillain, he proceeded to do this at some length, but Gillain's account cannot be taken at its face value. Gillain claims that he finally said: 'I am tired of hearing you insult General Walter and Colonel Putz. I'm not interested in their private life – I only know that with them the 14th was a crack brigade of which we are now ashamed.'

Not unexpectedly this came like a slap in the face to Colonel Dumont, who was thrown into a fury and stuttered out: 'And me – I have had enough of you veterans – you are all thieves, bandits. I have enough proof in my dossiers to have your Walter and your Putz shot! It's not courage you lack but order, discipline, respect for your chiefs, me above all!'

'Respect!' Gillain replied contemptuously. 'Respect for an officer who goes to the front once in eighty-eight days – who wouldn't budge from his headquarters in the battle of Escorial. . . . You want the respect of your subordinates – they prefer adventurers who have some guts.'[1]

The whole of this dialogue smacks of argument exaggerated in recollection, but there was no doubting the second arrest of Gillain which quickly followed.

[1] Nick Gillain, *Le Mercenaire*, p. 132.

Worse exposures were now made. Some seem incredible, but it is impossible to check any of the statements made since the documents have been destroyed. Gillain joined his old friend the Commissariat Officer in his prison cell, and the Commissariat Officer described to Gillain a system of double-entry bookkeeping practised, he claimed, by certain officers in the XIVth Brigade, which enabled the brigade to draw pay from the Spanish Treasury for men who were either dead, or had long ago deserted. He also admitted embezzling 20,000 francs himself.

On 14 December 1937 Gillain was once more brought before Colonel Dumont and relieved of the rank of captain, first for shameless squandering of the cavalry's food, second for something referred to as demagoguery, and third because his conduct was said to be undignified for an anti-Fascist officer.

Discharged from the I.B., Gillain developed a consuming desire for vengeance. He made his way at once to Madrid, and tried to find General Walter, believing that the general might be sympathetic enough to intervene and press for his reinstatement. Somewhere, he knew, the general had a villa in Madrid, a villa said to be luxurious. In the Madrid cafés he discovered the general's address and made his way to the Villa Paquita, a low, white, beautifully proportioned building surrounded by a garden. When he tried to approach it, bodyguards challenged him and told him that the general was away inspecting the XVth Brigade. Later that evening the general returned, but sent an aide to explain to Gillain why he could not receive him. As a former commander of the XIVth Brigade he was constantly criticized by his successor as the man who had caused all the trouble in its ranks, and he found himself in a delicate position where he could not take sides over the dismissal of an officer without exposing himself to fresh attacks.

Depressed and dispirited, Gillain drifted about Madrid for a time and then made his way to Albacete. There, fresh trouble developed. He discovered that certain members of the Belgian corps were opposed to his returning to Belgium in case he spread exaggerated stories of dissatisfaction among the Brigaders. His friends advised him to 'flee immediately' because there were some elements who regarded him as a traitor and were quite prepared to use violence.

An American ambulance driver finally smuggled Gillain into Barcelona, but repeated visits to the Belgian consul there did not help very much. Gillain complained that the consul adopted the tone of a judge interrogating a criminal. At last he decided to try his luck with the French consulate, and there he had a very different reception. An exit visa was quickly forthcoming and the long story of Nick Gillain's fight for the Spanish Republic at last came to this somewhat untidy, and from his point of view humiliating, end.

Chapter 17

The XVth at Brunete

In the early summer of 1937 the Republican Government suddenly launched two offensives in an effort to draw the Nationalist fire from hard-pressed Bilbao. One, under General Pozas, concentrated once more on Huesca on the Aragon front, and involved the Garibaldi Brigade led by General Lukacz.

In the terrible heat of a May day, Ilya Ehrenburg visited General Pozas's headquarters at Sariñena, and talked to one of the general's Russian advisers, a short, thick-set man with a morose expression who sat at a shaded table. Ehrenburg explained that he represented *Izvestia* and had to send back a report about the Huesca fighting. 'I don't think it's ever been so hot', the man replied and then went on swiftly: 'Have you heard the news? Tukhachevsky, Yakir, Uborevich are to be shot – enemies of the people.'[1] He referred, of course, to the latest news from Russia and obviously found it disturbing. If this offensive here, at Huesca, failed he might become one of those multiplying scapegoats so glibly described as enemies of the people.

He threw away a half-smoked cigarette, lit another and pointed to the map. 'The idea is to cut the road to Jaca – is that clear?' His face suddenly darkened again and he went on poring over the map as if he had forgotten Ehrenburg's presence. It was almost half an hour later when he said moodily: 'For *Izvestia* you say? And where's Koltsov? . . . The road to Jaca, here's the Dabrowski Brigade with Gerassi in command, here's the Garibaldi – Pacciardi – Lukacz will tell you all about it. I think he's still in Caspe. . . .'[2]

Ehrenburg already knew Lukacz well, and as a fellow-writer he had carefully re-read Lukacz's book *Doberdo*. According to Ehrenburg, this gay, good-humoured man who had spent no small part of his life within range of gunfire, loved quiet. He

[1] Ilya Ehrenburg, *Eve of War 1933–41*, p. 171.   [2] Ibid., p. 171.

slept constantly with 'his ear to the ground – but he could, he said, hear the beating of the human heart.' He lived in a world full of noise, action, danger, but spoke softly. Under his command were Italian émigrés, Polish miners, workers from the Communist suburbs of Paris, Italian seamen, Vilna Jews, Spaniards, callow youths, veterans of the First World War, and somehow he generated amongst a crowd of rough, tough, and hopelessly different men a much more genuine affection than was the luck of other Brigade leaders.

Lukacz's disposition was such that he could burst into song and once, in front of Ehrenburg, he seized hold of a Spanish peasant woman and danced with dashing abandon. 'You see,' he said, 'I can still dance. Don't forget I'm a Hungarian hussar.'

And then one day, on the Huesca front, Ehrenburg drove out towards Lukacz's new headquarters in the village of Apies, and suddenly they encountered a soldier who seemed in great distress. 'On a lower road – a shell – the general', he said.

Ehrenburg swiftly drove back to the big stone house converted into a hospital where they had taken Lukacz, and there he learnt that Lukacz, Regler and the Russian adviser had all been hit. 'Lukacz's condition is hopeless. Regler has had a blood transfusion, his life's not in danger but the wound is serious. . . . Your countryman's got off lightly. . . .'

The irony of the situation was that the offensive did not start until the next day and proved unsuccessful. Casualties were estimated at 10,000 Republicans, among them many Italians in the Garibaldi Brigade. George Orwell, who left such a brilliant account of fighting with the POUM, travelling in a hospital train, away from the battle, passed many Italians on their way to the front. He saw 'window after window of dark, smiling faces, the long tilted barrels of the guns, the scarlet scarves fluttering – all this glided slowly past us against a turquoise-coloured sea. . . . The men who were well enough to stand moved across the carriage to cheer the Italians as they went past. A crutch waved out of a window; bandaged arms gave the red salute. It was like an allegorical picture of war. . . .'[1]

Lukacz's death at 41 deeply distressed Ehrenburg. On his

[1] George Orwell, *Homage to Catalonia.*

last birthday Lukacz had written: 'I have been thinking about
destiny, about the vicissitudes of life, about past years – and I
am dissatisfied with myself. I have done too little. Too few
successes. Too little achieved.'

The whole of the XIIth Brigade mourned the death of its
general and the memory of the man moved Ehrenburg to write
about him in his memoirs: 'According to biblical tradition,
Sodom and Gomorrah might have been saved had ten just
men been found. This is true of all cities and all epochs. One
such just man was Mata Zalka, General Lukacz, dear Matrey
Mikhailovich.'

Almost simultaneously with the battle which killed Lukacz,
the Republicans launched a second attack on the Segovia
front under General Walter. The XIVth International Brigade,
led by Colonel Dumont, broke through the Nationalist lines
at San Ildefonso and reached La Granja before Varela managed
to contain it. This was the battle described by Hemingway in
For Whom the Bell Tolls and Hemingway suggests that spies
revealed to Franco where the attack would be launched.
Owing to André Marty's pig-headedness, when the betrayal
was discovered, the plan was still carried through. A savage
quarrel developed between Walter and Dumont as a result of
this, each blaming the other for the failure of the attack, and
when Walter protested against the vanity, and in his view
inefficiency, of Dumont, the French Communist Party came out
strongly in defence of their man. The result was that the XIVth
Brigade had to be transferred to another front and in future
Walter and Dumont operated in complete independence of
each other.

Events were now heading towards the Republican offensive
at Brunete which once again deeply involved the re-formed
International volunteers, but before that spectacular attempt
to cut off all the besiegers of the capital from the west began,
another small diversion intervened which brought an Anglo-
American company into joint action. Units of the International
Brigades were sent to reinforce Spanish troops defending the
mercury mines at Almaden, and the No. 1 section of the
20th Battalion – the most mixed battalion then existing –

consisted of forty British and Irish with an American and Spanish-American section. The remaining companies included Germans, French and many Slavs.

When the 20th Battalion reached the Pozoblanco front they found that a Republican counter-attack had already driven the enemy into a fast-moving retreat. So great was the pace and so unsuccessful the attempts to overtake them, that a spectacular new method became necessary which went down in the history of the Spanish Civil War as one of the most romantic rough-rides any battalion experienced.

The battalion commandeered a train, mounted machine-guns front and rear, piled the whole battalion aboard, and set out to chase the enemy by rail. The driver proceeded cautiously, checking every mile for signs of ambush, but it was not until they emerged from a cutting a few kilometres from Belmex that artillery opened up, and the driver put the train in reverse and drew into a siding. The men leapt out and deployed ready for action, but the enemy barrage pinned everyone down until darkness blotted out the landscape.

A few days later the Anglo-American company broke away from the main battalion to go to the assistance of a Spanish battalion engaging the enemy near Chimorra. There followed a ding-dong battle for a round-topped hill on the left flank of the Spaniards, with the battalion first taking it, then being driven off and finally, in a night-drive, retaking the hill and pushing the Moors back to their original trenches.

The Anglo-American company, now reinforced with Spanish troops, moved to another sector and took part in several actions before returning to Albacete in July, to join the XVth Brigade in preparation for the great Brunete offensive.

At a level quite remote from these activities, political dissension in the Government was now high-lighted by the May rising in Barcelona and an atmosphere of intrigue prevailed where the military situation demanded strong political unity. Malaga had fallen through sheer incompetence, the victory of Guadalajara could not be exploited because there were no reserves, and Caballero was now seen by his rivals as a vain old man who listened too closely to sycophantic advisers.

A remarkable meeting of the Spanish Communist Party executive revealed the explosive tempers just below the public surface. In line with the requirements of Moscow, Togliatti said that Largo Caballero must go, but Díaz and Hernández disagreed, and Díaz scorned the idea that they should always follow the policies put forward by Moscow. Marty agreed with Togliatti and someone interrupted to insist that actual events, not Moscow, had made Caballero's removal imperative. When Díaz accused Marty of behaving like a bureaucrat, Marty snapped back that he was a revolutionary and Díaz replied: 'We are all revolutionaries.' The argument became heated and Díaz suddenly said to Marty: 'You are a guest at our meeting – if our proceedings do not please you there is the door!' A fierce altercation now broke out, half the committee came to its feet and as the uproar grew La Pasionaria shrieked: 'Comrades! Comrades!' When the outburst had at last subsided, she then proposed that they should all accept Togliatti's proposal if he could command a majority vote. Togliatti won the day and almost at once he blandly suggested that Hernández, who had voted against him, should lauch the first attack, aimed to destroy Largo Caballero, at their next meeting in Valencia. Inevitably the choice of a successor fell on Juan Negrín who followed a policy midway between del Vayo's pro-Communist and Prieto's anti-Communist attitudes.[1] Dr Juan Negrín replaced Caballero as Prime Minister to form a government which quickly took the military situation in hand.

During the last weeks in June, General Miaja gathered together in the Brunete area two Army Corps including the Vth Army Corps under the Communist leader Modesto and the XVIIIth Army Corps under Colonel Jurado. Colonel Modesto embraced General Walter's 35th Division which took in the XIth International Brigade, and Jurado's corps included Gal's 15th Division which in turn brought in the XIIIth and XVth International Brigades. The whole army was one of the best equipped and most impressive ever put into the field by the Republicans, numbering over 50,000 men supported by 136 pieces of artillery, 128 tanks and 150 aircraft. The aim of the attack was to drive down on Brunete from the north of the

[1] Tomás Jesús Hernández, *Negro y Rojo*, pp. 66–71.

El Escorial–Madrid road and attempt to 'cut off all the besiegers of the capital from the west'.[1]

The comparatively new XVth International Brigade was under the command of Čopic, a man born of a poor family of small tradesmen in Croatia, who became a soldier in the Austrian Army during World War I, was taken prisoner in Russia, and while in prison read Marxist literature. The XVth Brigade was divided into two regiments, one led by George Nathan including the Abraham Lincoln, George Washington and British Battalions, and the other by Major 'Chapiev' embracing the Dimitrov, Franco-Belge and one Spanish battalion. Merriman once more commanded the Lincoln Battalion, Oliver Law, a Negro, had taken over the Washington, and Fred Copeman now led the British.

Before the attack began, away at 36th divisional headquarters, Pablo, Divisional Commissar, sketched the rough shape of a hand on the white wall of a farmhouse and held a candle closer for his officers to see the result. The hand closed over every rail and road into Madrid except for one slender line of communication along which passed all supplies to the beleaguered city. 'Here, on the wrist, below the thumb,' he explained, 'is Brunete; and beyond it, so, the heights of Romanillos. Those heights command the Fascist supply lines. If they are taken and held, the hand will be cut off at the wrist, the Fascists compelled to withdraw 20 miles and Madrid no longer be under artillery shelling. . . .'

It was a graphic crystallization of the aim of the attack. Before zero hour Prieto and La Pasionaria both delivered powerful speeches to Miaja's Army calling on the men to send the enemy reeling back and mark this day as the greatest Republican victory yet. Already, these two were fierce rivals, with Prieto trying to restrict Communist influence in the Army and La Pasionaria attempting to increase it. Within the last few months Prieto's influence had prevailed to the point where Army officers were not allowed to practise political propaganda or even to attend Party meetings and in November, according to Hugh Thomas, the post of Chief Political Commissar was abolished. When many of the commissariats at the actual front were also dissolved, it threatened the position of Anton, the

[1] Hugh Thomas, *The Spanish Civil War*, p. 460.

lover of La Pasionaria, and she came to hate Prieto even more, but that was not yet. For the moment, with her own miner husband and son at the front, her wonderfully rousing address to Miaja's Army had slightly ironic undertones for those who disapproved of the domestic arrangement whereby she, her lover and Togliatti occupied the same house in Madrid. It had its effect none the less.

Lister's 11th Division led the attack at dawn on 6 July with great dash, and within a few hours he had surrounded Brunete. At first they were met by depleted elements of Franco's 71st Division, supported by Moors, but presently the Nationalists called up reinforcements. As the attack developed, for reasons which still remain somewhat obscure – perhaps simple military ineptitude – the Republican High Command chose to pour through the small gap brigade after brigade until a certain confusion supervened and orders intended for one battalion were interpreted, in part, by another. Tanks, too, were wantonly used on what seemed the wrong targets – no less than 75 were flung at Villafranca. Within the next twenty-four hours, the Nationalists reacted swiftly and brought up battalion after battalion until 31 were thrown into the battle, with nine batteries of field artillery in support. The impetus of the attack slackened, every yard was now bitterly fought over and soon the scorched Castilian plain, burning hot under a torrid summer sun, became a place of terrible carnage, where no quarter was asked or given.

The XVth Brigade had been called into immediate action once again, after a long-drawn-out march through the night, and it was a tired, hot and thirsty British Battalion which attacked its first objective, the highly fortified town of Villa-nueva de la Canada.

At eight o'clock of a morning already fierce with heat, Fred Copeman led his men in an attempt to by-pass the town and cut the road behind. Working across country, they came under heavy fire but as the sun rose higher it was the relentless burning heat which troubled them most. The sun roasted the ground until it seemed red-hot to the touch, sweat saturated every garment, and thirsts could not be quenched because ten minutes before the order to advance came through a stroke of genius had sent all water bottles back to base for refilling. Where there should have been rivers there were dry beds, where streams once gushed was a gully of cracked crumbling earth.

Villanueva appeared on the horizon, a thick brown cloud of smoke, dust and explosions, looking like an approaching thunderstorm of concentrated horror as the Republican artillery pounded it to pieces. Casualties began to multiply among the English, but the great majority of the battalion reached the circumnavigating road and one company moved in close, trying to find cover in road ditches. At this point, a sweating excitement, with nerves jangled to fever-pitch, drove all thought of anything but the battle – and water – out of their minds. Still there was no sign of the missing water bottles, and the men dug into a dried river-bed to fill their gas-masks with a muddy liquid quaffed without regard for any consequences. As the church tower of Villanueva came into view the snipers and machine-gunners opened up, and now the advance companies lost man after man, until twenty were missing, and Copeman realized that they could not go on sustaining losses at this rate. There was, it seemed to him, only one thing left to do. Seek for the best temporary cover and wait until nightfall.

As dusk came down, the moans of the wounded trapped in no-man's-land drove many a man to risk his life to crawl back, carrying water in his gas-mask tin, but any movement drew the deadly accurate fire of the snipers. And then, as it was almost night, yet another piece of duplicity caused momentary confusion in the English ranks. Seasoned soldiers familiar with every kind of cunning, they should have known better; but when there suddenly burst out on the road from the town a score or more of women and children, all garbed in the brightest colours, a Cardiff seaman, Pat Murphy, hurried forward to discover what it meant. He quickly detected, half-concealed by the women and children, a group of armed Italian soldiers and at once ordered them to halt and drop their sub-machine-guns. The Italian group leader simply took a flying leap at Murphy, and they both fired simultaneously. The Italians then burst through the women, throwing hand-grenades and firing sub-machine-guns from the hip, and Murphy ducked behind the dead body of their leader, waited until they had overrun him and fired on them from their rear. The skirmish was short and sharp. Ten minutes later, Murphy slumped down as a splinter from a hand-grenade hit him in the groin, and the remaining Italians moved between the dead and wounded, shooting recklessly. Among the drab uniforms of the dead were at least two brightly coloured dresses.

The battalion had withdrawn slightly in the face of this totally unexpected sally, but Copeman rallied his men and they went into an attack which finally carried them into the streets of Villanueva de la Canada. The bursting of hand-grenades lit the streets with a red glow as the British made contact with the Dimitrovs, who had fought their way in from the opposite end of the town. A roar of trampling hooves suddenly sent everyone scurrying for cover as they anticipated what seemed an impossibility in that area – a cavalry charge – but as the Dimitrovs opened fire they found that they had shot to pieces nothing more lethal than two bulls running berserk down the burning street. When the British at last entered the deserted Nationalist headquarters and gave it a thorough 'going-over', according to William Rust they found a telegram from Franco which read: 'Hold Villanueva at all costs!'

As the night gave way to a perfect summer dawn with a breath or two of hot air which presaged the furnace heat to come, the cost to the British of taking Villanueva became clear. There were many gaps in the ranks. Among the dead was the tiny, soldierly, old-timer nicknamed Tich, who had come through a score of campaigns unscathed, but had at last succumbed to a grenade fragment which split open his chest.

Temporarily, the whole offensive was successful. Brunete itself had fallen and the XVth Brigade pressed on for the next two days, collecting every kind of spoil from food and ammunition to tanks and guns, while the enemy crossed the Guadarrama river and took up fresh positions on the heights of Romanillos.

Now began the attempt to take the vital Mosquito Ridge which was frustrated at the outset by a terrific artillery bombardment pinning the British to the ground. 'For two hours the shells whined and crashed, while the men, face downward, tried to burrow their way into the earth on both sides of the roadway, expecting every moment that the next shell would get them.'[1]

The shortage of water was now complicated by a shortage of food. Bombardment from the air and ground kept the field

[1] William Rust, *Britons in Spain*, p. 81.

kitchen well in the rear and presently some of the most heroic feats were performed by a series of figures, tiny at first to the men in the front line, but steadily growing bigger as they ran, who dodged, ducked and stumbled their way through the constant barrage, carrying on their backs sacks full of food. The stretcher-bearers, too, were forced to abandon daytime rescues and the wounded lay all day, sometimes unconscious for one hour and conscious the next, sometimes crawling a few yards only to collapse in their own blood, too weak and broken to move again. At night they were loaded like sacks on mules whose backs were soaked in human blood.

When the barrage at last eased up, the advance continued and ridge after ridge was fought over bitterly. The British pressed steadily nearer their objective, but within sight of Mosquito Ridge they were stopped once more by another terrific air and artillery bombardment. Pinned to the ground again they tore at the earth, burrowing shallow and inadequate trenches, crushed themselves face downward and for hours on end remained once more as near motionless as possible, with splitting heads and bursting eardrums.

The barrage eased once more and again they went forward, but this time more slowly and cautiously, with the opposition getting tougher and tougher. It took another hour to advance a hundred yards. The British had now relieved the Washington, with the Lincolns digging in on the flat ground to their left-rear, but the situation already revealed dangers because Campesino's Division had failed to pass the fortified village across the valley on their right flank. Worst of all, a limited Nationalist counter-attack had gained ground by the river-bed. The British were now dangerously far out ahead of everyone else and it became clearer every hour that without fresh support they would not reach the top of Mosquito Hill.

Within the next twenty-four hours it was even more certain that the impetus of the Republican advance had slackened and would presently come to a standstill. Already a number of counter-attacks were making it difficult to hold the line, and ammunition and food supplies for the British began to diminish. Another forty-eight hours of increasing resistance and mounting casualties at last forced them to withdraw.

The situation as seen from brigade and field headquarters

was now serious. Jock Cunningham tried to convince the High Command that fresh troops must be thrown into the Mosquito Hill sector, but the overall picture did not encourage Čopic to accept his advice. The single slender road to the front along which all supplies had to pass was continuously bombed; enemy planes had the mastery in the air; the enemy were pouring in enormous reinforcements and had a footing in the Republican lines at several points; the hold-up of Campesino's Division continued with little hope of a break-through; the best Republican troops had been fighting continuously for eight days and casualties in the 36th Division, which included the International Brigade, were so heavy that the British had been reduced from 630 men to 185.

Great bitterness was evident under the surface of the discussions which now took place between members of the High Command. Not only the Spanish Divisional Commanders but the leaders of the XVth Brigade, too, found themselves torn by dissensions. Some time during the battle, for instance, Nathan and Aitken pointed out to Jock Cunningham that he had his two battalions in the wrong place and he was so furious that he 'went on strike' – and for a time refused to issue any further orders.[1] A very highly strung man, Cunningham was jealous of Nathan and Nathan in turn was hated by General Gal. Indeed, after the Jarama battle, Nathan had left the XVth Brigade over some difference with Gal and joined the XIVth, but now, drawn too strongly by the presence of his own kind, he was back once more in the XVth Brigade.

What remained of the British Battalion had hardly taken up its new positions with the men in a state of bitter disillusion and exhaustion, when Copeman heard that Wally Tapsell, their Political Commissar, had been arrested. He rushed back to brigade headquarters to be told that Tapsell had criticized the strategy of the whole attack in a way damaging to morale and his arrest was inevitable. In fact, according to Walter Greenhalgh, Tapsell had said: 'Only stupidity or a deliberate disregard for life would keep men in such an exposed position. Gal isn't fit to command a troop of Brownies let alone a People's Army.'[2] Greenhalgh, a one-time painter and decorator from

---

[1] Verbal evidence, George Aitken.
[2] Greenhalgh, *Reynolds News*, 23 July 1961.

Manchester, had been involved in a number of battles and sympathized with Tapsell's comments. Not surprisingly, Gal was now demanding that Tapsell be shot for causing disaffection.

When Copeman spoke to Nathan about the situation, even the imperturbable Nathan seemed worried. British casualties apart, the virtual loss of a large part of the Washington Battalion had split the Command into at least two warring factions with many small subterranean struggles taking place at lower levels. Before he left the front line, Copeman had told his second-in-command, Joe Hinks, that if he did not return within two hours he was to 'bring the machine-gun company up to Brigade H.Q.' What would have happened if Copeman's fierce reaction and George Nathan's influence had failed to get Tapsell released, it is difficult to imagine. In the middle of a terrible battle with nerves at breaking point and death a commonplace, it is not inconceivable that Copeman – who had once before led a mutiny against a much more august body – would have trained his guns on the High Command and demanded Tapsell's release. Already he had broken all the rules by refusing, when he took command of the battalion, to accept the right of Political Commissars 'to influence military organization and discipline'. Now, at H.Q., he listened to demands for extreme punishment for those who caused disaffection or left the battle lines without authority. He heard warring strategies fiercely expressed and detected a savage struggle within a struggle not apparent to any of the men who were giving their lives for what they imagined to be a clear-cut, unified ideal. It seemed to Copeman, before he returned to the front again, that the fight against Fascism was being sadly confused by an internal struggle for Party political control. But Tapsell had been released and that was all that immediately concerned him.

Meanwhile Ralph Bates, American Commissar of the XVth Brigade, had set out on a tour of inspection of the front line from H.Q. and stumbled on a remarkable incident. He was, he later recorded, tired, tired, tired, and his brain 'like red glass that lacerated the inflamed cells. . . . Fatigue after that sleepless fortnight of red battle on yellow blazing hills was not weakness but pain, red glass in the brain, and glass dust in the eyes, splinters of glass in the muscles. . . .'

Coming upon some Spanish troops straggling back from a ridge which they had just abandoned, he went over to them: 'Hold the ridge', he shouted. 'Get back – it's this ridge we must hold.'

He pressed on again: 'At the top of the slope there was a wounded comrade writhing beneath the bushes, lips chewed to bleeding shreds. I drew my pistol and held it to his ear and blessed him with sweet death.'

Presently, he came upon a machine-gun crew with one of their number bent over a wounded comrade. 'I'll attend to him', he croaked, and took over nursing the wounded man. Suddenly he drew breath sharply as he saw, where the tunic was split open and the vest ripped away, 'the breast of a young girl, soft, pink-nippled. . . .'

'Comrade,' he whispered, 'you should not be here.'

Women had been forbidden to enlist in the International Brigades from the day when the Republican Government stopped any further women volunteers from entering the militia.

Now this girl, white-faced, full of fear, stirred and said: 'Number Two is my sister, send her away too if you must.'

The machine-gun leader ran over to Bates, and he realized that this, too, was a girl. She 'put her arm round my neck pleading mutely'.

The gunner himself was by now openly crying.

'She's your lover?' Bates said to him.

'No,' he said, 'Berthe is mine. Marie belongs to Paul.' He indicated the other man and all the time the second girl continued feeding the gun-belt skilfully and the firing went on. So the whole machine-gun crew was sexually and emotionally involved as one unit.

Bates turned to the gunner: 'Come, they shall go to the rearguard and work', he said. 'In fact you shall all go.'[1]

He knew he was robbing the brigade of what might be a most efficient team of machine-gunners, but something in him rejoiced at the thought of taking these young men and women to a place where they could serve the cause without breaking the bond which held them together.

When Bates returned to staff headquarters, he immediately

[1] Robert Payne, *The Civil War in Spain*, p. 258. Quoted from Ralph Bates's *Sirocco*.

received another commission. 'Go up to the Americans and find out how their left-flank contacts are. . . . The telephone is broken. . . .'

'Where's the American H.Q.?' Bates asked.

'Nelson reports it's in a gully near Jock Cunningham's post.'

In the attack on Villanueva de la Canada, three battalions – the Lincoln, Washington and British – formed a regiment with Martin Hourihan as adjutant-commander. The toll taken of officers in the action was heavy. Oliver Law, Negro commander of the Lincolns, died, and Steve Nelson, the Political Commissar, took his place. Martin Hourihan, Paul Burns and Hans Amlie were all wounded, and even the Brigade Commander Čopic was hit by a bomb splinter and had to be carried off to hospital. Among the English, the Battalion Adjutant, Charles Goodfellow, went down with a large piece of shrapnel in his head and died. Sam Wild replaced him, but within forty-eight hours, leading an attack on Mosquito Ridge a bullet in the thigh reduced him to a stretcher case, and when Malcolm Dunbar, Commander of the Anti-Tank Battery, collapsed before yet another bullet, Hugh Slater took over.

The story was monotonously repetitive. Key-man after key-man dead, wounded, missing. The Americans Moe Fishman and Al Robbins received bad leg-wounds and the two brothers Sam and Joe Stone died while the third brother Hy fought on. When he heard the news of his brothers' death Hy tried to leap out of the trenches to wreak a single-handed vengeance on 'some Fascist or other', but his companions forcibly held him down. There were literally, among the rank and file, hundreds of dead and wounded.

In a momentary lull, the commanders took a brief roll call to find that roughly fifty per cent of the Washington and fifty per cent of the Lincolns were still fit for active service. Brigade headquarters acted swiftly. The two truncated battalions were merged to form one complete battalion again, a battalion to become famous as the Lincoln-Washington.

The terrible casualties inflicted on the Americans were, according to Fred Copeman, largely due to their going into action in arrow formation, following some outdated military tradition. He also complained bitterly that their Negro commander, Oliver Law, was left lying out in the sun for two weeks, and when Copeman last saw him, presented a terrible spectacle of ballooning flesh, eaten away by decay and insects.

By 13 July, after fierce fighting around the old battlefield of Boadilla, orders were given to dig in and hold. The great attack which had been heralded with such passionate eloquence and high expectations had gained the Republic a pocket of land some fifteen kilometres wide and twelve deep, at the cost of very heavy casualties. One casualty above all stood out in the minds of those who had been associated with the Internationals from the beginning – George Nathan.

It was 14 July with the battle practically over. Early that day Nathan had once again performed his rallying feat, personally pulling together a battalion of fleeing Spaniards and leading them back to battle with his gold-tipped swagger stick swinging in his hand. The stick had acquired a mystical significance for thousands of men. It was his talisman. It had magic powers to protect him. Once he held the stick in his hand he could walk abroad and live where other men died. But this time something broke the magic spell and he was practically cut in two by a bomb fragment.

There are several accounts of what followed. According to Hugh Thomas, when he knew that he was dying, Nathan issued a last order to the men who surrounded him, half in awe that someone so sacred should be reduced to this pitiful condition.

He ordered them to sing him out of life. And they sang, uncertainly, out of tune, caps in hand. He was dead before they finished. As the dusk came down they made a rough coffin of some trench planks, and there, beneath the olive trees, close by the beautiful river Guadarrama, as they buried him, the Brigade Commissar George Aitken made a short, moving, funeral oration. In the small audience were two of the toughest men in the brigade, Jock Cunningham and Colonel Gal. As the earth closed over him there were tears running down cheeks which had not known tears since boyhood.

Steve Nelson added fresh detail to the story. After three weeks in the line, the new Lincoln-Washington Battalion was to be withdrawn and sent back to rest. The relief battalion arrived late and instead of moving at night, the Lincoln-Washington was forced to travel after sunrise in full daylight. Inevitably, the column became an ideal target for air attack, and very soon the bombers were threatening fresh death and disaster at the very point where the Americans thought they had escaped. As the first wave came over, in an instant the whole road was bare of men and lorries, but immediately the first bombers had gone the men poured back on the road again, hurrying towards the village of Ibanez. Major Nathan, in charge of the withdrawal, strolled across a field in his casual, don't-give-a-damn way, and greeted Nelson with his upper-class English accent. According to Nelson these are the words he used: 'Steve, old chap!... Come along, you old Yank, and have a bit of a snifter. I've been saving this for you. An Englishman's drink.'

He handed Nelson a tin cup, filled it, and then in turn filled his own from what appeared to be a water bottle. 'To our new Brigade Commissar! Mud in your eye!'

'You mean me?' Nelson said.

'Certainly – you'll have official notice shortly but I assure you – I say!'

The second wave of bombers coming over had made him break off.

'Best hit for cover, eh? Over that wall – a ditch.'

They ran swiftly, leapt the wall, fell into the ditch and lay there as the planes came over, flying very low. A few seconds later a high-pitched whistle was followed by a tremendous crash which deafened and momentarily blinded Nelson. It felt to him as if the bomb had burst right next to him, and in one sense he was right, because he suddenly heard Nathan's voice calling, 'I'm hit, Steve!'

Nelson rushed to him and at first saw a gash in his breast with very little blood, but Nathan's face was twisted in agony and he began clawing at his Sam Browne belt. It was a strange reflex action and as he dragged the belt off he seemed to Nelson to be saying: 'Take it – I'm through.'

When the first-aid men had bandaged Nathan they rushed him to a nearby ambulance but a Spanish major, with a red cross on his sleeve, came hurrying up shouting a protest as they pushed the stretcher into the rack.

'Stop! You can't have my ambulance. I order you to stop.'

A man called Garland, another American, had leapt into the

driving seat and now Nelson bawled back at the major – 'A brigade officer has been wounded.' He turned to Garland: 'Drive on', he snapped and as the Spanish major leapt for the running-board he found himself staring into the muzzle of Nelson's automatic.

In the evening, Nelson telephoned the hospital and a voice told him that Major Nathan had died – ten minutes before.

Nelson later wrote: 'The words were a blow across my heart. Nathan, good and wise and capable, cheerful and jaunty. Strolling blithely along under the heaviest fire, swinging his foolish little cane, his pipe cocked up at an angle, drawing smoothly – the rawest recruit couldn't be afraid when Nathan was around. . . . Nathan had taken the most outrageous chances, exposed himself hundreds of times in the grandly arrogant manner. And now death had found him, in the tragic accident of a bomb splinter – a pure, blind, bloody chance.'[1]

After a three days' lull, the Nationalists gathered all their heavy reinforcements together and launched a counter-attack which stretched the resources of the Republicans to breaking point. The new Lincoln-Washington Battalion not merely found itself full in the path of the counter-attack, but without machine-guns or reserve ammunition. By an extraordinary piece of bungling, when the battalion was first withdrawn, the machine-guns and ammunition were loaded into carriers and rushed from the front to be stored in the armoury. Now, with the enemy breaking into their positions, the machine-guns remained several miles away in a useless state of storage.

An American called Sergeant Lamb commandeered a truck, drove madly back to the armoury and returned with the guns, only to find the road blocked by great columns of retreating troops, lorries and ambulances. The front line had given way under tremendous attacks and now the Americans, ostensibly in reserve, faced the full fury of the attack. Sergeant Lamb forced his way through the overwhelming tide and arrived just in time to get the guns into dominating positions behind the infantry.

For forty-eight hours the Lincoln-Washington fought on stubbornly, only retreating in the classic manner, inch by inch.

[1] Steve Nelson, *The Volunteers*, p. 193.

Time and again they seemed to be surrounded and under enfilading fire from three sides, and time and again they fought their way out and straightened their lines.

John Koblick recorded in his diary for 14 July: 'A little while later a row of Fascist bombers attacked us. The bombardment was so heavy we thought we were all doomed. As I lay on my belly I heard a terrific explosion, a bomb landed about ten feet away. Three men were killed and five wounded. . . .'

Milton Wolf, then a machine-gunner, many years later recalled the campaign: 'Everyone agreed with us that we, in the machine-gun company, were performing a Herculean task. We were loaded down with pre-World War Maxims, the shields of which were Colt, vintage 1914. The men not engaged in carrying the guns carried 500 rounds of ammunition in addition to their rifles and 150 rounds of rifle ammo. I was grateful for the ten months I had spent in a CCC camp, for I had developed the strength, if nothing else, to make me almost equal to the task. I couldn't help marvelling at the sight of men like David McKelvy White, a college professor who had probably never performed a day's manual labour in his life, struggling gamely and silently under their loads. . . . During the fighting the hills stank of burning sage and scrub oak, of dead men and animals cooking in the fierce July heat.'[1]

Thirst and heat. These were the two extra and invisible enemies which took a toll of strength and nerves no less than the incessant strafing and bombing. At least one man staggered out of his trench groaning in the classic manner – 'Water! Water!' – as the sun seared everything to a bleached whiteness and he could no longer fight or even think of his own safety in his craving for something to drink. The sun made an obscene mockery of corpses, blowing them up like balloons and roasting them until the air smelt of scorching human flesh.

Before the battle of Brunete was finally over, the Americans faced the worst test of all. Briefly relieved by a battalion of *marineros*, they were lying utterly exhausted among a group of pines, when a dispatch rider came racing across the field sending up a cloud of white dust. He asked for Major Nathan and when they told him that he was dead, he handed a message to Colonel Gal. The colonel's face stiffened as he read the

[1] Edwin Rolfe, *The Lincoln Battalion*, p. 100.

message. Immediately he summoned a staff meeting of all commanders and commissars, and they crowded into a small tent, where the air was even more suffocating than outside.

'I have here orders from Division Headquarters,' the colonel said, 'that we immediately march back to Quijorna where there is now desperate fighting. The Spanish divisions are almost surrounded – in a most dangerous situation. We are the nearest troops who can get there in time to influence the battle.'

There were gasps of amazement. 'Christ! Jesus! It's madness.' The men of the Lincoln-Washington had been fighting continuously for three weeks; they had marched for six hours to occupy their present position; and now they were asked to march another 14 kilometres back to Quijorna and immediately go into action again. The commander of another battalion broke the silence. 'I'll never be able to present such an order to the men. They'll bloody well never go back. Not now. Christ, man, you can't get blood out of a stone!'

The colonel listened imperturbably and jerked his head towards another commissar. 'And you?'

The interpreter went to work on his answer. 'He's not sure if he has the weight to put it across', he said. At last it was Nelson's turn. 'If the order is explained to the men,' he said, 'I think they will go back.'

One battalion commander burst out, 'You know bloody well your men won't go back any more than ours, Steve.'

'Okay – what do you propose doing?' Nelson demanded.

The colonel called for order, and Nelson now suggested that they should see the reaction of the Americans when he explained why the order was necessary. No other army in the world would have gone through this subtle attempt at democracy with any hope of success, but now the colonel and Nelson went along together to address the Lincoln-Washington Battalion. The men were a dim mass of subdued humanity gathered in the star-lit open air around a rock, and as the colonel read out the order there were uneasy murmurs until one man shouted: 'For Christ's sake, Steve, you're not telling us to go back, are you?'[1]

Nelson now put the whole order in a wider perspective, explained the precise nature of the general crisis and appealed to his men to respond to a call which came in desperation. A

[1] Steve Nelson, *The Volunteers*, p. 202.

dark, deep silence greeted his speech and then at last one man growled out: 'You're right, Steve!' – and that short comment was the beginning of a change in the general reaction. Battalion by battalion, the order was explained, debated, and finally accepted, and the men formed up to begin the appalling trek back to Quijorna again, in a state of silent, clumsy, total exhaustion. Of course, considerable time had been lost in the interests of democratic procedures, and the Spanish might have become the victims of these refinements, but the brigade had hardly reached the main road when another motor-cyclist came tearing along with fresh news. The Spanish had fought their way out and were safe. The XVth Brigade could relax once more in its chosen camp. For the Americans that was the last episode in the long tortured story of the Brunete campaign.

Once again both sides claimed Brunete as a victory. Certainly the Republic gained an area fifteen kilometres long and five deep and retained Quijorna, Villanueva de la Canada and Villanueva del Pardillo, but their very limited successes were achieved at the cost of 25,000 dead and 95 aircraft lost. The Nationalists lost half that number of men and only 23 aircraft. Hugh Thomas regarded the action as a defeat for the Republicans because it failed to achieve its main objectives. It was also very depressing to the Communists dominating Republican military strategy, since they had insisted on launching the attack and had personally chosen the Brunete area.

The ever-watchful German and Italian military experts saw the action as a fascinating test of tank strategies. The Czech Commander Miksche later wrote in *Blitzkrieg* that French theories dominated the use of Republican tanks and dissipated their power by spreading the limited number available in support of infantry. The German von Thoma insisted that Varela, the Nationalist commander, should concentrate his tanks, discover a tactical thrust-point (*schwerpunkt*) and then strike. This proved highly successful. The French might easily have anticipated German tactics in the Second World War from the small-scale model of Brunete.

As for the International Battalions, most had fought gallantly, and some had suffered terrible casualties. The Dabrowsky Battalion lost 121 killed, 320 wounded and 50 unaccounted for.[1]

[1] *Polacy w Wojnie Hiszpańskiej*, ed. Michala Brona, p. 28.

There were several episodes of serious insubordination. Deserters totalled over 250, Copeman had threatened to blow hell out of his own brigade headquarters and it was in the Brunete struggle that the XIVth Brigade refused point-blank to return to battle and Colonel Kriegger shot one of the mutineers. Kriegger himself narrowly escaped death at their hands and the XIVth Brigade had to be re-educated and completely reorganized. Add the dramatic desertion of Captain Alocca – in command of the XIIIth Brigade's cavalry – who suddenly turned away from the battle and headed for the French frontier, and it becomes clear that a spirit of disillusion had spread more deeply than anyone cared to admit. Absurdly, Captain Alocca returned to Madrid later, and was promptly shot for cowardice.

Most of the British leaders, disturbed by quarrels over political control in the British Battalion, left for England after the battle of Brunete, and men like Fred Copeman, Jock Cunningham and Walter Tapsell were presently involved in violent arguments with the Central Committee of the Communist Party in London. Cunningham's forceful manner, partly the result of his passionate belief in what he had to say, led to hints of a Fascist temperament, and in due course a disgusted Cunningham left the Party.

With Tapsell, Aitken and Copeman, it was different. After a stormy scene with Rust and Pollitt, Copeman and Tapsell were leaving the King Street Communist Party headquarters when Copeman suddenly said to Tapsell: 'Listen – they're sending us back – but how do we know it isn't a death sentence?'

This remark was inspired by a new awareness of the ruthless political manœuvring now going on between the British, Spanish and Russian Communists. Rust himself had come to believe that the Russian supplies entering Barcelona were only released for use when the Republican Government satisfied the political demands of the Russians.

Copeman and Tapsell thereupon burst back into the meeting. 'I want a letter,' Copeman said, 'giving us your full backing in Spain.'

When they did return to Spain in late September, they were equipped with the highest credentials from the British Communist Party which carried them through many a nasty situation.

George Aitken, who had returned to England with Copeman and Tapsell, found himself assigned to a job in Manchester and when Tapsell was reaffirmed as Political Commissar to the British Battalion, it looked as though Aitken – a very steady, reliable man, quite different from the flaring, temperamental Tapsell – had been sacrificed to political expediency.

Kitty Wintringham, wife of Tom Wintringham, also returned to confront the Communist hierarchy in London. Her husband had been wounded a second time and had developed typhoid. She brought a specially memorized message from him, but all Harry Pollitt said was: 'Tell him to get out of Barcelona, go up to the front line, get himself killed and give us a headline.'[1] For reasons of their own, the Communist Party had come to hate Tom Wintringham.

[1] Verbal evidence, Mrs Wintringham. Will Paynter, who became political commissar to the British Battalion, thinks it unlikely that Pollitt would have said this.

Chapter 18

The XVth on the Aragon Front

ANOTHER diversionary offensive was launched by the Republic on 24 August along the Aragon front and once again the XVth International Brigade played a part. The Americans were now beginning to dominate the command of the XVth Brigade with Robert Merriman as Chief of Staff, Steve Nelson as Brigade Commissar, and Malcolm Dunbar the only Briton among them in the higher ranks. Nelson, the tough ex-shipyard worker, contrasted oddly with Dunbar, an elegant young Scot who a few years before 'had been leader of an advanced aesthetic set at Trinity College, Cambridge', but no one knew better than Dunbar how to subdue his background and iron out class differences.

The situation in the American Battalion had changed too, and the Lincoln-Washington was now led by Hans Amlie, an engineer from Wisconsin, once a member of the Irish Republican Army. Americans similarly dominated the command of a newly formed battalion, the Mackenzie-Papineau, which was said to be Canadian, named after the leaders of the Canadian rebellion against the English in 1837, and originally drawn from Canadians serving in the American ranks. In fact, its numbers were so heavily made up by Americans that only a third remained Canadian. Joe Dallet, who had fought his way through the French courts with his band of volunteers, was now Political Commissar of the Mac-Paps, and the commander, Captain Thompson, also came from the States. It was Joe Dallet who had written home to his wife: 'This is a funny place. Some of the most prominent people back home . . . turn out badly here, while some insignificant people like Johnny Gates rise to the top.' Gates was destined to become Brigade Commissar in succession to Nelson.

The XVth Brigade now constituted a small part of the very considerable forces which were assembled for yet another attack under the new name of the Army of the East led by General Pozas. General Walter's Division included four International Brigades, excluding the XIVth because, as we have seen, he had quarrelled with Colonel Dumont. At Brunete, the International Brigades made up roughly one-fifth of the total army, but now they were less than a twentieth part, and the Spaniards claimed that General Pozas commanded what was really a Spanish people's army which for the first time represented all shades of political opinion from all parts of Spain. Socialist battalions stood cheek-by-jowl with Anarchists, and Communists marched beside liberals, but the officers remained mainly Communists. At the outset of the war, 90 per cent of the higher-ranking Army officers had gone over to Franco and left a gap which it was hoped the Brigades would help to fill. They were also intended to give the Republicans a chance to play for time while the militiamen became efficient soldiers. This, now, had largely been achieved, and the importance of the Brigades diminished proportionately.

On 25 August, the new diversionary offensive was directed against eight separate targets on a front which consisted mainly of fortified strong-points strung along a series of strategic heights. The Dimitrov Battalion, consisting mainly of Yugoslavs, went in before the Lincoln-Washington, to attack a hill known as Purburell, and a battalion of Lister's men attacked and tried to silence machine-gun emplacements which threatened the advance. When heavy machine-gun fire stopped the Dimitrovs, the Americans went in to support them, but they, in turn, were pinned down. By ten o'clock in the morning, the Listers had at last mastered the machine-gun posts and now the advance moved according to plan.

As one American eye-witness wrote: 'The tanks came on, blasting the Fascist fortifications and over the top we went following the tanks. The Fascists ran back to the town and we followed closely on their heels capturing the trenches outside. . . . The tanks pursued the fleeing foe right into Quinto, firing at fortified houses and destroying machine-gun nests. Most of the enemy took refuge in the church. . . . By the time our battalion reached the cemetery night was fast approaching. . . .'

The following morning, the Lincoln-Washington Battalion broke into the streets of Quinto, fighting with every kind of close-in weapon from hand-grenades to dynamite bombs. It was necessary to force their way from house to house, and suddenly a warning came that the enemy were weaving back along the outlying buildings, trying to re-encircle the attackers. Captain Thompson ordered his men out of the town again.

On the third night, the first and second companies of the Lincoln-Washington turned their attention to the heights over-looking Purburell Hill, and the third company reached the bottom of the hill itself. There they made contact not with two companies from the Dimitrovs as they had expected, but with some of the English Battalion which had replaced the Dimitrovs. Volunteers were now called for to attack the main church converted into a powerful strong-point, which was still holding the Brigades at bay in front of Quinto. Led by an American longshoreman, Carl Bradley, ten Americans armed themselves with nitro-glycerine bottles and wriggled their way to within ten yards of the church which had walls three feet thick and machine-gun emplacements at regular intervals.

'Out of our ten men,' Bradley said, 'two were wounded as we snaked our way to the building. Three of the gang had to carry them back. That left five of us to carry on. We took our bottles, filled with this deadly explosive glycerin, picked windows and threw them in with well-directed pitches that came from good baseball arms. Tremendous flames exploded inside the building. We came back twice with the bottles, and then rolled a big drum of gasoline into the structure with a fuse attached to it. It exploded inside.'

Quinto fell the same day.

When the attack began on the morning of 24 August, the British Battalion was disgruntled to find itself placed in reserve. Then they realized what was afoot. While the Lister Brigade cut the Nationalists' communications in the rear of Quinto and the American, Spanish and Dimitrov Battalions moved in to occupy the town, the British were gathered ready to launch the final assault on the towering stronghold of Purburell Hill itself. The attack began, and as one man wrote: '. . . hell broke loose. The Fascist trenches near the summit became one line of continuous crackling machine-gun fire.'

The Irish commander, Peter Daly, was wounded almost at once, and later died in hospital. The Political Commissar had to retire from the battle with another less serious wound. Presently, with casualties mounting, the attack was suspended until dawn the following day. Arthur Ollerenshaw, a former R.A.F. pilot, recently appointed adjutant to the battalion, gave this description of what followed: 'The anti-tank battery did marvellous work. They sent over salvos without a pause, raking the Fascist trenches, searching out the machine-gun nests and destroying them one by one. . . . Cheered by the visible damage our guns were doing we began the advance down the slope again like the previous night, and across the road, with the Fascist machine-guns spitting fire at us. Then the upward climb against Purburell. It was, I think, about nine o'clock when our guns suddenly ceased. There was a deathly stillness. Then, over our heads, we heard a familiar humming that soon became a roar – Fascist planes.'[1]

Fortunately they were too near the Nationalist lines for the bombers to drop their load without the danger of blowing up their own troops. They dropped them, instead, harmlessly on the other side of the hill. The anti-tank battery continued firing its small shells at the enemy machine-gun nests, and the English made another dash forward, but one gun in particular took a heavy toll and O'Daire ordered everyone to take cover while they pinpointed its precise position. They then discovered barbed wire protecting the site and O'Daire asked the artillery to smash a way through before he attempted a storming manœuvre. A few hours later the battalion renewed the assault and this time carried everything before them. Several Nationalist officers committed suicide, but scores of prisoners were taken. Miles Tomalin wrote in his diary:

'*August 29. Sunday.* A bunch of Fascists held out in the church long after the village was ours. . . . Thirteen men surrendered; five officers remained, knowing that they would not save their lives by giving in. Officers are shot. What else can you do? Every convinced Fascist alive adds to the danger in which their kind has placed the world.'

Presently final mopping-up operations were proceeding in Quinto, and the attack on what was said to be the impregnable

[1] William Rust, *Britons in Spain*, p. 91.

fortress of Belchite began. Certainly, for a small-scale defence system, the fortifications in Belchite were a magnificent justification of German throughness with an interlocking network of pill-boxes, trenches, iron stakes, steel prongs, and machine-guns, perfectly placed to cover every avenue of approach. Even Napoleon had failed to conquer Belchite, and now the town had enormous strategic importance because it commanded the crossroads from which a deeper penetration of Aragon became possible.

Approaching Belchite, the Spanish XXXIInd Brigade suffered heavy casualties and it became necessary to throw in the XVth Brigade. The Lincolns filtered through the lines of the XXXIInd Brigade in an attempt to recover the impetus of the advance, and by nightfall they were entrenched in shallow ditches not more than 100 yards from the cathedral on the Belchite–Azaila road. During the night, special bombing parties made stealthy attacks on the cathedral, but its solid rock construction seemed to brush off hand-grenades and nitro-glycerine bombs like flies. The approach of dawn brought devastating fire from the cathedral and the Lincolns were forced to move back to what appeared to be the protection of a natural ledge. Still the snipers continued to pick off man after man.

Dave Engels was one of the men trapped in the quickly improvised trenches, and he described what it meant as the day wore on and they remained pinned to the ground:

'They were very shallow, just deep enough to give us cover if we lay flat. Once in, we had to lie there all day without food or water. The position was . . . completely exposed: it was impossible to bring up supplies. The Fascists in the outlying houses raked us with enfilading fire; everybody who as much as sat up in the trench was certain to draw fire immediately.'

Bravery – sometimes cool-headed, sometimes foolhardy, sometimes the result of blind rage – had become commonplace, but it needed a very special brand to face up to a frontal assault on the main cathedral strongpoint. Several attacks were launched with unpleasant results. Safe behind rock walls three feet thick, peering from narrow doors and windows, the Nationalists brought every attack to a standstill with terrific fire. When the C.O. was wounded in the head, and Steve Nelson, Brigade Commissar, wounded in the face and groin, matters seemed bad enough, but within a short time the whole battalion had been reduced to no more than 100 effective fighting men, and the situation became critical. Leonard Lamb, who took over command from Hans Amlie, decided to try repeated small-scale assaults by squads of five riflemen armed with as many grenades as they could carry, on the principle that a dozen or so squads converging from different points should dissipate the enemy's fire.

While these squads went to work, Carl Bradley led a larger contingent of thirty men towards Belchite itself.

'We charged uphill some 350 metres under enemy machine-gun fire. . . . Three of our men were killed, seven wounded. . . . We took a street to a point where Charlie Regan was killed . . . we built a barricade of bags of grain taken from the cellars of abandoned houses and gave the Fascists hell from behind it with bombs and rifles. Then we decided to move the barricade forward a few feet at a time. Two volunteers were needed for this and two stepped forward immediately. One of them was Ephraim Bartlett of Colorado, a man with some Indian blood, a miner who had been a soldier in the United States Cavalry. . . . Back to the sides of the building he took sack after sack from the barricade, and holding them in front of him in direct fire of the enemy, he piled them in position. . . . Then we began to advance through the buildings. . . .'[1]

At last the many assaults on the cathedral drove the Nationalists back through the cathedral itself, down the open streets into the plaza. As the Americans penetrated deeper into the town, scores of Nationalists surrendered, and suddenly the deep rich strains of the 'Himno de Riego' burst from the brigade's propaganda truck. The volume was now increased to such a pitch that even the explosions from rifle and hand-grenades did not drown it. A short, eloquent appeal to the Nationalists to surrender followed, and then, once more, the national anthem rang out.

It was one of those occasions when those who believed in propaganda triumphed. An uncanny silence followed the anthem. Firing had ceased and everything was unnaturally quiet. A few scattered shots now broke out once more – said by Edwin Rolfe to be part of a mutiny among the Nationalists.

[1] Edwin Rolfe, *The Lincoln Battalion*, p. 126.

And then cries of 'Viva la Republica!' came from the enemy, and men began to appear with their hands above their heads, surrendering.

Ernest Hemingway was at the Aragon front in September and gave a different picture of the taking of Belchite: '. . . for three days they fought from house to house, from room to room, breaking walls with pick-axes, bombing their way forward. . . . Finally they made a juncture with the Spanish troops advancing from the other side and surrounded the cathedral where four hundred men of the town garrison held out. These men fought desperately, bravely. . . . Then, after some fighting of the sort you never know whether to classify as hysterical or the ultimate in bravery, the garrison surrendered.'[1]

Robert Merriman, now Chief of Staff of the XVth Brigade, was one of the leaders in the last assault. Wounded six times by splinters, he arrived at the cathedral with a smoke-blackened, delighted face and only then would he have his wounds dressed.

Prisoners told Hemingway that the Nationalists lost 1,200 killed in Belchite alone, and certainly, when the Lincolns entered it, the town had such a smell of death from corpses squashed beyond identification in broken and collapsed masonry that 'the Government burial squads digging to reach them were unable to remain there without gas-masks.'[2]

The XVth International Brigade now withdrew from the front and underwent a period of 'resting' which still meant moving from place to place. For the first time the Mackenzie-Papineau Battalion moved into Aragon and was incorporated in the XVth Brigade. Already the brigade had drawn on special groups from the Mac-Pap Battalion to replace casualties at places like Brunete, but the battalion was still predominantly American with only one Canadian rifle company to two American.

On 12 October the XVth Brigade received fresh orders to move up to the Fuentes del Ebro front, and the plan of action was explained by General Walter to the battalion commanders. This time, an attempt was to be made to sweep past the Fascist line of fortifications which intervened between the Republicans and Saragossa on the south bank of the Ebro.

[1] *Fact*, July 1938, p. 35.　　　　[2] Ibid., p. 36.

The attack began on 13 October across open ground, climbing slowly towards the enemy trenches, and as the men fanned out in the first few hours they waited for the plane support which they had been told to expect. It did not materialize. Nor was there any sign of the heavy artillery barrage which would disorganize the enemy's defences and enable the XVth to try a direct assault on one strong-point after another.

There were now four battalions with the XVth, the British, the Lincoln-Washington, the Mackenzie-Papineau and one Spanish battalion, the XXIVth. This was the first action of the Mackenzie-Papineau Battalion and before they took up position, Staff officers discussed whether Dallet should be removed from his job as Political Commissar because his fanatically disciplinarian methods had made him unpopular. In the event he remained Commissar.

On one sector of the front, as the battle began, a spectacular new technique with tanks was tried out. The Republicans amassed all the tanks they possessed, totalling 100, and drove them straight through the enemy lines with one battalion of infantry actually riding on the tanks. This was an early attempt at the blitzkrieg technique, and in theory a column of trucks carrying the main body of the infantry would be poised ready to follow through the breach and rush to Saragossa, fifty miles behind the enemy lines. The tanks were light tanks manned by Slavs, the infantry which they carried Spanish, and the follow-up infantry British, Canadian and American. The breakthrough proved comparatively simple, but before the infantry could follow up the fast-receding tanks the Nationalists recovered, poured an appalling concentration of fire into the gap and stopped the second wave of infantry dead in its tracks. The infantry never really got into its stride and the now-distant tanks were cut off, surrounded and finally captured or destroyed. Partly it was a failure of communications; partly the problem of orders which had to be translated into many languages. The Spanish created military history by going into action mounted on the tops and turrets of these whippet tanks, travelling at 40 miles an hour, clinging desperately with one hand and firing – equally desperately – with the other. Once again European observers took sharp note of the terrible casualties they suffered.

On their sector of the front the Mac-Paps moved in across the central area below the main line of Fascist fortifications, the Lincolns advanced on their right flank and the English covered the Lincolns' flank towards the river. When they were near enough to the enemy to make bombing impossible, the long-expected Republican planes suddenly came sweeping over and simply had to return to base again with their bombs intact. Brigade H.Q. was furious.

The machine-gun commander of the Mac-Paps afterwards wrote: 'The attack started at 1.40 p.m. Joe Dallet, battalion commissar, went over with the First Company on the left flank, where the fire was heaviest. He was leading the advance when he fell, mortally wounded. He behaved heroically until the very end, refusing to permit the first-aid men to approach him in his exposed position.'

By four o'clock in the afternoon it became clear that the attack could not achieve its objective. By then the advance had long come to a standstill and the Lincolns and Mac-Paps were merely taking whatever cover they could find, and waiting for nightfall to get back to their lines. In the mixed-up character of the American, Canadian and English Battalions, it was not unexpected to find Sam Kaplan, a New York boy, going into action with the British Battalion, and saving the life of John Patterson, an Englishman.

But once again the attack had failed. It carried the XVth Brigade a bare kilometre nearer the objective at heavy cost, and then they were forced to dig in, establishing all the paraphernalia of a new line less than a mile from their old one. On 3 October they were relieved by a Spanish brigade and once more came out of the line.

Chapter 19

More Trouble in the Brigades

By the autumn of 1937 there were two Spains, each with an army of about half a million men occupying clearly defined zones which had established their own kind of order, and the savage atmosphere of July 1936 had changed. In the north, the existence of three comparatively independent states in the Republican area remained a source of great weakness, because each had its own theory of government and each was torn by political strife. Franco had the advantage of much greater political unity and controlled two-thirds of Spain under what was virtually a military dictatorship. Franco's victories in the north gave him 18,600 square kilometres of land and nearly 1½ million people 'including many war prisoners who were put to work in conditions little better than those of concentration camps'.[1] It also freed 65,000 men from the northern campaigns to fight in the south.

In Republican Spain, the Cortes met on 1 October, continuing the policy of preserving the outward form of democracy. Two hundred of those members elected in February 1936 were present, and the Communists, whose sixteen members did not any longer accurately reflect their following, clamoured for new elections which Negrín refused. Díaz, at the Communist Party conference of 12 November, pressed for new elections, but it would have meant the Party leaving the Government and this seemed dangerous because it remained powerful out of proportion to its representation in the Cortes. The POUM leaders, arrested six months before, were still languishing in jail and the Communists continued to arrest many political enemies on one ground or another, some genuine, others partisan. A new secret police organization known as the SIM (Servicio de Investigacion Militar), directed by Communists, was set up ostensibly to investigate spies, and did not hesitate to use certain

[1] Hugh Thomas, *The Spanish Civil War*, p. 481.

NKVD methods. Many documents drawn from captured Republican archives with photographs and dossiers are included in *The General Cause*, and unless these have been faked, baths with which to freeze prisoners, irons to burn and clubs to beat them were part of an equipment which also included cells made small enough to threaten suffocation.[1]

According to Fred Copeman, high-level political conspiracies between such conflicting parties as the Communists, Socialists and Anarchists were reflected in new troubles within the International Brigades. The Brigades' periodical, *The Volunteer for Liberty*, published on 1 November the text of an announcement which formally incorporated the Brigades into the Spanish Army.

'The units constituted by Spanish and foreign volunteers were organized by the decree of 31 August 1920[2] developed in the circular order of 4 September of the same year. . . . Even though the units now existing under the name of International Brigades are legally those which the Spanish State, using its sovereign rights, has constituted to take the place of the units which revolted in July 1936, and are analogous to those which under different names exist in the armies of almost all countries, it is necessary to lay down fresh norms which should regulate their recruitment, organization, administration, etc. . . . To meet with this necessity I have determined:

'To take the place of the Tercio de Extranjeros (Foreign Legion) formed under the decree of 31 August 1920, the International Brigades are formed as units in the Spanish Army. At the present time five of the above-mentioned brigades should be constituted on the basis of those formed spontaneously in the course of the present war, adapting their constitution to the norms indicated in the present order.'

There were many other complicated clauses in the pronouncement, including: 'Petitions for leave abroad will be noted by the brigade commanders and forwarded to base. In no case will the applicant be authorized to absent himself from the ranks of his unit before the leave has been granted.'

[1] *The General Cause*, p. 436. According to Carlo Penchienati the SIM had its counterpart in the International Brigades. The Italian Communist Vittorio Vidali, who went under the name of Commandante Carlos, was its first chief. *Brigate Internazionali In Spagna*, pp. 39–43.

[2] *Diario Oficial*, No. 195.

The number of deserters had increased in recent months and now new attempts were made to instil fresh disciplines. Another weekly paper, *Our Fight*, published by the XVth International Brigade, printed an article which made self-conscious attempts to justify the habit of saluting, a habit referred to in earlier days as bourgeois snobbery. It seemed that saluting, one of the contributory elements in disciplined behaviour, had deeply tainted bourgeois sources which now had to be explained away at any cost.

'1. A salute', the article said with fatuous naïveté, 'is the military way of saying "hello". For either to omit it when a soldier meets an officer is as insulting as for two men who know each other to pass without greetings in civilian life.

'2. A salute is the quickest, easiest way for a soldier to say to an officer: "What are your orders? I am ready to carry them out."

'3. A salute is not undemocratic. Two officers of equal rank when meeting on military business salute each other.

'4. A salute is a sign that a comrade who has been an egocentric individualist in private life has adjusted himself to the collective way of getting things done.

'5. A salute is a proof that our Brigade is on its way from being a collection of well-meaning amateurs to a precision instrument for eliminating Fascists.'

Everyone was now exhorted in periodicals, speeches and Commissar pep-talks, to learn Spanish, and everyone received instructions intended to improve dress and appearance. It might look as though the military principles by which a bourgeois army lived had revealed characteristics worthy of imitation, but other forces were at work as well.

Numbers of volunteers had now succeeded in returning to their home countries and had taken with them embittered stories of indisciplined confusion and exploitation among the Brigade. Those who were not Communist resented the fact that Communists dominated the Brigades; those who were liberals spread the story of the liquidation of the POUM rebellion; and those who were individualists complained that the voluntary status with which they set out had been ruthlessly removed. It became increasingly difficult to get volunteers from abroad who brought that brand of idealism which was prepared to face up to anything.

The present Spanish Government claims that at this stage a number of deceptions were practised by what they refer to as 'Republican consuls' in different countries. They go further. 'The communist propagandists . . .' they state 'now had recourse to fraud.[1] They made candid persons believe that they were contracting high-salaried workers for the Spanish industry. Many, thinking that they were going to work in the potassium mines in Cordova, crossed the frontier and upon reaching Spain were sent to the deposit [sic] of volunteers in Albacete.' Edward Knoblaugh's evidence is given in support of these allegations. Knoblaugh was an American foreign correspondent who returned from Valencia in a British destroyer, and two of his travelling companions were Lawrence Mullers, a Canadian, and Tim Keenan, an Irishman, both deserters from the Brigades.

According to their evidence, originally they had volunteered for work on the Spanish railways, but when they arrived at Albacete their passports were confiscated, and they were given rifles and 'ordered to go to the front'.

Vigorous protests merely brought a warning that without passports they came under Spanish law and 'would be shot if they attempted to desert'. They did succeed in deserting and sought the protection of the British Embassy in Valencia, only to be told that nothing could be done for them. In danger of arrest at any moment, they were tipped off that the consul in Valencia had smuggled several Irish deserters aboard warships and they hurried off to see him. He managed to get them aboard the torpedo boat *Brazen*, and later had them transferred to a destroyer. Both men informed Knoblaugh that there were scores of Brigaders who would 'desert tomorrow' if they possessed passports and could avoid instant arrest.

The interesting story of John Coope now came to light. On 28 April, Coope's father received a letter in England from the International Brigade Committee in Albacete saying that his son was missing on active service and that they had no exact knowledge of his fate. In great distress, Coope senior sent the letter on to Captain Heilgers, his M.P., who contacted the Foreign Office, and a search began.

[1] *The International Brigades*, Madrid, 1952, p. 121.

Meanwhile further news came through. Coope was found to be the sole survivor of a small group of men who had been blown to pieces by mortar shells, and he now wrote a letter to his parents. 'Being under 18 can't you possibly get me out of this?' His father sent a strong letter to the I.B. authorities in Valencia, but without result. Coope now deserted and managed to make his way, with seven other Brigaders, to Barcelona, where they boarded a British ship. Suddenly the military police arrived, demanded to search the ship, found six of the eight hidden men, lined them up on the quay and without further question – according to Coope – shot them. John Coope had the advantage of the others. As a student of marine engineering he knew the precise layout of the main 'cubby-holes' in the ship, and he found a very obscure and remote one, where he felt certain he would be safe. He was right. The search did not penetrate to their hide-out.

Back in England, Mr and Mrs Coope, now even more disturbed, were searching their son's belongings one day when they found a letter which Ellen Wilkinson, M.P., had sent to Coope at the outset. Convinced that an illicit traffic was being carried on under the guise of the Dependants' and Wounded Aid Committee in London, and furious that his son should have been a victim, Coope senior set out to expose the 'fraud'. Giving the name of Smith, he followed exactly the same procedure as his son and first wrote to Ellen Wilkinson. Presently he received a request to attend an interview at Bury St Edmunds, and now it was necessary to nominate someone much younger than himself who could successfully pose as a candidate for Spain. At this point, suddenly and unexpectedly, John Coope himself turned up in England, having at last broken through the Spanish security net, and he agreed to adopt the name of Smith and follow through the proceedings once more, with one big difference. The interview would take place, this time, in a room divided from a second room by a thin partition, and in this room a typist would take down every word said.

Once this evidence became available, the whole matter was brought out into the open in the British House of Commons, and Captain Heilgers made a speech in which he said: 'I think that if I can prove that this society [The Brigade Dependants' and Wounded Aid Committee of Lichfield Street] which purports to deal with benevolent activities in connection with the pensioners and wounded of the I.B. is really sending people to Spain . . .'

But he never did prove it. Ellen Wilkinson replied in the House that her secretary had merely supplied an address as she might to anyone seeking information, and she doubted the evidence of six men being callously shot, since it came from one man – a very young man – with a vested interest in the whole affair. It was up to the Foreign Office to inquire into the story. After several vain attempts to break into the debate, William Gallacher at last managed to growl out the vital piece of information that there were two addresses at Lichfield Street, and each was engaged in different activities.

As the flow of volunteers for Spain diminished, where the battalions threatened to fall below strength Spaniards were transferred from their own still-growing and steadily more disciplined army. Whether the Spaniards were selected to fill the gaps because they were Communists or not is difficult to establish, but mostly they *were* Communists which led to fresh friction with those volunteers who still had not succumbed to the faith.

The XVth Brigade Commander Čopic now permitted himself these reflections on his troops: 'Despite the splendid accomplishments of the Brigade at Belchite, its military preparedness was not up to the required level. The grade of workmanship was low . . . in a tactical respect units were not sufficiently trained. Discipline and order in the various units was poor. This was hardly surprising. The American comrades who became a very important factor in the reorganization of the brigade, had at that time almost no military experience and training. . . .'

A general reorganization of the Brigades coincided with these remarks to remove the more highly trained and experienced Dimitrov and Franco-Belge Battalions from the XVth Brigade. This was very important because despite the scant attention paid to the Dimitrovs in this book – a shortcoming enforced by sheer space – they were one of the best battalions in any of the Brigades, and their long record of service, casualties, bravery and single-minded devotion remarkable.

The Franco-Belge Battalion was another matter. It, too, had performed feats of heroism which were characteristic of the whole fantastic story of the International volunteers, but the pulse of Latin individuality constantly broke out to cause fresh trouble.

There was, for instance, the incident on the heights above Sesena with the 9th Division. The French had managed to procure and drink large quantities of champagne and it was an extraordinary body of intoxicated men who suffered a terrible mortar bombardment. Gillain describes how, caught in a deluge of fire, they fell back, and the enemy, feeling their fire weaken, launched an assault, the full brunt of which finally fell on the Franco-Belge Battalion. Astonishing scenes followed. Still completely drunk on champagne, the men hurled themselves into the open, recklessly attacking the enemy with handfuls of grenades. As Hugh Thomas said, 'the battle eventually became a massacre of the intoxicated'.

This added fresh fuel to the troubles within the International Brigade High Command. A committee was set up to investigate the episode and the activities of Colonel Dumont, commander of the Franco-Belge Division. The committee later alleged that Colonel Dumont spent his time in 'meetings, celebrations and the persecution of Trotskyists'.

Worse trouble had developed back at the Brigades base in Albacete. The second-in-command, the Frenchman Gaymann (known as Vidal), had been accused of embezzlement and after a preliminary investigation was found to be suffering from 'ill-health' and sent off to Paris. The already fierce rivalry between the German and French Communists at Albacete, intensified when a German, not a Frenchman, who went under the name of Gómez (actually Zeisser) was appointed to take the place of Gaymann. Suspicions multiplied and presently the embezzlement charge was hurled at one person after another until the chain of accusations came closer and closer to the great André Marty himself.

A French Communist, Grillet, and his wife were presently alleged to be involved, and as close friends of Madame Marty, suspicion at last fastened on her husband. Now came the cry that Marty had himself 'volé les soldats de la Liberté', and as the pressures mounted, and German Communists saw their chance to challenge his authority, Marty found himself hounded to the point where he was forced to go to Moscow to justify himself.

Meanwhile Copeman returned from England with 350 new recruits to take over command of the English Battalion once more and found that 'most of the older volunteers were so fed up that unless a tighter grasp could be kept, the new recruits would be likewise affected.'

He discovered two causes for discontent and poor discipline. First a number of deserters had vanished in Republican Spain without trace and this unsettled those who had applied for 'repatriation' unsuccessfully. Second, rumours of political plots and conspiracies between Anarchists, Socialists and Communists in the Republican Government had spread throughout the rank and file, disrupting their sense of unity with a new cynicism. Copeman tried to counteract the first by announcing a drive to round up all British deserters in Spain, and the second by reaffirming the central purpose of their fight as quite unchanged by local political squabbles.

A third conflict had arisen in the English Battalion. According to Copeman, the Americans were placing American leaders and Commissars in the battalion, with the indirect aim of achieving complete political control over the exclusively English-speaking units in the Brigades. Copeman deliberately changed the senior commands in his battalion, appointing an Englishman, Bill Alexander, a very self-effacing, conscientious intellectual, as commander, and Sam Wild as adjutant, while Tapsell remained Political Commissar. Another reason for these changes centred around the insistent Communist call for the death penalty in certain cases. Copeman was flatly against the death penalty. 'I have never changed my opinion on this matter', he said. 'I believe that any political belief or any religion must depend on righteousness if it is to be successful. Force only engenders force and in the end may be the means of destroying the idea which uses it.'

He insisted that once the battalion went into action again, Tapsell was not to be permitted in the front line, and the decision on the death penalty for cowardice, desertion or refusal to obey orders was to be left in the hands of Bill Alexander and Sam Wild, both of whom, he felt sure, were equally opposed to it. In all these activities Copeman was now aided and abetted by Alexander Foote, a man who had stolen one of General Gal's staff cars, resprayed and disguised it, fitted machine-guns fore and aft and now drove Copeman round like a Staff general in royal splendour. Foote's personal story finally took an amazing turn, but that was not yet.

Copeman himself now fell seriously ill. On the eve of the Teruel offensive a series of bilious attacks culminated in the worst bout of sickness he had known, and what at first looked like a serious appendix case, presently revealed other complications which necessitated a three-hour operation. He arranged for reports of the battalion's activities to be sent to his hospital, and it was here that he pieced together the story of what happened in the Teruel battle. At the outset Tapsell and Sam Wild visited him almost daily, but there came a day when Bob Minor, the American Political Commissar, arrived instead, and 'I sensed that something was seriously wrong.' Astonishingly, Minor was 'a grey-haired old chap who looked a good seventy', and he now explained to Copeman that the battalion had suffered serious casualties with Bill Alexander wounded and Wally Tapsell almost certainly dead, although the exact nature of his death was not known. Nor was that all. The very penalty which Copeman had tried to avoid at any cost had been imposed in his absence. 'The Brigade had demanded a court-martial of two of our men, sentence was passed and they were immediately shot. I asked what Sam's attitude had been to all this, and was told that British volunteers had formed the firing party. Life seemed to stop. Somehow too much had arrived at once, and I had reached the end of further physical effort.'[1]

All unaware of these internal troubles, in December a group of British Labour leaders came to visit the British Battalion, and Clement Attlee, Ellen Wilkinson and Philip Noel-Baker were royally entertained to a great dinner. The usual speeches with the obligatory phrases perfectly in place were made, and then came a spectacular torchlight procession with a stirring demonstration of the battalion's strength and discipline. Henceforward Attlee agreed that the No. 1 Company of the British Battalion

[1] Fred Copeman, *Reason in Revolt*, p. 147.

should be known as the Major Attlee Company, and Attlee announced: 'I would assure you all of our admiration for your courage and devotion to the cause of freedom and social justice. I shall try to tell the comrades at home of what I have seen. Workers of the world unite!' He set off back to England quite unaware of the covetous eyes which were watching every quarrel in the battalion in the hope of turning the next one to political ends.

Chapter 20

The Battle of Teruel

TOWARDS the end of December the lull in the fighting broke once more. Franco had intended to take the initiative by launching an attack first upon Guadalajara and then on Madrid, but his plans were betrayed and these campaigns cancelled. It is interesting to recover the sense of surprise and shock that the Republican forces should still have the ability, after a long history of attack, stalemate and slow defeat, to emerge suddenly with a sledge-hammer blow when everyone expected the next offensive to come from Franco.

They chose Teruel for three surface reasons. First it was thought to be lightly held, second its capture would threaten the road to Saragossa and third the town had come to have a special place in the minds of the Republican forces. Underneath the surface more complex motives were at work. Prieto wanted to demonstrate the ability of the Army to operate successfully without a Commissar-General, and rumour also had it that once Teruel was conquered, he intended to sue from this small position of strength for a possible armistice. Once again, mainly for political reasons, the original plan made no provision for the employment of the International Brigades. This was to be a purely Spanish victory with Spanish arms, men and prestige.

The bleak, walled town of Teruel enshrined the fatalistic legend of the Lovers of Teruel and each winter it knew the worst weather that can be found in Spain. The winter of 1937 was no exception. Four beautiful cathedral spires rose from the town and three tree-lined roads led into the surrounding sugar-beet fields. In the middle distance, the remarkable red cliffs were sculptured by erosion into columns which looked like organ pipes.[1] With its great ridge on the west side offering natural protection, and the heavily fortified hillsides thrusting out of the

[1] *Fact*, Hemingway, 15 July 1938, p. 37.

plain, Teruel gave the impression of a natural fortress, and it was easy to understand why the Anarchist columns had remained in the hills around it, carefully avoiding contact with the enemy for no less than eight months. Ernest Hemingway described the stalemate: '. . . In many places the old lines, we saw, were from one to three kilometres from the enemy wire . . . and the only contact made . . . was on the purest friendly basis . . . when Anarchists would issue invitations to the rebel forces for football matches. Until the notorious Anarchist Iron column was disarmed . . . they often ran an excursion column of trucks to Valencia over the week-end, leaving the lines practically unheld.'[1]

Now, before the Teruel offensive began, everything was changed. In the middle of a terrible winter a new army of Levante, commanded by Colonel Hernández Sarabia, a regular army officer, took the place of the old army, and everything was keyed to the highest possible pitch on a strict disciplinary basis.

So it came about that in a dim ghost world of falling snow, on 15 December, Lister's XIth Division was, as usual, the one which sallied out from its positions, silently, with artillery and aerial bombardment suppressed to avoid warning the enemy, and advanced rapidly towards the ridge on the west side known as La Muela de Teruel – Teruel's Tooth. Simultaneously Heredia led the XVIIIth Brigade in a similar attack. By seven o'clock in the evening they had encircled Teruel and the Commander of the Garrison, Colonel Rey D'Harcourt, began to withdraw his outlying defences into the town. Barcelona Radio prematurely announced the fall of Teruel when 4,000 defenders were still firmly established in the Bank of Spain, the Civil Governor's office, the Seminary and the Convent of Santa Clara. Protected by the German air squadron of the Condor Legion, Franco launched a counter-offensive to relieve Teruel on 29 December and pushed back the Republican lines. Still official policy forbade the use of the International Brigades but they were now brought up in reserve.

At this point the weather did its best to bring even the most heroic fighting to a standstill. A blizzard came down, with snow obliterating the roads to a depth of four feet and the cold became so intense that many went down with frostbite and some

[1] *Fact*, Hemingway, 15 July 1938, p. 37.

cases were so bad that limbs had to be amputated. Temperatures fell to 18 degrees below zero, the machines of war simply froze to a standstill, fighting died out as ice clogged engines and boots, icicles formed on guns, supply lines were smothered out of existence, and hordes of vehicles were trapped, snowbound on and off the roads. Only inside the city did the fighting continue. The Nationalists were reduced to defending piles of ruins, with no water, diminishing ammunition and iron rations, and when the blizzard reached a new intensity in January, this stopped the relief forces from pressing their advantage. Colonel Rey D'Harcourt at last surrendered. The Republicans now evacuated the civilian population, occupied the town and in turn became the besieged.

As the International Brigades waited in reserve an episode occurred which remained in the minds of everyone who heard and witnessed it. Paul Robeson arrived at the front and there, surrounded by snow-clad hills and valleys, he began singing Negro spirituals in the open air. It was said by one man present that as his voice gathered power and began to echo and re-echo down the valleys, the shooting in the area died away, men paused in the midst of battle and cocked their heads to listen to what seemed for those who could not see him a great Russian choir of a voice, singing strange, lilting melodies which yet struck a familiar chord, until some openly wept and men were silent with a deeper awareness of what it meant to be alive.

In the wider, outside world the ambassadors of Franco's 'hidden' allies, Italy and Germany, were now considerably worried. Count Ciano, the Italian Foreign Minister, recorded in his diary the fear that a Republican offensive would 'push back the whole nationalist front'. 'Either', he wrote, 'we strike the first blow or skilfully disengage ourselves, and rest content with having inscribed on our banners the victories of Malaga and Santander.'[1] Stohrer, the German Ambassador in Salamanca, was equally disturbed by the increased economic and military strength of the Republic and told Berlin that 'if Franco was to win the war he would need more aid, especially in the form of officers and technical personnel.'

As for the battle itself, on 17 January it entered a new

[1] Ciano, *Diaries – 1937–38*, pp. 64–5.

phase as the Nationalist Generals Aranda and Varela launched a second counter-attack aimed at capturing the heights overlooking Teruel. Italian artillery prepared the way for their advance, and constant dog-fights developed in the air between Italian Fiats and Russian fighters. Suddenly and dramatically, on 18 January the Republican lines broke, and now for the first time the International Brigades, under General Walter, were flung into the battle.

The British Battalion took up their positions in three feet of snow, occupying separate mountain-tops connected only by field telephones. The cook-house lorry stuck half-way up the mountainside and each company had to send out runners to collect the food and reheat it on the return journey. When the meals seemed to diminish in size Walter Tapsell, the Commissar, discovered that the 'grub parties' were having little snacks, which sometimes approximated to a banquet, on the way.

On 19 January the Nationalists attempted to advance down the valley leading directly into Teruel. The Major Attlee Battalion was posted on top of a high cliff overlooking the valley and the main road into Teruel. Rust gave a more detailed description of their position. It 'was divided by a gully in the cliff face. The left half of the Battalion faced a similar high cliff on the edge of which the Canadian Battalion of the XVth Brigade was in position. It was possible for the British to engage the enemy with machine-gun fire over the heads of the Canadians. The right half of the Battalion on the other side of the gully, faced, over the valley, rolling open ground which was commanded by two high hills. If the Fascists took these hills it would open up the advance up the valley (of which they held one side) and would catch the Canadians on the Fascist side of the valley between two fires.'[1]

A terrific artillery bombardment drove two Spanish battalions off these hills and they were forced back under the cliffs held by the British. When the Nationalists tried to occupy the hills, British machine-gunners at first held them, but the Nationalists then began a second attack which threatened to reach a point in the Canadians' rear. Orders came by field telephone from Brigade H.Q. for three companies of riflemen to go down into the valley in an attempt to recapture the hills.

[1] William Rust, *Britons in Spain*, p. 110.

It was a desperate manœuvre which, in the event, delayed the Nationalists' advance but could not reoccupy the hills.

In the early dawn of the next day, the Nationalists let loose a terrific artillery bombardment and attacked the Canadians who made a stand which saved the British from encirclement. Then the direction of the attack changed and the British machine-gunners on the cliffs were forced to watch their comrades, the brave handful of riflemen who had sallied out the previous day, being mown down in the valley below. Some of the British now retreated into a fortified block house which 'controlled' the valley, but as others feverishly dug fresh trenches, enemy gunners found their range and trench after trench collapsed in crumbling mounds of dust and rubble before it was completed. When the Nationalists at last flung their infantry at the block house, the attack, according to Rust, 'was completely repulsed'. He went further. He claimed that they brought to a standstill the attempt to drive down the valley into Teruel.

On 15 January the Mac-Pap Battalion came up to relieve a badly hit battalion of the XIth Brigade, which had just repelled a savage and prolonged head-on attack by the Nationalists. The Lincoln Battalion replaced another battalion of the XIth which held the line of hills on the left flank and to the rear of the Mac-Paps. The Spanish XXIVth was thinly spread across the outskirts of Teruel from the Saragossa road to La Muela de Teruel. Teruel itself, once an ordered town of 12,000 inhabitants, had now become a battered heap of ruins.

The Americans took advantage of a collapsed hat shop to substitute huge black sombreros for tin helmets which had proved incapable of stopping bullets. As they took possession of one shop after another, fantastic clothing began to replace worn and ragged 'uniforms'. The Americans had constantly protested that their rags would soon fall off and leave them naked, and now they took the opportunity to don patent-leather shoes, striped vests, pin-striped trousers and a brilliant variety of ties. It was nothing to see a man crouched behind a machine-gun, with a savage determination to slaughter anything within range, wearing striped morning trousers, heavy and expensive riding-boots, a brilliant blue shirt and black sombrero, the whole apparition offset by a huge .38-calibre pistol tucked in the top of his trousers.

Such was the garb of one section of the International Brigades which now faced a series of fresh assaults. Unable to smash their way directly into the heights of El Muleton the Nationalists moved southward and advanced towards the Thaelmann, Lincoln and Mac-Pap positions. They inflicted terrible casualties on the Thaelmanns and then turned, and at last overwhelmed El Muleton. Caught in a steady raking fire from the hills, the Mac-Paps retreated slowly, but once the Nationalist artillery found the exact range it kept killing and maiming man after man. The trench mortars' shells, which arrived silently, exploded with a sound like tearing paper, and threw malignant steel splinters in all directions, took the worst toll of all. The Lincolns protecting the walls of Teruel were subjected to many kinds of fire and Phil Detro – an enormously tall Texan – was killed trying to cross a street between two factories. Relieved by the Spanish Campesinos on 3 February, the XVth Brigade was supposed to retire for rest and reorganization but on 9 February they were recalled into action. The Nationalists had launched yet another counter-attack, broken through the Republican lines and taken Argente, Perales and Alfambra north of Teruel.

At this point, a new and daring plan of action was carefully explained right down the line of command to individual Republican company commanders and men. Edwin Rolfe was present at the battle which followed and later wrote: 'The Thirty Fifth Division composed of the XVth and XIth Brigades was to strike from Segura de los Baños at the heart of the Fascist communications over which poured the troops and materials for their Teruel counter-drive. The two brigades were to assault the rebel fortifications at Atalaya and Sierra Pedigrossa which overlooked the town of Segura and from there to battle southward, sweeping over enemy forts, and taking possession of the apex formed by the three main roads converging. The task of the assault was given to the XVth Brigade which was in far better condition than the XIth. The latter had been practically cut to pieces in the defense of Teruel and El Muleton, and was assigned the job of acting as a rear-guard against any surprise flank attack that might develop after the movements of the XVth Brigade got under way.'[1] It sounded

[1] Edwin Rolfe, *The Lincoln Battalion*, p. 175.

a big and, if successful, devastating operation, but in the event once again it merely captured 'four important hills over a small but strategic two-kilometre front.'

The final battle for Teruel began on 17 February. The Nationalist commander Yagüe crossed the Alfambra and fought his way along the east bank, cutting off the city from the north. Aranda now joined him in an attempt at encirclement, and by 20 February Republican rail and road communications to Valencia were seriously threatened. As the defences in Teruel itself began to break at certain points, Hernández Sarabia gloomily decided that there was only one thing left to do – withdraw – but he delayed the order dangerously long and over 14,000 men were trapped as the Nationalists harried the retreating Republicans. El Campesino (The Peasant) the famous Spanish commander and his staff, were surrounded in Teruel itself and had to fight desperately to break through the ring. In his book *Listen Comrades*, he later claimed that Communist political conspiracies had deliberately withheld ammunition from the Teruel defenders in order to discredit Prieto, and he himself had been left to die in Teruel by the rival Communist commanders Lister and Modesto.

Since no other man had simultaneously succeeded in gaining the support of the CNT, the Communists and the UGT, the Communists had until now been forced to conceal their hatred of Prieto's leadership, but they decided at this point to launch a full-scale campaign against the War Minister, blaming him for the loss of Teruel, large quantities of guns and ammunition and no less than ten thousand Republican dead in Teruel itself. This campaign followed the return to Spain from Moscow of the Comintern representative Stepanov, with the news that Russia intended to intensify her aid to Spain providing Prieto was replaced. La Pasionaria now publicly attacked his direction of the war, and Hernández adopted a pen-name to criticize him in *Mundo Obrero*.

Once again the rank-and-file members of the International Brigades did not immediately know of these conspiracies. Political Commissars and their newspapers kept them fully alive to changes in Party policy, to a number of movements in the outside world, to the iniquities of German and Italian aid to Franco, but the bitter struggles within their own political leadership were only revealed in any detail after the campaigns had reached their climax. Thus, as Togliatti announced that Negrín would have to take over power from Prieto, the end result came as something of a shock to many of the comparatively simple-minded men in the Brigades who, like any other army, had a limited immediate vision of what was happening.

Chapter 21

The XVth Defeated

FOLLOWING what had become a victory for the Nationalists at Teruel, Franco launched a new offensive in an unexpected area. William Rust claimed that officers who were really Fascists had succeeded in penetrating the highest ranks of the Republican General Staff and now passed information to Franco which revealed the weakly-held and badly-fortified areas in the Aragon region where hilly and variegated country made a formidable natural defence system.

On 9 March the new attack began with the heaviest artillery and aerial barrage which the Republicans had ever encountered. German and Italian men and planes now swelled Franco's forces in great numbers. The German fliers included two Messerschmitt groups of four squadrons, two Heinkel 51 groups of two squadrons, a reconnaissance group of three squadrons and four bomber groups of three squadrons. The German Tank Corps under von Thoma involved at least four battalions with fifteen light tanks to each company, and no less than thirty anti-tank companies with six guns each. Hugh Thomas records that some doubts had entered the minds of the German rank and file about whether they were fighting on the right side, and the slogan – we are fighting on the wrong side – now gained some currency, but in the battle which followed they played a powerful and in some cases overwhelming role.

After the thrust and counter-thrust, attack and retreat of the Teruel battles, the Republican troops were weary, and replacements for battered and lost equipment inadequate. On the very first day of the offensive the Republican lines broke at several points and General Yagüe advanced swiftly down the right bank of the Ebro. The Black Arrows under Berti ran into trouble at Rudilla, but motorized units overcame it and another break in the line occurred.

Back in Rome, Count Ciano, the Italian Foreign Minister,

recorded in his diary 'It's full speed ahead', and for once his jubilation was not premature. Stiffer resistance occurred at Montalban, and by 13 March Rojo was reorganizing his forces to make the full weight of the defence felt. Naming Caspe as the new centre of the defence system, Rojo threw in all the International Brigades in an effort to interpose an impassable barrier, but before they could establish themselves the news came through that the Italian motorized battalions were already approaching the next town of Alcañiz. Republican battalions fought valiantly for brief spells, but the retreat of flanking units constantly drove them back, and slowly it became apparent that one swift thrust after another had broken not merely each new defensive line, but lines of communication, control between Battalion H.Q.s and their troops and any ordered disposal of one Brigade in relation to another. What began as a series of break-throughs for the Nationalists swiftly became for the Republicans a rout.

When the International Brigades first moved into position 'the Mac-Paps and English proceeded towards Calaceite while the Lincolns went beyond Batea. The XIth Brigade had already placed its two remaining battalions at strategic points, one defending the Caspe road, the other, the Edgar André Battalion, establishing lines in defense of the winding road from Nonaspe. . . .' The Lincolns were in the hills, loosely connecting the gap between the scattered battalions of the XIth Brigade. '. . . To the Americans' right another two kilometres of wooded hills were a possible entry point for the enemy as far as the road itself, where the Edgar Andrés, with a total strength of only eighty men and a few officers, anchored the Lincoln's flank.'[1]

In position for one night only, the Americans suddenly received the sensational news that the Nationalists had smashed the Republican lines in the Calaceite sector. The British had been caught still marching in formation, and had come under point-blank fire from a company of Italian whippet tanks. Before they went into the line André Marty had addressed them, saying: 'You English are incorrigible. I ask you at the last retreat what's happened and you say "Oh nothing much!" ' But now even the English gift for understatement was hard-pressed. Dr Königsberg remembers this action clearly: 'There

[1] Edwin Rolfe, *The Lincoln Battalion*, pp. 206–7.

was criminal lack of expertise. No scouts were sent abroad. Our march was suddenly cut by the Italian whippet tanks. Over 100 British were captured in two minutes. But the machine-gunners behind gave a good account of themselves. They set two whippets afire before they had to surrender in turn. . . . Walter Tapsell I last saw arguing with an Italian officer – he would! I believe he was killed that day. . . .'[1]

What the Americans did not immediately know was that they too were surrounded in one of the swiftest and best-executed manœuvres which the war had yet produced. The truth quickly became apparent, and the new Commandant of the American Battalion, Melvin Offsink, decided that they must break through the ring of besieging troops, enter Gandesa and join the defending forces. They attacked at 10 a.m. and one company seemed to penetrate towards the town in running combat with the enemy, but the remainder were brought to a complete standstill by a hail of machine-gun fire. They withdrew to a small hill in the north and planned to await the cover of darkness before making another attempt in a different direction.

This time there was no attack. Instead they moved off the hill in many separate lines, single file, avoided the flaring bonfires which indicated enemy encampments, and began the highly dangerous process of trying to infiltrate the enemy's lines in darkness. As Captain Milton Wolf later said: 'It would be useless to describe my feelings or the feelings of the men as we made our way through the dark in hostile, unknown territory. But this I believe: that there wasn't a man who made that trip who didn't feel death walking by his side.'

There was no moon, but a glimmering half-light made every man a shadow which might be a bush or tree, and as they entered the groves around Corbera, everywhere the enemy lay in small groups, some sleeping, some snoring, some still talking with their guards. It seemed incredible that even the few men who remained intact from the original battalion could seep through this semi-sleeping host with its awareness of a nearby enemy. 'As they slid across the Villalba road and began climbing the cliffs its groups disintegrated again and one handful completely lost touch with another.'

[1] Letter to author, 18 April 1964.

Thirty-five men led by Robert Merriman, Lamb and Dave Doran suddenly encountered another group which they took to be American. A terrified guard let out a weird wail: 'Cabo de Guardia. Cabo de Guardia! Rojos! Rojos!' (Corporal of the guard – Reds! Reds!) A second later he opened fire and the Americans scattered. Unwittingly Merriman and Doran rushed in the direction which they thought was away from the Nationalists only to find themselves running straight into their line of fire. Two other Americans who had dashed in the opposite direction heard shots ring out, followed by the command 'Manos arriba!' (Hands up!) and that was the last ever heard of Major Merriman, the highest-ranking American officer in the XVth Brigade, a man who had come through a dozen campaigns unscathed and was the oldest and one of the bravest veterans among them.

Similar confusion reigned everywhere. Running, hiding, scrambling up cliffs, racing across gullies, the scattered groups of men threw away their arms, but even unburdened, the terrible race to escape death was exhausting. After twelve hours of constant running and scrambling one man collapsed on the ground sobbing: 'I can't go on . . . even if they kill me. . . . I can't do it', and a second man seemed to go quite mad, raving unintelligibly to himself.

John Gates led another column which was more successful. An hour before dawn they filtered between two hills on which the Nationalists were waiting, and when the sun rose and occasional glimpses of scrabbling figures came to light, they were out of machine-gun range. There remained a number of forward Nationalist patrols to contend with. They reached the very wide, very swiftly flowing Ebro river and could find no trace of a boat and no sign of any materials for building a raft. By now the group had split and divided until Gates had only four companions. Utterly exhausted, their chances of swimming across seemed slim, but they decided to risk it. Only three of them succeeded – Gates, Watt and a man named Joseph Hecht, later to distinguish himself in World War II. The bodies of the other two were washed up on the shore two days later. By now none of the survivors felt that they could take another step without collapsing into unconsciousness, and when they realized that they had to cross a field of cockleburrs on

naked, bruised feet, even Gates, who had 'sworn never to surrender to the Fascists', began to waver in his resolution. They
crossed the field and collapsed beside the road, too exhausted
to care any longer what fate overtook them.

The impossible happened then. A car drove up, two men
stepped out and Ernest Hemingway and Herbert Matthews
(*New York Times* correspondent) leapt out, shook hands and
hugged the three naked men. Hemingway explained in his
explosive phrases that the main body of the Republican Army
had successfully crossed the Ebro and was busy regrouping to
make another stand. Turning towards the river, Hemingway
shook his burly fist: 'You Fascist bastards!' he said. 'You
haven't won yet. We'll show you.'

When the new set of raw American recruits, with the novelist
Alvah Bessie among them, approached the battlefield, they
encountered a number of men sitting on a stone wall, 'their
faces streaked with dirt, their beards long, a look of desperation
in their eyes.'[1]

The recruits had been warned against talking to subversive
influences whose morale had broken, and when these men spoke
to them they 'smiled with the superiority of ignorance'. A
small, bedraggled half-grinning Finn began to speak: 'You go
Fifteen Brigada. . . . No more Fifteen Brigada: all killed, all
dead; I get away lose gun and ammo; everybody dead; you
no believe? Hell up there; we no do anything, no can. You got
to smoke! Everybody blow to pieces, everybody kill.'[2]

When someone had the nerve to bawl at him 'You ran away!'
the Finn replied: 'Sure I run; you run too . . . all over; all gone,
no use no more. . . .'

At two-thirty the following morning the recruits began a
march of fifteen kilometres towards the XVth Brigade H.Q. In
the early morning they reached a point where they were re-
directed up the side of a wooded hill, and there they were told
they would find the Lincoln Battalion. Once more the men they
first encountered were a dishevelled band sprawled over the
ground in a state of filthy and actively lousy exhaustion.
Scattered on the hillside which looked across to a magnificent

[1] Alvah Bessie, *Men in Battle*, p. 80.   [2] Ibid.

mountain view, these men, too, were not merely exhausted but disorganized and demoralized. 'They stank; their clothes were in rags; they had no rifles, no blankets, no ammunition, no mess kits. . . . They had nothing but the rags in which they were dressed and the filth with which they were covered. . . .'

A few of the fresh, young recruits bawled greetings at the stragglers but all they got in answer was a contemptuously cynical look. Then the recruits asked questions. If they got an answer at all it was in the form of grunts or obscenities. At last, with great reluctance, a man bigger and even more bearded than the rest admitted to being in command, and with a kind of surly, staring indifference, he tried to assign the recruits to different companies. Companies! No one seemed to know where one stopped and another began; no one seemed quite sure whether these crushed remnants could be divided into companies at all.

Gradually the recruits pieced together the terrible story of the remaining one hundred men. They had been on the run – with the Brigade – for five days, and had witnessed the humiliating spectacle of Lister's Spanish Brigade stopping what threatened to become a rout. Five times the enemy had surrounded them and they had fought their way out at the cost of heavy casualties. The battalion kitchen had been blown up; food was almost non-existent; and finally rifles and ammunition became pointless encumbrances to be thrown away.

Their demoralization appeared to be complete. They tore into the behaviour of their commanders, they spat at the mention of courage, they laughed when someone talked of something called morale. 'These men seemed to be licked; if they had had tails they would have been between their legs. They barked at each other and at us; they cursed continuously, making accusations that horrified the new replacements.'

There was more reason for this than at first appeared. In the savage retreat from which these remnants had emerged, the three key battalion commanders had been wiped out – Chief of Staff Robert Merriman, the Political Commissar Dave Doran and the Brigade Commander Čopic. The slaughter had been even worse than the laconic comments of these men conveyed, and when one of the recruits was tactless enough to talk of cowardice, of the wickedness of throwing guns away, a dirty, bearded, huddled figure muttered 'Shit', and spat. Bessie, who watched this scene, would not have been surprised if the young recruit had been torn to pieces on the spot. And then one of the closely similar ghouls opened its mouth and spoke for the first time with the voice of reason: 'Comrades,' he said quietly, 'we've been through hell the last few days and do I understand you're accusing us of being cowards?'

'Well!' said the tactless young man. 'I don't want to be misunderstood –'

A swarthy Corsican with a huge pair of handlebar moustaches, named Joe Bianca, interrupted him. 'Haul your ashes,' he said and repeated 'haul your ashes', before he too spat noisily.

Chapter 22

The Battle of the Ebro

AFTER the terrible retreat and rout around Teruel, each of the old international battalions had witnessed harrowing scenes as the survivors waited for friends and comrades to come in long after the battle. Some arrived singly, some in tattered exhausted groups. 'Two close companions reunited after one of them had been given up for dead would stand silently, hands clasped, each fearing to speak lest the words break the tension of pent-up fear and joy and shock, and end in tears. Many wept unashamedly.'[1]

Captain Wolf returned after eight days behind the enemy lines and was the centre of embraces, kisses and tears worthy of a lost lover returning to the arms of a stricken counterpart. Wolf took over command, but when he came to muster the men the Lincolns 'consisted of one section of Americans, numbering fewer than forty men, and a Spanish section with about thirty-five others.'

That was all that remained of the Lincoln-Washington Battalion. Over four hundred men were dead or missing and those who came back alive were 'precious beyond any possession. . . .'

The shattered remnant took a long time to accustom itself to what seemed like a new kind of brutality in this terrible war, and any lofty commotion about fighting the Fascists to the death was now met with a series of obscenities. As the days went by a number of men drifted back to the battalion from hospital, rest-camps and dissolved units. Slowly the battalion rebuilt itself, but now like many counterparts in the Brigades, the majority of the new recruits were Spanish, until for every one American, there were at least four Spaniards. Wolf remained Commander and Watt Commissar, with Lamb, leader of the first shock company, as second-in-command. Like the Lincoln

[1] Edwin Rolfe, *The Lincoln Battalion*, p. 130.

Battalion, the XVth Brigade, too, slowly rebuilt itself on quite different lines.

The new Brigade Commander was José Antonio Valledor, a man who had led part of the famous Asturian Revolt of 1934 and was once sentenced to death by the Lerroux-Robles government only to be set free when the People's Front won the elections of 1936. He had fought in the Army in Asturias, become a Brigade Commander, suffered imprisonment and escaped, and late in May had succeeded Lieutenant-Colonel Čopic as Commander of the XVth.

Thirty-one-year-old Valledor and twenty-four-year-old John Gates, the American Political Commissar to the Brigade, quickly responded to each other, and together they spent long hours in passionate discussion of the Brigade's future.

Gates later admitted that at this period he behaved in an extraordinary way. His nerves were raw and edgy and 'I used my new authority to denounce and even jail men who dared to dispute my word, convinced that this was necessary for military discipline.'[1]

A friend who, in turn, was brutally frank said to him one day: 'You know you are a Brigade Commissar and if a private says something you don't like you can do anything you want, even jail him. But if you say or do something a private doesn't like, there is absolutely nothing the private can do to *you*.'[2]

Gates admitted later that it was a short, sharp lesson in the corruption of power which he did not fully appreciate until he had left the Brigade and finally the Party. For the moment he exhausted a great deal of eloquence as Political Commissar, in disillusioning those Americans who thought that repatriation was close at hand. He spoke with brutal frankness. Such matters, he said, were for the Spanish Government to decide, not some alien non-intervention committee which had never had the interests of the Republic at heart.

Fresh difficulties arose between the new Spanish recruits and some of the old Brigaders. The first fine flower of international fervour had withered as the war advanced, and Alvah Bessie recalled that familiarity had bred distrust as well as

---

[1] John Gates, *The Story of an American Communist*, p. 62.   [2] Ibid.

contempt. A new Spanish *teniente* in charge of Section Three of the re-formed American Battalion quickly made it clear that he distrusted foreigners on principle and American volunteers in particular. He could be found, many a day, telling a group of young Spaniards what a drunken, degenerate lot the Americans really were. In some cases there were elements of truth in the accusations. Bessie admitted that: 'By and large the quality of the American rank and file seemed none too good. We had a couple of drunks, a couple of known deserters, some guys who had served time in labour battalions, some weaklings, some *inutiles*.'

The Spanish *teniente* made great play with the fact that Americans got drunk and Spaniards did not. In the end his agitations and scandalmongering became so bad that he was removed, first from the company and then the battalion, but the Spaniards got back at the battalion command by having Bessie himself replaced with a Spanish adjutant rejoicing in the name of Teopisto Perich Salat.

Similar troubles appeared in the re-formed British, French, German and Polish Battalions. They were now getting towards the tail-end of the volunteers and literally thousands of the best-quality men had been killed or badly wounded. The repatriation plans of the Non-Intervention Committee were widely discussed and hardly a day passed without one Spaniard or another putting the question – 'You are going home soon?' Often it was more a desire than a question. Bessie wrote, 'This was a real and growing situation and when we talked of it – we shook our heads. The future was none too bright to us.'

At this point a new young American recruit arrived to join the Lincoln-Washingtons. He was Jim Lardner, son of Ring Lardner, the famous American writer, and he brought with him spotless new clothes, a brand-new rucksack, a French grammar, a Spanish-English dictionary and a copy of *Red Star over China*. He could not know that he was doomed to die very soon after he entered his first front-line battle.

Deep in a natural cave at the head of a barranco lay the new command post of the re-formed XVth Brigade. Once the natural home of a family of peasants, they had filled the mouth with rocks and stones, and divided the enormous cavern into many gloomy, damp-dripping, eerie rooms. Now, each of the network of rooms had its array of candles and every room was crowded with men, some working the crude telephone system, some sleeping, some poring over reports and maps. From each of the rooms 'there rises a hum of sound, the droning of conversation, the rattle of typewriters, the buzzing of the "control", and the separate voice of one or other of the jefes on the phone'.[1]

Spilling out of the mouth of the cave, disappearing in the half-light of a not quite dark night, runs a spider-web of wires, twisting down the mountainside, over the barrancos to the individual command posts of the four battalions – the Lincolns, the Mac-Paps, the British and the 59th Battalion. Messages are flashing along the wires co-ordinating the Brigades' activities and at the centre, in the big cavern, near the mouth, overhung by enormous bosses of rock, with a rough field-table, maps and a specially concentrated array of thick, old-fashioned candles splashing a heavy, golden light, is the man who now holds all the wires in his hands, the new commander of the XVth. 'He is a small man as stature goes: he does not offer the stereotyped picture of the military man.'[2] His name is Major José Antonio Valledor.

There is a moon outside scurrying among clouds, and in the distance a huge black hill, held by the enemy, reveals a creeping line of flame moving across it. Almost precisely at midnight a voice echoes slightly in the cave, saying: 'Pongame con el cincuenta y ocho.' Then 'Wolf . . . four hundred zapadores are coming up there; use them as you see fit. Hello! Oiga oiga! Central. Yo estaba hablando con el cincuenta y ocho. . . .'

A machine-gun opens up, shattering the silence of the night with a sharp authoritative voice and Valledor, standing near the entrance of the cave, gives one of his little laughs. 'He wears a short leather jacket that hangs open; he wears no hat. . . . He is always cheerful; he gives the appearance of possessing a boundless fund of good humour; he laughs frequently, talking . . . in short, staccato sentences. . . .'

'Digame', says the voice. 'Quién? El capitán Dunbar? Un momento. . . .'

Enemy pressure is building up to the south. . . .

The men lying in blankets against the rock walls have the grotesque postures of the dead because total exhaustion brings a kind of temporary death, but the hum of the 'central' is continuous and life remains while its note is unchanged.

'Damn it all,' a voice says, 'Goddard was there to show them where to place that anti-tank. Get busy on it.'

There is a hum of conversation from a point on the dirt floor where Valledor and Gates are talking. They are huddled close together, Gates's voice low, indistinct, Valledor's sharp, accented. Very soon now, this slowly ticking-over headquarters of the XVth will burst into new life because yet another great offensive – against all reason – has been planned.

On the morning of 24 July 1938 a meeting of the Republican War Council in Barcelona agreed to Colonel Rojo's plan to launch a diversionary attack across the river Ebro to relieve the pressure on Sagunto and Valencia.

It was a very bold scheme which at its lowest aimed to confuse the communications between the Nationalists in the Levante and Catalonia, and at its highest to 'restore land communications between Catalonia and the rest of Republican Spain.' One big weakness did not deter them. The French frontier had been closed, reopened and now closed again over the last eighteen months, and supplies had ceased to flow in from this source once more, but the indomitable Colonel Rojo and the War Council refused to be dismayed. Hugh Thomas believed that they would have been wiser to learn the lessons of Brunete, Belchite and Teruel and remain on the defensive, but more audacious counsels prevailed.

The elegant, ex-Trinity College Scot, Malcolm Dunbar, now Chief of Staff of the XVth Brigade under Valledor, recommended the point of crossing, and at a quarter-past midnight on 24–25 July the Republicans once more amazed the world by launching yet another offensive over the Ebro from what seemed to be a position of weakness. And once again part of the initial assault was carried by a not-very-international battalion – the Hans Beimler Battalion of the XIth Brigade. Now composed mainly of Scandinavians and

Catalans, it went across crying incongruously 'Forward, sons of Negrín'.[1] As usual, too, the officers led their men into the attack. A small invasion fleet of over 110 vessels, each capable of carrying eight men, moved off on a moonless night across the swiftly flowing, hundred-yard-wide river, and returned at once for more men and materials. Pontoon bridges were rapidly strung out and before the enemy quite realized it hundreds of men were safely over. Much of the bridge-building had to be done at night because enemy air superiority made it possible to smash the bridges in the day.

The inevitable happened at one point. A tank stuck half-way across a pontoon bridge and of course it was the very bridge which carried some of the most essential material. Malcolm Dunbar believed that this episode seriously reduced the effectiveness of the attack.

The area from Mequiñenza to the sea came under the command of the Nationalist General Yagüe, and the Mora sector was held by part of the Army of Morocco under Colonel Peñarredonda. From the point of view of the Internationals there was no worse commander. Colonel Peñarredonda singled out for his special loathing all international volunteers, and without any higher authority had issued orders that any such person captured in battle should be shot out of hand. This was no idle threat. He had already forced Peter Kemp, an Irishman serving with Franco's troops, to shoot a fellow-Irishman captured from the Brigades as a special blood protest against intervention on either side.[2]

An ironic coincidence had for the past few months brought Peter Kemp on Franco's side in direct confrontation with Malcolm Dunbar on the Republican side, both being contemporaries from Trinity College, Cambridge, but novelties of this kind were quickly overwhelmed in the battle which followed.

The Canadians were one of the first battalions of the XVth Brigade to cross the river, but they were preceded by thousands of Spaniards from other Brigades. The British followed the Canadians, mostly in rowing-boats, and the Lincolns, too, went across in boats with one enemy bomber gliding right over their

[1] *Reconquista* (newspaper of the Army of the Ebro), August 1938.
[2] P. Kemp, *Mine Were of Trouble*, p. 43.

National memorial gathering of the British Battalion of the International Brigades at the Empress Hall, London, 8 January 1939.

James Phillips Lardner, son of humorist Ring Lardner, went to
Spain as a war correspondent for the Paris edition of the *New York
Herald-Tribune*, and later joined the International Brigades.

American volunteers at the Austerliz Station in Paris, December, 1938, enroute to Le Havre. The main body of American volunteers from the International Brigades sailed on the liner *Normandie* from Le Havre on December 3, after escaping a last bombing from insurgent planes as they crossed the Franco-Spanish frontier the previous day.

Wide World Photos

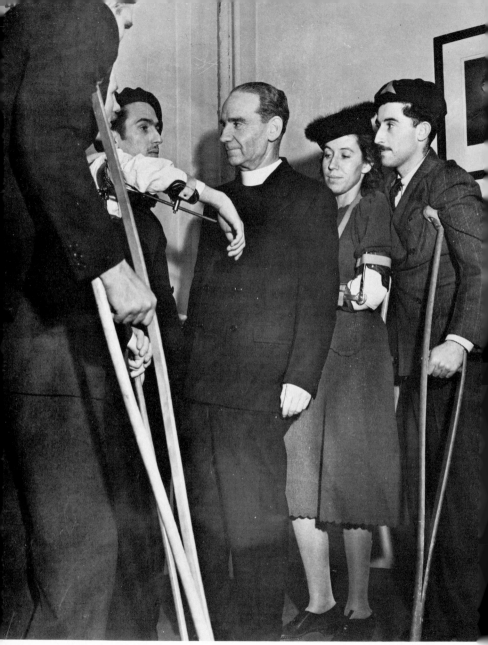

American members of the Abraham Lincoln Brigade, wounded while fighting in defense of the Spanish Republic, receive a visit in New York City, March 2, 1939, from Father Leocadro Lobo, a Madrid priest. Left to right: Alvin Van Arsdale of San Francisco; Ricardo Triana of New York City; Father Lobo; Helen Freeman, a volunteer nurse who lost her arm, and Moe Fishman, both of New York City.

Wide World Photos

heads. Bob Cooney recorded in the British Battalion's diary:
'Revolutionary songs and old-time choruses were sung and in
each one you could sense the feeling that the singers were on the
eve of a great adventure. . . .'

It was a romantic interpretation of what followed. Certainly
the British got across with no casualties and proceeded rapidly
in the direction of Corbera, but by now Nationalist planes
continuously bombed every moving thing. At four o'clock, on
the outskirts of Corbera, they made contact with the XIIIth
Brigade who hesitated to enter the town because a number of
Moors held the hills on their left. The British Battalion went in to
attack the Moors and the battle continued all night, eventually
driving the Moors back. The XIIIth then occupied Corbera.

The Republicans had by now established a large bridge-head
before the Nationalists recovered from their first surprise, and
if the XIVth Franco-Belgian Brigade quickly found itself on
the losing side in a fierce struggle which lasted without pause
for eighteen hours, the XVth pushed on inland to 'outflank,
surround and capture the demoralized troops of Colonel
Peñarredonda.'[1] At the centre, Lister pushed swiftly forward
twenty-five miles and came within range of Gandesa, while
Tagüeña managed to advance five kilometres from the Ebro.
Everything at this stage was still proceeding splendidly with
most of the heights between Gandesa and the river in Republican hands, and several thousand Nationalist prisoners taken.
The vast elbow formed by the bend of the river Ebro taking in
its sweep four hundred square miles had, in fact, fallen to the
Republic, but Gandesa became the centre of the key battle,
as Franco moved up massive reinforcements to try to contain the
rapidly deploying Republicans. The weather was suffocatingly
hot. A brilliant sun turned the earth to dust, made every metal
object burning to the touch, drove men to desperation with
thirst, sucked up what water the earth contained and converted the slightest physical effort into a sweat-flooded burden.
Day and night, in the terrible heat, Lister assaulted and re-
assaulted Gandesa without success.

Then a series of savage Nationalist counter-attacks began.
The majority of the fighting took place around fortified hill-
tops and it was against the key Hill No. 481, known as the

[1] Hugh Thomas, *The Spanish Civil War*, p. 547.

Pimple, that the XVth Brigade threw themselves time and again. Day after day for five consecutive days, the British, Americans and Canadians of the XVth, the Slavs of the XIIIth and the Spaniards under Lister tried to reduce this impudent pimple of such absurd geographical consequence. On the last day of the assault the British continued the attack for twelve hours, crawling nearer and nearer to the topmost ridge under paralysing fire.

No. 2 Company had five acting-commanders within five days, the first one killed, the other three wounded and Lieutenant Lewis Clive – 'a Labour Councillor, Oxford man, author, sportsman and cheerful giant' – took over on the last day of the assault. Two documents he wrote in the heat of the battle have been preserved. 'Time 10.15. Your message just received. You seem to visualize the Company giving covering fire only while the message also just received from Battalion gives orders to advance taking advantage of artillery barrage. Assume the latter to be correct and will look out for opportunity so to advance. Please let me know if I have not understood position correctly. Lewis Clive.'

And much later:

'Time 16.15. I had orders some time ago to contact you re assault. The runner I sent has not returned. Our position was then and is now: we are 150 metres from 481 and cannot advance further without coming into fire both from 481 and cross-fire from our left flank. Understand some of your men within 15 metres 481. Have you further plan? L. Clive.' In the midst of such a battle these extraordinary civil-service messages had a hopelessly outdated ring.

The Americans suffered equally rough handling in what came to be known as Death Valley. Edwin Rolfe wrote in his notebook: 'The place stank with the smell of dead and decomposing bodies. . . . Sounds of men screaming "Socorro! Socorro!" (Help!) and groaning "Madre mia" kept up all night . . . always the noise of rifles, machine-guns, hand-grenades and artillery. Men were dead by the hundreds – mostly the enemy's – and the bodies stank when you came close.'[1]

By 2 August the Republican advance had been checked and now, in a desperate effort to hold the territory they had won,

[1] Edwin Rolfe, *The Lincoln Battalion*, pp. 268–9.

Lister issued an order – 'if anyone loses an inch of ground he must retake it at the head of his men or be executed.'

Among the captured Republican records are several orders of the day which report men shot for dereliction of duty or self-mutilation. Aznar quotes one which reads: 'The following have been handed over to the Tribunal – 1st Commander José Sánchez López, 2nd Commissar Camilo Peiro Miro. Because of their negligence, the forces they commanded abandoned the positions they held. Also the following have been shot dead because of voluntary self-mutilation – Angel Coll, 3rd and 4th Battalion, 1st Brigade, and Fernando Guitare, 3rd Company, 4th Battalion of the 100th Brigade.'[1] According to Copeman two internationals were summarily dealt with in this way.

Excerpts from the diary of Captain R. Smrcka, Chief of Information for the XVth Brigade, reveal something of what followed. 'Sept. 6th. We are standing by. Hectic night. The enemy continues its pressure accompanied by tremendous concentrations of fire. Counted more than 100 Fascist planes in the air. Front has been boiling since dawn.

'Finally our orders. We are to move in immediately to prevent a threatened breach. Within twenty minutes the Brigade is on its way.

'I am leading one of the Battalions into position. On the way back I am caught in an artillery barrage. . . . I feel I am about due to get it again – I have been too lucky for too long. . . .

'The enemy pressure increases. . . . The troops of another unit unable to hold out any longer gave way. . . . The Lincoln Battalion is rushed into the breach and succeeds in stopping the Fascists. . . . A small advance on a narrow sector – this has been the result so far of the much-heralded – decisive – Franco offensive on the Ebro.'

Luigi Longo wrote on 5 September 1938: 'More than a month has gone by since the soldiers of the Republic victoriously crossed the Ebro. Time has only confirmed and emphasized the importance of this great victory . . . we obliged the Fascists to discontinue their offensive on the Levante. . . .'[2]

*   *   *

[1] Manuel Aznar, *Historia Militar de la Guerra de España*, p. 744.
[2] *Volontaire de la liberté*, 5 September 1938.

The Republic had reacted with exaggerated enthusiasm to the early successes of the Ebro and even the pessimistic Azaña almost came to believe that the tide was turning at last, but Negrín's attempts to secure a peace settlement with Franco, which he had carefully concealed from the Communists, came to nothing and early in August 1938 he continued to compromise with the Communists, forming a new government at the request of Azaña. As Hugh Thomas said: '. . . the most efficient and tenacious advocates of the policy of resistance remained the Communists', and they had to be used. On the other hand 'the fact that Negrín did not take the Communists into his confidence in his search for a negotiated peace proves that he was not absolutely their tool'.[1]

About this time, a gathering of internationally famous writers at the Hotel Majestic, Barcelona, in August, paid a farewell tribute to Theodore Dreiser. 'André Malraux was there, his face convulsed in dreadful tics, his handshake limp, his hair damp and matted over his forehead. Ernst Toller was smiling his sad refugee smile. . . . There was Bolesłaskaya of *Pravda* . . . and Louis Fischer, dark and saturnine and . . . James Lardner drifted in, looking pale and ghostly from his wounds.'[2]

After a lavish dinner, Robert Payne, a newspaper correspondent, left the dining-room with Toller to help him pack, and they were plodding up the stairs when a huge American Negro guard from the International Brigades challenged them, waving his gun at Toller.

'You don't have to wave that thing at me', Toller said. 'I'm Ernst Toller.'

The black fingers fumbled at the trigger of the gun and the waving barrel moved closer. 'You're just a fuckin' liar! – Ernst Toller, sah! I'se read about dat feller! Writes poetry. How do I know youse the same guy?'

He now jabbed the gun into Toller's stomach in the most dangerous manner and for a horrible moment Payne feared he was going to shoot. Instead he said: 'Let's hear some of your fuckin' poems.' So Toller began quoting a poem from his *Book of Swallows*, closing his eyes and swaying gently to the rhythm of the words. The Negro listened with his ebony head on one

---

[1] Hugh Thomas, *The Spanish Civil War*, p. 551.
[2] Robert Payne, *The Civil War in Spain*, p. 320.

side, and as the words and voice took possession of him, the barrel of the gun ceased to stick into Toller's stomach, his voice dropped and he said: 'Ernst Toller, sah – pass on.'[1]

In the end the battle of the Ebro became a classic example of artillery conquering the ground which the infantry then proceeded to occupy, with the difference that Franco developed the tactic of concentrated air and ground bombardment on small areas followed by one or two battalions occupying the 'saturated' ground. By this means, on 6 and 7 August Serrano reoccupied the northern pocket between Mequiñenza and Fagón, and the Republic left a thousand dead in the wake of their retreating battalions. Two more counter-attacks were pressed home, and by the 14th even the indomitable Lister had been forced off the high point of Santa Magdalena. By now the Republicans had completely lost command in the air and raids which were then considered huge – 300 planes at a time – were launched against the Republicans with little interference. Every day from now on, for nearly four weeks, the Nationalists unloaded 10,000 bombs on the Republicans, but many of them were completely wasted and 'it was estimated in Barcelona that as many as 500 bombs were needed to destroy one pontoon bridge.'[2]

[1] Robert Payne, *The Civil War in Spain*, p. 322.
[2] Hugh Thomas, *The Spanish Civil War*, p. 549.

Chapter 23

The Volunteers are Withdrawn

THE long, tortured negotiations to find some means of withdrawing volunteers from each side without giving serious offence to the other reached a climax in September 1938. A plan devised by the Non-Intervention Committee suggested that two commissions should be sent to Spain, first to make some assessment of the actual number of 'aliens' and second to supervise their withdrawal. The Republic accepted the plan in principle but proposed that Moroccans in Franco's Army should be described as foreign volunteers and that any subsequent control check should be exercised by air. The Nationalists counter-proposed the withdrawal of a preliminary 10,000 from each side, after they had been granted belligerent rights, and strongly resisted the idea of foreign observers who 'would usurp in a humiliating way the sovereign rights of Spain'. This amounted to rejecting one of the most important parts of the plan. There was considerable coming and going behind the scenes and Francis Hemming, the Secretary of the Non-Intervention Committee, set off to see Franco in an attempt to modify his views.

With the terrible battle of the Ebro approaching its grimmest moments for the Republic, the announcement of the withdrawal of the International Brigades suddenly came through: 'The Spanish Government wishes to contribute not only in words but also in deeds to the appeasement desired by all, and resolves to dispel all doubts as to the completely national character of the cause for which the Armies of the Republic are fighting. To this end the Government has decided upon the immediate and complete withdrawal of all non-Spanish combatants now participating in the struggle in Spain, in the Government's ranks, and it is to be understood that this withdrawal will apply to all foreigners, without distinction as to nationality, including those who may have assumed Spanish nationality since 5 July 1936. . . . We are overcome with a feeling of the deepest pain at the idea of being separated from this body of brave and self-sacrificing men who, with an impulse of generosity that will never be forgotten by the Spanish people, came to our assistance during one of the most critical hours of our history.'

The battle was still raging when the news reached the XVth International Brigade. Their last action occurred on 22 September when Jim Lardner, the newest and youngest American recruit, was killed at the very point of withdrawal and most battalions again suffered heavy casualties. The English Battalion diary recorded these words: 'What a day it was! Such artillery bombardments as I had never seen before. They literally churned up our positions. Under the cover of the artillery the Fascists advanced with infantry and tanks. They were on top of us before we were aware of their advance. Our lads were mown down. We retired in as good order as possible and formed a line on the next ridge. The artillery bombardment continued with continuous bombings added. Somehow or other we managed to hold on till dark when we went out to get our wounded. It took us four hours to evacuate our wounded. That night we were relieved.'

Shortly afterwards the American Sandor Voros was summoned from the battle-front to Barcelona by the Italian Luigi Gallo, now Inspector-General of the International Brigades, and told to take over the editorship of the last issues of the Brigade paper *Volunteer for Liberty*. He proceeded to write an editorial assuming that many Brigaders would eventually find refuge in the Soviet Union: 'They have fought the Fascists, the foes of mankind: now they will have a chance to help build Socialism in the only socialist country in the world – the fulfilment of the Communist dream! History is working out well for them the only reward worthy of aspiration.'

When this article had been set up in type an urgent summons came from André Marty for Voros to see him at once in his new Barcelona office. Marty received Voros with a ferocious outburst. Waving the proofs under his nose he began to shout: 'Who gave you the right to formulate the policy of the Soviet Union!'

He knew most Americans were arrogant or congenital idiots, he said, but he had not expected to encounter quite such political

presumption in a leading member of the Party. Voros left
Marty's office in some confusion, and the following day found a
note on his desk stating the new official line to be followed by all
editors. The volunteers were now seasoned anti-Fascist fighters,
it said, and they must return to the democratic countries where
they would lead the fight against Fascism in their own lands.
Puzzled at first by this announcement, Voros discussed it with
a German comrade who burst out – 'But you see what this line
actually means – it means that the Soviet Union has shut her
doors in our face, you fool!'

One other experience now produced an even more chastening
effect on Voros. John Gates, the Brigade Commissar, summoned him to his office one day and Voros encountered a quite
different Gates. 'The once modest and indifferently dressed
young comrade, whom I knew to be a non-smoker, now sported
a fancy tailored uniform topped off with the highest officer's
cap ever displayed in Spain. He was puffing on a fat, expensive
. . . cigar, sprawled back with his feet on the desk.'[1]

He did not shake hands but came to his feet and poured out a
torrent of words. Voros was in trouble, he said, and he didn't
know Gates well if he thought he would let him get away with
it, and he'd have him court-martialled and so on. He then
insisted that the Commissariats' missing funds be returned to
him at once. In God's name, what missing funds, Voros demanded.

There followed a long wrangle about depositing a large sum
of money with various people, and one of the 'witnesses' was
called in without any conclusive result. Voros now realized
that his situation had become delicate. An accusation of embezzlement in the Party at home in the States was the first step
towards political liquidation, but here in Spain, under what
now amounted to a military dictatorship, it could lead very
quickly to the firing squad.

The Finance Officer of the Brigade was many miles away
and for two long, uneasy hours Voros tried to reach him by
telephone. The agonizing delay reached a pitch where 'I had
never felt such acute distress even in the tightest situations in
the field.'

At last they traced him and he acknowledged having the

[1] Sandor Voros, *American Commissar*, p. 439.

money safely on deposit from Voros, who then expected some sort of apology from Gates. It was not forthcoming.

On Sunday, 17 October, a day regarded as the second anniversary of the International Brigades in Albacete, with a crisp autumn morning flooding the streets and courtyards in steady sunshine, the 35th Division began its great farewell festival with a tremendous parade of International Brigades through the streets. The men came marching down from around the bends in the mountain road, with a band blaring Spanish military music, the Germans stolid, the Poles gay, the Americans and British mixed in their reactions, while a handful of Cubans refused to keep in step, and a huge standard-bearer led the long, motley, proud procession. Thousands of Spaniards lining the route roared out '*vivas*' and a great dinner followed with all the current leaders present – André Marty the founder, Luigi Gallo, Commissar Inspector, Lieutenant-Colonel Hans, until recently commander of the 45th Division, and Ludwig Renn. What the Spaniards called honour-cards for valiant service were presented by José María Sastre, Commissar of the 35th Division, first to André Marty, then to Gallo and later to John Gates, Commissar of the XVth Brigade, and Majors Milton Wolf and Cecil Smith. Among the British, Sam Wild and Malcolm Dunbar were similarly decorated.

Gallo made a speech in which he said: 'I want to thank this brave people for giving us the chance to fight shoulder to shoulder with them', and Marty concluded a passionate, rousing address with: 'We cannot fool with a mad dog. We must annihilate it. Fascism is a mad dog and we shall kill it.'

Final speeches came from Lieutenant-Colonel Tagüeña and Commissar Fulsimaña, chief of the 15th Army Corps, which incorporated the 35th Division. Towards the end, a great roar of cheering rose, with a cloud of clenched fists, and then music broke out from somewhere and spontaneous singing and dancing began.

Another great farewell parade to the Brigades took place in Barcelona on 15 November and this time no less than Negrín himself and La Pasionaria were there to give thanks to the remaining thirteen thousand men. 'Comrades of the International

Brigades!' La Pasionaria said. 'Political reasons, reasons of State, the welfare of that same cause for which you offered your blood with boundless generosity, are sending you back, some of you to your own countries and others to forced exile. You can go proudly. You are history. You are legend. You are the heroic example of democracy's solidarity and universality. We shall not forget you, and when the olive tree of peace puts forth its leaves again, mingled with the laurels of the Spanish Republic's victory – come back!'

A wave of plainly visible emotion ran through the vast crowd as it cheered and cheered again, and there were tears in many eyes as a mass of flowers fluttered down on the Brigaders, and the bands broke into stirring military music. Standing there among it all one veteran felt that 'something which could never happen again in the history of the world had come to an end – I felt that my heart would never beat quite like that again. I had to turn away. . . . I couldn't stand it.'[1]

Repatriation, when it came, was not very satisfactory. The League of Nations' Commission headed by the French Colonel Homo, the British Brigadier Molesworth and the Finnish General Jalander made a count of foreigners in the Republican forces and arrived at the figure of 12,673 drawn from no less than twenty-nine nationalities. By the middle of January the repatriation machinery, which worked reasonably well, had sent on their homeward journey 2,141 French, 407 British, 347 Belgians, 285 Poles, 182 Swedes, 194 Italians, 80 Swiss and 548 Americans. This still left a total of nearly 6,000 men who were involved in the Catalonian battles which followed and suffered hardships even worse than anything they had encountered before.

The Spanish Office of Information in Madrid claimed, in 1953, that the Republicans evaded the international agreements of the League of Nations Commission by granting, fraudulently or voluntarily, Spanish nationality to thousands of Brigaders. They quote a number of captured Republican documents which do show that Spanish nationality was granted to each of the men mentioned, but it was inevitable that Poles and Germans, who would be arrested and shot if they returned to their own countries, should welcome Spanish nationality.

[1] Letter to the author, 16 January 1964.

As the Nationalists pushed swiftly into Catalonia and the end of the war became imminent, they claimed 500 international prisoners, and the French newspaper *Le Matin* listed large numbers of American, English, Germans, French and Poles. Many remaining International Brigaders were finally driven across the frontier into France.

The frontier presented a scene of tragic chaos. The French authorities found themselves trying to cope with a great tide of hundreds of thousands of people pressing against their boundaries and although at first they refused, for sheer financial reasons, to permit entry, in the end they relented. 'The fugitives were worn out by hunger and fatigue. Their clothes were damp from rain and snow. Yet there were few complaints. Crushed by disaster, the Spanish Republicans walked on upright, erect and dignified.'[1]

A makeshift organization known as a clearing camp was set up at Le Boulou and larger camps at Argelès, St Cyprien and four other places. Any pretence at shelter or services was abandoned. The camps were simply open sand-dunes near the sea, marked off into limited areas by barbed wire, and for the first ten days disaster threatened as more and more men, women, children, soldiers and some Brigaders poured into the camps without an adequate water supply, and no sanitation whatever. Men were reduced to digging holes in the sand-dunes like animals to provide some sort of shelter. Among the 400,000 refugees at least 250,000 were men of the Republican Army and, of those, roughly 5,000 were International Brigaders. No one who was in the camps for the first ten days wants to remember the hunger, thirst, and exposure which the sand, whipped off the dunes by the wind, sometimes made even more intolerable.

In France a private member's Bill, granting an amnesty to those French volunteers who were classified as deserters because of their absence during the September mobilization, was passed in the Chamber. Among the Germans and Italians – what was there left to do? They could not return to their own countries, now dominated by the ever-more successful dictators Hitler and Mussolini; Russia offered refuge only to the top Republicans like La Pasionaria and some 200 members of the

[1] Hugh Thomas, *The Spanish Civil War*, p. 575.

Brigades;[1] those with influence or money made their way to Mexico and some drifted across to North Africa to be finally enlisted by the Long Range Desert Patrol into Field-Marshal Montgomery's Second World War forces. Russia took no more interest in the rank-and-file members of the Brigaders and a number of appeals for help were made in vain. Some were reduced to bumming their way from one town to the next, and one at least ended up sleeping on the gratings of the Paris Underground, once more a workless, homeless nobody. Thousands of Italian and German members of the Brigades were finally interned in French concentration camps where they led a miserable, restricted existence until World War II set them free to join various Allied Army units. Others were less fortunate.

Dr Königsberg told me how the Gestapo came to the camp where he was a prisoner-of-war in Palencia, selected those Germans who belonged to the Thaelmann Battalion, and carried them off in trucks – where to, no one ever knew. Dr Königsberg is now an English schoolmaster and he has turned to scholarship as a way of escape from bitter memories of the days when he was repatriated to England 'like a criminal in a sealed train', while the Italians who fought for Franco were returned to Italy with full honours by a British destroyer.[2]

In Poland the Government announced that it would deprive volunteers of their citizenship and this may have been one reason why the Dabrowsky Battalion demanded to go back into action in Catalonia as late as 29 January 1939. Finally the Poles were sent to camps at Gurs and St Cyprien, and when the Second World War broke out they prepared and delivered endless petitions to the Polish Government asking for permission to return home and fight. It was useless. The Polish Government wanted nothing to do with them. When Poland was finally overrun, some Brigaders managed to get away and join the free Polish forces, but a hard core of 500, under Vichy policy, was transferred to North Africa, perhaps, in the circumstances, humanely, since certain death would have followed the German occupation. Some of those who spoke French well enough remained to join the French resistance. Many more were still in

---

[1] Verbal evidence, Hugh Thomas.
[2] Verbal evidence, Dr Königsberg.

prison camps in North Africa when the Allies landed in 1943 and it was due, this time, to the Russian repatriation Commissions that they were transferred to Russia and given a chance at last to join the Polish Army.[1]

The fate of the Americans was mixed. In Washington, during December 1938, the Immigration Commissioner James L. Houghteling refused to drop deportation proceedings against fifteen aliens (some Germans and Italians) held on Ellis Island after returning to the United States from Spain. All were former residents of the United States who volunteered to fight in Spain without taking out the necessary re-entry papers, and they had not lived long enough in America to qualify for citizenship. On 3 December, 327 American volunteers came singing into the border town of France, LaTour de Carol, and as they left the train and stood on the platform the war almost caught up with them again as five Nationalist Junkers dropped bombs on the railroad tracks over which they had just passed. Although the French authorities finally sealed the train and they were not allowed to leave it again until they reached Le Havre, they were relatively happy men. They were embarking shortly for America and by an odd quirk they were to travel in the self-same luxury liner, the *Normandie*, which had brought the first main group of 96 American volunteers to Spain.

The British, too, eventually came home to a tumultuous welcome at Victoria Station, but not before 309 were temporarily trapped in a remote Pyrenean village only a few feet below the snow line. They included 146 British-born Canadians, 125 foreign-born Canadians and three Palestinians. For six weeks they all lived in a disused theatre with thin mattresses spread in a close mosaic where once there had been theatre seats. Most were eager to be back to eat English food again, to smell the dusty air of London and see the merry-go-round of Piccadilly Circus, but there were those who viewed the future with apprehension. They had known the more subtle and in some cases prolonged hardship of unemployment, debt and the sense of being unwanted in a society which seemed incredibly rich at many points. There was a former 'burglar' who came back feeling that his only chance was to – stick to his trade. Ironically the Civil War had replaced the missing purpose in these men's

[1] *Polacy w Wojnie Hiszpańskiej*, ed. Michala Brona, pp. 44–45.

lives, and given them that form of security which goes with belonging to a like-minded group.

At least one man felt that there was a conspiracy to delay their return home. M. Stang wrote from Barcelona: 'I have received Tanner's letter about the importance of retrieving our passports and I am persevering in attempts to get them. . . . I have made repeated applications but frankly there is not much hope; a large portion of the passports have been lost or mislaid.

'We are stuck here much longer than we expected and it is now perfectly clear from the evasive nature of the consul's replies that Chamberlain is attempting to hold us up as long as possible . . . to avoid the effect of our re-appearance in England. . . . It depends on the protest raised in England as to when we get home: so if you want to see me again in the near future, set to work agitating your M.P. etc. etc.'[1]

Now it was all over. Now the war was coming to a certain end and in Madrid the astonishing way in which those grand, terrible human passions can suddenly change the object of their attack became clear, as what was left of the Republican Central Army turned and fought the Communists and a civil war within a civil war slowly brought to an end the prolonged and savage struggle – for what? Appallingly both sides had claimed to be fighting for freedom, truth, righteousness, and each had generated greater hatred, greater heroism with phrases which had a sinister similarity. But the Republicans stood for a for-ward-looking, humanist world, where religion would cease to exercise what they regarded as its stranglehold, and the scores of fragmented political parties would somehow reconcile the interests of Socialists, Communists and Anarchists in a society where class distinctions were severely modified and the interests of the common man became paramount; and the Nationalists for a static world where religious principles remained intransi-gent, where beliefs which stemmed from feudal times were carefully preserved and an aristocratic hierarchy dominated the social scene for what it considered society's good.

[1] 30 November 1938.

Chapter 24

The Return Home

WHEN Chamberlain finally signed his notorious appeasement agreement with Hitler at Munich in 1938, Russia immediately recast her foreign policy. Stalin saw an international war of catastrophic proportions threatening him and decided to try to turn the threat away from Russia towards the West. This meant scrapping the Litvinov policy of a Western alliance against Germany and involved dropping his commitments in Spain without any ceremony, while preparing the way for the Hitler-Stalin pact. His commitments in Spain had always been heavily controlled. His arms and supplies were generally earmarked for Communist units or those controlled by Communists, and military strategy was sometimes enforced by withholding or granting vital items. Now Republican Spain slipped into limbo for Stalin, no longer a useful pawn in the game of international power politics, and until the final catastrophe when Franco swept the remaining Republican Spaniards back to the borders of France, the atmosphere of Republican Spain was charged with conflict, hypocrisy and fear.[1]

Perhaps that exaggerated the brutal expediencies of Stalin. He had, at one stage, hoped the Republicans might win, but when Franco swept into Catalonia and the democracies still remained aloof, he sought to save face and adjust as rapidly as possible to the new situation. A Machiavellian element was inseparable from power politics and in the face of Britain's abandoning Czechoslovakia it was difficult to complain too loudly that Stalin had set the example in Spain.

Immediately after the Spanish Civil War, liberal commentators argued that the International Brigades 'never amounted to more than a useful marginal addition to the fighting forces on each side', and that supplies were far more important than

[1] Valentín González, *Solidaridad Obrero*, 11 March 1951.

manpower. Intervention was decisive because of guns, tanks, ammunition and aircraft, not men.

In the first place the external forces, Moors, Italians and Germans, which supported Franco's troops, were more than marginal and numerically far greater than any steady accumulation of International Brigaders, no matter how one may juggle with the statistics.

As for the Brigaders, they may have been marginal in numbers but they served three vital purposes. They arrived at the crucial psychological moment in the defence of Madrid and stiffened the morale of the whole population even if their inspiration was modified for some by the delusory belief that the Russians were coming to Madrid's aid in considerable numbers. They also stopped a possible break-through on 9 November which might have crumbled the whole defence of Madrid. And as Manuel Aznar wrote to me: 'I believe that the presence of the XIth and XIIth Brigades, especially the XIth Brigade in Madrid, during the first fifteen days of November 1936 were decisive to the resistance of the . . . Republican Army.'[1] The Brigades also played a vital part in preventing the encirclement of Madrid and helped to win a breathing space while the Spanish militia were properly trained, and the missing officers who had deserted to Franco were replaced. The new Republican Army also copied the organization of the Brigades.[2,3]

Finally, the Brigades carried a message for mixed forces today. It is often suggested that any attempt to form an international striking force under the control of UNO, ready to rush to outbreaks of violence which threaten world peace, must fail because different political indoctrinations and training would induce different reactions to on-the-spot emergencies and commands would become confused because of language difficulties. The Brigades grappled with these complications and in most cases overcame them. One man in each company had a rudimentary knowledge of several languages and could quickly translate commands. The common purpose of fighting Fascism modified, if it did not remove, political differences among the rank and file in the early stages, although from time to time

[1] 14 May 1964
[2] Eduardo de Guzmán, *Madrid Rojo y Negro*, pp. 164, 200.
[3] *Politica*, 11 November 1936.

these led to conspiracies within the middle and high command.

However, what may well have been the last crusade in the romantic tradition of the past finally turned into something of a sham. In the early 1930s a great upsurge of social conscience and idealism had spread throughout large parts of England, Europe and America, inspiring men of totally different nationalities and class, but what came out of the thirties in the end? Idealism seemed to reveal a fraudulent face, social conscience led to disillusion and treachery. The justification of any means to the desired end brought about the farcical gymnastics of the British Communist Party in the early stages of World War II, and the Hitler-Stalin pact of 1940. What had happened to sheer common sense if the forces which inspired the International volunteers to pour into Spain to fight Spanish Fascism now came to terms with German Fascism? In many eyes it was abject betrayal. They were incapable of accepting the Machiavellian manœuvre by which you temporarily embraced the object labelled 'Fascist beast' in order to survive to destroy it under more favourable circumstances. Even the most expedient philosophy, they believed, must have certain principles which remained unchanged if it was to work. High inspirations had suffered sad inhibitions but at least conscience had been awakened throughout the world and the plight of the poor, the unemployed, the under-privileged and the forces which conditioned their lot had been subjected to fierce scrutiny and attack.

By the 1940s many British and American intellectuals had finally abandoned their Marxist convictions. Sharp Party practice had depressed many a fanatical spirit. What happened to the Communist convert when he renounced his faith? Stephen Spender and André Gide were briefly members of the Party, but were never involved with the inner hierarchy. Both quickly left the Party and Spender's reaction was typical of many:

'My conclusion is – that the Communist Parties of the world, as they are organized today, could not make a better world. They might even make a far worse one. The reason why I think this is that too much power is concentrated in the hands of too few people. These few people are so protected from criticism of their conduct on any except Party lines, that neither they themselves nor anyone else is protected from their worst human qualities: savagery, vindictiveness, envy, greed and lust for power.

'Because I do not believe that the central organizations of the Communists are capable of making a classless society or indeed of doing anything except establish the rule of a peculiarly vindictive and jealous bureaucracy, I do not feel that I should surrender my own judgment to theirs, however powerful or effective theirs may be, however ineffective my own.'[1]

Despite widespread denunciations of this kind, there were a number of key-members of the International Brigades who remained intransigent Communists. No one expected that big, bluff caricature of a French Left-Wing politician, André Marty, to modify his views. Shortly after he returned to France and became a Communist deputy he was involved in a typically French scene in the Chamber of Deputies. Marty went to the tribune to defend himself against accusations by Nationalist deputies that he had made 'French volunteers dig their own graves before being shot'. M. Herriot had in fact stated that M. Marty ordered back to the front line 67 French volunteers who were to have been repatriated, with express instructions to expose them to enemy fire. M. Herriot concluded his accusations with the words: 'A mysterious atmosphere of blood surrounds M. Marty. The witnesses against him must be heard by the judges.'

Indignant shouting from the Nationalists and prolonged cheers from the Communists drowned out half of Marty's opening sentences in reply, and then at least 60 Right-Wing deputies came to their feet and left the Chamber almost *en bloc*. Marty continued speaking but another interruption followed. 'Are you an assassin – yes or no?' someone shouted.

'It is for the prosecutors to furnish proof', Marty said. 'It is not for the accused to prove his innocence – the facts have been distorted on purpose.' He proceeded to defend himself against the more specific charge that he had been responsible for shooting Major M. De Lasalle. He was, he said, a spy, convicted of intelligence with the enemy, and had been executed by order of the general in command of that sector. 'As for me,' Marty went on, 'I was neither one of his accusers nor a witness.

[1] Stephen Spender, *The God That Failed*, p. 269.

Hundreds can testify to this. I was with them in the midst of battle.'

It did not correspond with the facts as other people knew them, nor did it satisfy the Chamber. A Radical deputy suddenly came to blows with M. Quenette, a Nationalist, behind the Ministerial bench, and M. Campinchi, the Minister of Marine, tried to separate them. A tremendous uproar now drowned out every word until at last the voice of the President of the Chamber broke through shouting, 'I suspend the sitting.'

Marty's reputation has waxed and waned, suffered savage criticism and recovered again, but some of the veteran Brigaders still cling to the belief that he was well intentioned and foolish, a remarkably charitable interpretation of what seem to be the facts. Even the French Communists quarrelled with him in the end, and expelled him from the Party. He died, so far as I can establish, a completely natural death in 1955 although towards the end he became increasingly unbalanced.

Several French veterans of the Commune de Paris Battalion became leading members of the French resistance in the Second World War only to be trapped and shot by the Germans. E. L. Champion was arrested on 11 July 1942, tortured and finally shot at Issy-les-Moulineaux. He left a brief letter to his wife which finished: 'I die certain of having worked well for the future of our child, for the future of all working humanity, for progress against barbarism and slavery. . . .'

Julien Hapiot, who was badly wounded in the Ebro battle, became a resistance organizer in the Nord region until he was arrested and shot on 13 September 1943. He wrote to his wife: 'A brave comrade, Rolt Henri, has been condemned to death this morning for having harboured a partisan. His attitude is exemplary. I recalled to him the couplets of the *La Marseillaise* because it is to the song of our forefathers that we go to the place of execution.'

Joseph Epstein, executed in Fresnes Prison on 1 April 1940, wrote: 'My beloved Paula, Faithful to the last breath to my ideal this afternoon, at 5 I shall be shot. Have courage my beloved Paula. Our dear son has to be brought up and must be made a good and courageous man. His father leaves a name without stain. In moments of discouragement think of me and my love for you both, of my immense love which will never leave you, which will accompany you everywhere and always. My best beloved do not give up. You will be, at the end of 15 hours, the father and the mother of our child. Vive la liberté.'[1]

In 1947 'General Walter' became Minister of National Defence in Poland's provisional government and was subsequently killed in an ambush prepared by Polish patriots. Colonel Roy Tanguy, ex-Political Commissar of the XIVth Brigade, returned to the French Army, and the one-time leader of the Dabrowsky Brigade, Colonel Tedeusz Oppman, became Poland's Military Attaché in Paris.

Lieutenant-Colonel Hans Kahle, former commander of the Thaelmann Battalion, came first to England, where a number of sympathizers with the Spanish Republicans volunteered to house him for a few weeks or months at a time. He stayed, for one period, with Mrs Charlotte Haldane, and despite her resistance to Germans and his supremely ugly face, Kahle succeeded in charming her out of her prejudice. The Nazi-Soviet Pact of 1939 came as a great shock to both of them, but more so to Kahle, who as a German Communist was certain to end up in a concentration camp if he returned to Germany. However, like good Communists, there was no questioning the eternal truth of Stalin's edicts and they dutifully 'spent a long week-end working out the new Soviet line'. When the Second World War broke out Kahle was rounded up with all German refugees in England, and sent to Canada. Two years later he came back across the Atlantic without any trace of bitterness and he and his wife, who was now expecting a child, once more stayed in Charlotte Haldane's flat. When the war was over they returned to Germany. Hans Kahle finally became Police Chief of Mecklenburg and died in 1952.

The other German leader, Ludwig Renn, wrote to me from Berlin-Kaulsdorf, where he still works as a writer. Some of his books have tremendous sales, one of them, *Nobi*, reaching 300,000 copies. He commented: 'I have not changed my views since Spain. In the first year of the war, 1936-7, the Brigades were of great importance because they included a lot of people with military experience. . . .'

A sinister cloud of confusion surrounds the final fate of other leaders of the International Brigades. The Russian

[1] *L'Épopée de Espagne*, pp. 187-8.

General Berzin, along with Kléber, Gal and Čopic all vanished in Stalin's series of purges between 1937 and 1941. In his famous speech denouncing Stalin in February 1956 Khrushchev said: 'Very grievous consequences, especially in reference to the beginning of the war, followed Stalin's annihilation of many military commanders and political workers during 1937 to 1941 . . . the cadre of leaders who had gained military experience in Spain and in the Far East was almost completely liquidated.'

Ehrenburg has written: 'Of all these men I was the only one to survive. . . . As for the others, they were destroyed for no reason at all by their own people.' As far back as 1937 those Russian advisers who had first arrived in the dramatic days of 1936, Antonov-Ovseenko, Stashevsky, Kol'tsov and Berzin, left Spain and presently vanished from history. Krivitsky too – the ex-chief of Military Intelligence in Western Europe – came to an unpleasant end. When those generals who had been his friends for years were executed by Stalin in 1937 he abandoned his job and first took refuge in France where two attempts were made on his life. Later he went to America and in 1941 he was found dead in a Washington hotel in mysterious circumstances. He had been shot in the head and his hand grasped a revolver, but despite a letter addressed by Krivitsky to his attorney Waldman, in which he said that he felt he was being persecuted, Waldman refused to accept the obvious explanation of suicide.

Luigi Longo (Gallo), Political Commissar of the XIth International Brigade, disappeared in France when the Civil War came to an end, was arrested by the French, repatriated to Italy, and exiled to Ventolene. Released in 1943, he took a leading part in the partisan struggle as Vice-Commander of the Corpo Volontari della Liberta, and once again came through every kind of hazard and adventure with many less well-known survivors of the Garibaldi Battalion. Today he is a Communist deputy in the Italian Chamber and Secretary of the P.C.I. Between them Togliatti and Longo ruled the Italian Communist Party until Togliatti died recently, and Nenni, of course, has led the Italian Socialists for some years. Pacciardi became a leading figure in the Italian Republican Party and joined the coalition Cabinets of De Gasperi as Defence Minister.

Among the French I can find no trace of Colonel Putz or

Dumont, but Malraux, of course, is now Minister of Culture under de Gaulle, a régime he might once have found distasteful.

In Eastern Europe, the pattern of Moscow repeated itself. László Rajk, once Commissar of the Rakosi Battalion in the XIIIth International Brigade, became Foreign Secretary to Hungary, but the witch-hunting trials of Stalin finally selected him as their next victim and another purge took place in 1949. Embracing the current fantasies of all the accused, he admitted that he went to Spain under instruction from the secret police of Admiral Horthy in order to 'find out the names of those in the Rakosi Battalion . . . and to bring about a reduction of the military efficiency of the Rakosi Battalion'. As if that were not enough, he made sure no court could acquit him by adding: 'I also carried on Trotskyist propaganda. . . .'[1]

Following the execution of Rajk, no veteran leader of the International Brigades in Eastern Europe was safe. The witch-hunt gradually spread its net until, as Hugh Thomas says, most of them were arrested and many shot.

In contrast to the Germans, Italians and Poles, none of the British and American Brigaders returned to high office in their own lands, but interesting new evidence has now come to light about some of their leaders. Two were homosexual, one committed suicide recently, and another went from one mental home to another for treatment, shortly after he returned to England.

Richard Bennett carried out prolonged research which seemed to connect the legendary figure of George Nathan with two unsolved murders in Ireland. It seems clear that Nathan, like many another distinguished man, was homosexual. More certainly, in 1921 he became a member of an organization known as the Dublin Castle Murder Gang which combined the duties of intelligence officers and gunmen. In March of the same year two masked men shot dead the Lord Mayor of Limerick, George Clancy, and the ex-Lord Mayor George O'Callaghan. As Richard Bennett wrote: 'Nathan, I was told, came down to the Auxiliary mess at Killaloe, a few miles from Limerick, and said he had a job to do that night. . . . In the end it was another officer from the Auxiliary Company at Killaloe who went with Nathan. They came back to the mess

[1] *László Rajk and his Accomplices Before the People's Court*, p. 6.

at six o'clock the next morning boozed up and looking like death. Nathan told the Auxiliaries at breakfast, to their horror, that he had killed Clancy and O'Callaghan.'[1]

It is possible to read into Nathan's incredible bravery under fire and the deliberate way in which he exposed himself to every kind of hazard, a guilty desire to sentence himself to death, but it is equally possible that Nathan just happened to be a completely fearless and ruthless individual who did not fit into – indeed loathed – bourgeois society. It was inevitable that a high proportion of leaders in the Brigades should be men who had openly rebelled against bourgeois society and found a new kind of purpose and fulfilment in the bohemian-military society created by the Brigades. Others undoubtedly solved their problems at one remove or smothered them by replacing psychological with much greater, physical, hazards.

An element of mystery continued to surround Malcolm Dunbar, the Scot who became Chief of Staff of the XVth Brigade. A man who rarely talked about himself, when he came back to England he remained uncommunicative except to one or two very close friends. He did not change his Marxist views although he had severe qualifications about the British Communist Party. Extraordinarily, in a man who had led an open-air life of fierce action for eighteen months, he undertook detailed, microscopic research work for the Labour Research Department. From there he progressed to the actors' trade union, British Equity, and once more plunged into painfully detailed research about actors' income tax, producing an erudite little book full of impossibly complicated tables which did not carry his name. No one would have known from the book that it had any connection with a man called Dunbar which was in itself a remarkable piece of – modesty? His habits were unexpected in a person working for research departments. No one could ever persuade Dunbar to arrive at Equity's office in Harley Street before eleven in the morning; he hated attending any form of committee meeting and even some who worked closely with him never penetrated his flat in Kensington. Of course, all this becomes much clearer when one knows that he was homosexual.

Towards the end a close friend of Dunbar's rang him casually

[1] *New Statesman*, 24 March 1961.

one day and was disturbed to hear a monosyllabic voice which spoke almost incoherently with long silences between each word or phrase. He admitted that he wasn't feeling well and after long hesitation said, 'All right. You'd better come round.' She called on him at once, and he then admitted that he had tried to kill himself. She never discovered the precise reasons.

It seemed, on the surface, idiotic. Here was a good-looking man with enough capital to give him a private income of £2,000–£3,000 a year and relationships with working-class young men which were to him satisfying. Underneath, the picture was very different. His capital, it seemed, had almost disappeared. Perhaps he made generous and continuous loans to his working-class friends; perhaps, as a Communist, his guilt drove him to dispense with his comparative wealth over a number of years, but there a contradiction arose. He had left the Communist Party and his whole world seemed to break apart from that time onwards. At one point, he was reduced to borrowing money from one or two friends and by then his appearance had degenerated from the always smart, always immaculately dressed person into a somewhat gross man with a puffy face and narrow eyes. The good looks were gone; the introversion had become deeper.

Another change overtook him before the end. He became thin, tired, hypochondriac. And then one day he removed all means of identification down to the laundry marks on his clothes and disappeared from London one night in 1964. When a body was washed up on the Welsh coast the police were puzzled. No one came forward to identify it and there was nothing on the body to help them. A brief report appeared in the newspapers which mentioned a handkerchief with a special letter in one corner, and a woman who had known him for years suddenly realized that this must be Dunbar because she had made a habit of giving him such handkerchiefs every Christmas. She went to the police, and finally identified the body.

Dunbar, she says, was, until the last, an idealist who could not bear the sight or sound of suffering. He may also have himself suffered the fate of the ageing homosexual, who no longer finds it possible to attract the young men he needs and cannot face the combined horror of sexual deprivation, loneliness and poverty. One other fact remains to be recorded. The coroner's court did not describe his death as suicide. It gave an open verdict.

Fred Copeman's disillusionment with the Communist Party began when he went to Russia. Among the many exciting possibilities of the trip was the opportunity of meeting the great Spanish woman revolutionary, La Pasionaria, again. After a few days of sight-seeing, Copeman pressed his request to meet her, but it was received without enthusiasm. 'I had expected to find her on the stage at the Bolshoi Theatre holding the hand of Stalin and being introduced as one of the greatest living Communists.' Instead, she was nowhere to be seen and when he repeated his request, various excuses continued to be made. At last he insisted on seeing her, and was escorted to a small room in the Luxe Hotel where she paced up and down with Red Army guards at the door. 'Once again my loyalty to the Party based on the deep human feelings which Communism in its initial stages produces had suffered a shock. If any living creature had the right to everything we had, to me it was Pasionaria.' Now he found her alone in a room under what seemed to be house arrest. When he left her he thought she was in tears. He was next introduced to two English people: Jimmy Gibson, who worked in the Moscow Radio Station, and Doris Hart, who had married a Russian prince. Once again: 'You couldn't help noticing that their movements outside the hotel itself were not – free.'

Another unexpected oddity now troubled Copeman. He quickly became aware that in all the speeches made by the Russian leaders there was no single reference to the International Brigades or the part they had played in the Spanish Civil War. This he deeply resented. Presently he discovered what seemed to him a considerable gap between the standards of living of the common people and the politicians, executives, and technicians. Within a few more days, 'A visit to the Soviet which I had hoped would give me renewed inspiration, was making me, if anything, cynical. . . . The gilt was wearing off the gingerbread.'[1]

[1] Fred Copeman, *Reason in Revolt*, p. 150.

The Stalin purges had not yet reached their height but already an atmosphere of suspicion and mistrust had grown to the point where most members of a British delegation to Moscow were afraid to express anything dimly resembling heretical views. All attempts to prevent Copeman speaking his mind, however, were in vain. When at last the delegates entered the Kremlin to gather round a conference table with Stalin at the head, Bill Rust, the British Communist Party Secretary, leaned across and whispered fiercely to Copeman: 'For God's sake, mind what you say – they wouldn't think twice about taking us outside and shooting us!' Stalin noticed this conversation going on, and through his interpreter said to Copeman: 'What has the big Englishman got to say on the question of who would be best to lead the English in a war?' Without hesitation Copeman named Churchill and half the English froze in their seats. To name an aristocratic capitalist as a war leader! Many men had been shot for less. But Stalin merely nodded impassively. Of course, much later, the interpreter confessed to Copeman that he was in the habit of revising speeches to suit the delicately attuned ears of one of the most ruthless dictators in history, and his message might have read – 'As a true trade unionist the Englishman will fight to the death the Fascist dogs under whatever leader the Party chooses!'

Back in England, Copeman spent the next few months travelling round Britain, visiting the mothers and wives of some of the 500 men who 'went from these islands to Spain never to return again.' When he reached London once more, a man named Robson – a member of the Party Control Commission – called on him with a proposal from Harry Pollitt that the Brigade Dependants' Fund should repay to the Party £1,600 'which he claimed was a loan'. The root source of the £1,600 was, in fact, the Paris Liaison Committee, a subcommittee interconnected with the Comintern. This, in turn, did not please Copeman. There followed an incident when some absurd piece of bureaucracy from one of the leading Communists drove him into such a fury that he 'tore into him like a thunderbolt and he finished up unconscious'. When the man regained his senses he suddenly began screaming 'Murder! Help!' and rushed out of the room. This was not the first time Copeman had concluded a political argument in this way.

Not unexpectedly, soon afterwards Copeman left the Party. Since then, he has fulfilled a number of jobs and embraced some very different faiths. In 1939 he received a letter from Lord Wigram of the Royal Household inviting him to lecture to the staff of Windsor Castle on the dangers of aerial bombardment. He gave the lecture in the great Banquet Hall and several members of the Royal Family were present. One, at least, was delighted by the paradox of a man who had started a mutiny in the Royal Navy, become a member of the Communist Party and an officer in a revolutionary army, only to end up teaching the staff of Windsor Castle and members of the Royal Family how to protect and prolong their lives.

Early in 1945 he found himself drawn more and more towàrds Catholicism. 'The flying bombs had been falling on London for some weeks and my above-ground staff controlling the deep shelters was beginning to dwindle. I began to notice one member of it – Mrs Margot Burridge – who, although obviously terrified when the sirens sounded, stuck to the job in spite of her fears.'[1] He discovered that Mrs Burridge and her family were members of the Catholic Church.

It was far more than Mrs Burridge's bravery which finally drove him to visit Father Martindale in his small, bare room beside Farm Street Church. A working-class aristocrat, with enormous talents and an explosive temperament, not even the discipline of the Navy had quite contained his fiery nature and now, where materialistic restraints failed, he turned to spiritual ones.

Following many months of preparation, Copeman made his first Communion in Farm Street at midnight on Christmas Eve 1946. It was extraordinary to hear this explosive rough diamond, whose language could be forcefully obscene, saying that: 'The beauty of the Mass is always an inspiration – High Mass in Westminster Cathedral or in a chapel on a mountainside in Switzerland.' He adds, 'My belief in and worship of God is intimate and personal.'

This was not the end of it. That mysterious body of seemingly very rich people known as M.R.A. who so successfully work to bring into their ranks influential men from all walks of life, set out to win over Fred Copeman. What a marvellous catch

[1] Fred Copeman, *Reason in Revolt*, p. 202.

he would be. The Moral Rearmament Movement could claim to have fresh support from a most distinguished member of the trade unions and working classes if it could number Fred Copeman among its – adherents. He now carried almost royal credentials since he had won the O.B.E. for his war work. At first he had serious doubts about M.R.A. 'After all to live to your absolute moral standards is all very fine. . . . Absolute honesty – impossible! There are some things that only I must know; Kitty [his wife] wouldn't understand. Absolute unselfishness – hadn't I ordered my life for the cause? Surely I had no selfish ways. I gave in the church as much as most – Absolute love – nice but sloppy. Absolute purity – well, after all – I'm still a sailor, aren't I?'

In the end, the combined effects of careful thought and prolonged propaganda swept away his objections and he joined the ranks of what seems to be a naïve simpleton's world-faith, but is, in effect, a highly sophisticated political organization.

Today Fred Copeman works for the Constructional Engineering Union. Today the long search for a discipline which could mould and contain his tremendous energies to the best ends has taken him full circle from mutiny and Communism to the trade unions and God. But latterly he has come to question M.R.A. again.

Mrs Charlotte Haldane was similarly tempted by the Catholic Church when the Spanish War came to an end. She had never officially been a member of the Communist Party but reconciled the roles of member of the Labour Party and crypto-Communist. Her disillusionment, too, really began when she returned from a trip to Russia. 'As soon as I could . . . I asked J.B.S. [Haldane, her husband] to come and see me. He arrived in due course. During the next three hours I told him in considerable detail of . . . my inability to get any definite information regarding Vavilov, of my failure to obtain the royalties due to him . . . of my disillusionment and disgust. I said that on returning to the Soviet Union thirteen years after our visit there in 1928, I had naturally expected to find great progress and improvement. But, on the contrary, I found few advances and many retreats from the high idealism of the earlier period.'[1]

When she finally went to see Bill Rust, Secretary of the C.P.,

[1] Charlotte Haldane, *Truth Will Out*, p. 255.

he said sarcastically, 'I suppose you will now write a book about Russia?'

She acknowledged the intention.

'Would you', he said, 'be willing to accept Party collaboration in writing your book?'

She politely but firmly declined the offer. 'And that', she said, 'was the end of my connection with the Communist Party of Great Britain.'

She immediately became a leper to all her Party friends who were warned that she had turned traitor and must not – in the technical Party phrase – be contacted.

One witty member found a satisfying explanation of her defection: 'You know, I don't really believe that Charlotte was "got at" or that she is Trotskyist. She was probably embittered at not meeting Stalin. But Stalin decided that rather than run Charlotte, he would prefer to continue running the Soviet Union.'

Her son, the pale acne-ridden youth who went into the International Brigade all those years before with such youthful panache, had survived with a slight wound and joined an infantry regiment in the Second World War. During the Battle of Caen he received a piece of shrapnel in one lung, but again survived to marry and become a father. Meanwhile Mrs Haldane was divorced from her famous Professor husband J. B. S. Haldane, and the Party seemed pleased to see him freed from her. The customary procedure from Communism to Catholicism did not finally occur with Mrs Haldane. Today she has left London and lives at Brighton, earning a living as a writer.

When Tom Wintringham returned to England he was still a very sick man from typhoid and he and his wife Kitty retired to an old vicarage, rented for a song from a friend. There they lived on a few pounds a week while Wintringham hammered out chapter after chapter of *English Captain*. As the Second World War drew closer the demands for articles from someone so recently familiar with modern war grew, until the telephone never ceased ringing and from earning nothing Wintringham's income leapt to over £100 a week. The declaration of war intensified the demand still more. Tom Hopkinson gave two whole issues of *Picture Post* to articles by Wintringham on how to fight a modern war, but the War Office disdained to notice. By now Tom Hopkinson and Edward Hulton felt that the time had come to set up some training centre which would illustrate the skills which Wintringham had acquired in Spain, and Hulton, with that magic available to the rich, conjured up Osterley Park as a base. There followed a dramatic interview at the War Office with a top-brass general who quickly indicated that although Hulton might have plenty of what he called *it* – meaning money – this did not qualify him to launch a training centre with any military efficiency.

Wintringham was highly suspect, of course. By now his quarrels with the Communist Party had driven them to expel him, but the stain of Communism remained ineradicable in the eyes of the War Office. When at last the early units of the British Home Guard appeared, Wintringham became an instructor, but he never rose to higher rank and took no part in the actual fighting of World War II.

His views changed to some extent. The original concept of a Popular Front had gone sour, he thought, but if only it could have preserved its original inspiration, a new, modernized version would have made a planned world on broad socialist lines much more possible. Before he died in 1949 he explored the possibilities of an entirely new party – the Common Wealth Party – which flared to momentary success and involved the deeply religious Sir Richard Acland, but mightier forces were required to challenge the entrenched giants of the Left and Right in England.

Of the other leading figures in the British Battalion, Peter Kerrigan remains an intransigent Communist and has become National Organizer of the Communist Party. Albert Digges, who runs the British International Brigade Association, still holds the same views as he did in Spain and works now as a wages clerk. Miles Tomalin has become a free-lance writer, also without changing his views. John Sommerfield describes himself as a 'grey-haired old codger who does a bit of writing on the side'. He has, in fact, written an excellent book on his experiences in Spain and two novels, but he has withdrawn from active political life, dismayed by its cynicism. Esmond Romilly became a fighter pilot and was killed in the Battle of Britain.

Today George Aitken looks the part of an elder trade-union

Accordingly I left the job and the Party and broke completely away. . . . Not long after that the War started and I was in the Army. There I was soon identified as a "premature anti-fascist" and although I received no positive evidence that this discriminated against me I sensed that I was not completely accepted.'

Today Walter Greenhalgh has built up a thriving scrap-metal business of his own but he has a second and more significant life. He is a member of a Borough Council and chairman of a Town Planning and Libraries Committee. He comments: 'I like to think that by relegating the way I earn my living to a minor "intellectual" role I can retain some sort of independence in the work I do – that is politics.' Mr Greenhalgh is also a member of the Co-operative and Labour Party today, and has been offered full-time work in politics, but he feared that this would take away his freedom as well as the fun.

Was he right to volunteer for Spain? 'I firmly believe – we were right – and if we had won a little more success, history would have been completely different.'

When the survivors of the Lincoln-Washington Battalion first poured back into America, more than 2,000 men gave the V.A.L.B. (Veterans of the Abraham Lincoln Brigade) many headaches. The secretary's job seemed to occupy every waking hour. Today the V.A.L.B. occupies one room on 21st Street, New York ($35 a month for rent and telephone), and Moses Fishman goes there on Wednesday evenings only, from six till eight. He himself took part in World War II as a radio operator and now earns a living 'allied to the printing trade'.

The V.A.L.B. attempted, in the forties, to issue cards to all its members but did not meet with very warm response and now all they have as record of those tremendous years is a ledger with names and addresses, and even that has gaps when some of the dead are remembered by Christian names only. Every International Brigade veteran was issued with a medallion struck in silvered alloy with a map of Spain, a clenched-fist salute, a five-pointed Red Star, the dates 1936–37 and encircling it, *Voluntarios Internacionales de la Libertad*. Moses Fishman still has his medal. Scores of others can't remember what became of it. Some threw away what degenerated into a smooth and almost characterless piece of alloy; some, like Alvah Bessie, have it carefully wrapped in tissue, tucked away inside a wallet.

There were three or four courses open to American volunteers when they returned to America. They could work politically for one or other of the unions, go back to their old trades, or remain militant and active members of the C.P. Inevitably John Gates chose the last course, but he was also one of the first to enlist in World War II. Christmas of 1941 found him at Fort Sill, Oklahoma, the Army's Field Artillery Training Centre, and he quickly graduated from private-first-class to battalion operations sergeant, but when the order alerting his division came in 1942 he discovered that he was to be left behind and 'transferred forthwith to the service unit permanently stationed at the camp'. Officers and men were equally dismayed, since he had become an integral part of his particular unit. He appealed to his commanding officers who assured him that they would make a powerful plea for him. Some of the men thought him mad to press the point. Here was a marvellous opportunity to enjoy a luxurious war safely ensconced at a well-supplied base, and instead he went about pressurizing everyone to get himself sent into the front line.

However, nothing came of all this activity, and he then decided on a dramatic approach to none other than President Roosevelt himself. Army regulations permitted a direct appeal by letter to the President under certain circumstances. He wrote a long letter and subsequently learnt that Roosevelt sent a copy to his Battalion Commander asking for his comments. Gates went on furlough shortly afterwards, and when he returned he was delighted to hear that he had been transferred back into his battalion. Unfortunately, at this point, a celebrated columnist published the whole story in his coast-to-coast syndicated column, including the name of Gates's battalion and the fact that it was earmarked for overseas service, both matters of a confidential military nature. Some friends had hoped that the publicity would improve Gates's chances, but the violation of military secrecy brought about the immediate countermanding of the order restoring him to his battalion. Gates was now a married man and he poured out all his feelings and frustrations in long love letters to his wife Lillian.

Finally he could see only one way of getting into active combat; by volunteering for a paratroop regiment. He reported to the Army Parachute School at Fort Benning, Georgia, and became one of a class of 1,600 men, only five of whom – including himself – were over the age of 30.

He arrived in France late in March 1945, and early in April joined the 17th Airborne Division in Germany only to find that 'the Division had jumped a few days earlier on the east side of the Rhine. This was the last combat jump in the European War and I had missed it.'[1]

Throughout the war he remained a Communist and a few years after the war he became one of the Foley Street eleven who reported daily to Room No. 110 in the Federal Court House on Foley Square, New York City, to face continuous interrogation about their associates in Communist activities.

Gates made some fine distinctions about the charges: 'The average person thought and still thinks that we were tried and found guilty of espionage, sabotage, treason and planning to overthrow the government by force. None of these crimes was even charged against us. We were actually accused of "conspiracy" to organize a political party which would teach and advocate the duty and necessity of the violent overthrow and destruction of the United States Government.'[2]

Whatever the distinction, the verdict remained harsh – five years' imprisonment and a $10,000 fine. It was the maximum possible sentence, which the Judge refused to mitigate in view of Gates's honourable war record. Even worse, immediately after he had dealt with the eleven defendants, the Judge turned to what he termed 'some unfinished business' and proceeded to charge the defendants' lawyers with wilful contempt, almost in the same breath convicting and sentencing them to terms of imprisonment ranging from one to six months. The early symptoms of the McCarthy hysteria were now unashamedly coming into the open.[3]

In retrospect Gates's martyrdom seemed wasted. By 1957 he was beginning to become restless under the Party yoke and in September of that year he published, in the *Daily Worker*, a letter of resignation from a man called Clark which sharply

[1] John Gates, *The Story of an American Communist*, pp. 94–5.
[2] Ibid., p. 121.   [3] The *New York Times*, 30 June 1950.

criticized Party policies. This, in itself, represented an unprecedented step in Party history, since no one was given space in official organs to explain publicly why he had resigned.

Then came what he described as a shameless piece of distortion in the Soviet theoretical magazine *Kommunist* which published a long analysis of Gates's pre-convention article – 'Time For a Change'. The writer, a man named Ponomarev, claimed that Gates wanted to convert the American Communist Party into a debating society and Gates counterclaimed that he had said exactly the opposite. Since Ponomarev's quotations from Gates's article were, in his view, 'simply inventions', he proposed that the American Communist Party should 'publicly correct these falsifications'. It was useless. The voice of the *Kommunist* was sacrosanct. James Jackson, the Negro Communist leader, thought the whole proposition ill-timed when it coincided with that amazing feat which Russia had just accomplished, the launching of a Sputnik into fathomless space.

The change in policy which Gates advocated was, in effect, revolutionary, and went to the roots of Party thinking. Continuously they had subscribed to the proposition – 'The Soviet Union right or wrong' – and now he wanted to replace that with the counsel of a great American of Lincoln's day: 'When right, to be kept right: when wrong, to be set right.'

Two further events showed Gates that his days in the Party were numbered. The first was the dogmatic retreat to the rigid policies pursued by the Comintern when it held sway over external affairs in a 12-Party statement at the Moscow celebration of the 40th Anniversary of the Russian Revolution and the second the sudden death of the Party's paper, the *Daily Worker*.

He attended a New Year's Eve Party at the national headquarters in 1957, and told a comrade that when the *Daily Worker* finally ceased publication he would 'go with it'. On the evening of Thursday, 9 January, he finally wrote his letter of resignation.

Later, at the age of 47, he graduated from Brooklyn College, and in 1962 became a student in economics and social science at the Massachusetts Institute of Technology. Life has begun again for him, and who knows what the education he originally missed may finally produce in him?

Steve Nelson, today a man of 60, is the same toughly attractive personality, but he has gone back to his roots. Originally a carpenter by trade he became a carpenter again, but the
old, hand-manipulated tools had given place to electric ones
and there was a period when he wondered whether he could
adjust to the new methods. The last I heard of him it was working out successfully.

When the Second World War involved America, invisible
barriers prevented many veterans from reaching the fighting
line. This war was against Fascism too, and at a certain stage
Russia, with all its Communist commitments, became an ally,
but these men carried the stigma of American Communism
which involved a different brand of subversion. More than
500 ex-International Brigaders eventually served in the American forces, but the overlapping subtleties of their loyalties
produced a surrealist confusion. They might be seasoned
soldiers who knew what modern warfare meant; they might
be familiar with tank techniques and know how to survive
dive bombing; they might be prepared to volunteer once
more to fight an even more evil and wily old bird which, for
them, displayed the same sinister plumage; but most of them
encountered a new form of segregation. They could serve, yes,
but when it came to being shipped overseas to actual battle-
fronts they were singled out time and again to remain at home.
Not that, in the end, some did not break the service bar. There
were others who felt that they had done their share; men who
knew what it meant to be mutilated for life in the service of an
ideal which went sour on them, and were only too happy to
stay at home.

After the Second World War the slow and tragic inversion of
values quickly converted war-time heroes into suspect persons
whose involvement twenty years before in an anti-Fascist
struggle, which aroused democratic enthusiasms throughout
half of Europe, made them possible subversives. The stale
shadow of McCarthy overwhelmed mitigating facts until, in
1955, the Subversive Activities Control Board ruled that the
Veterans of the Abraham Lincoln Brigade must register with
the Attorney-General as a Communist Front organization.
Fishman claims that of his membership forty per cent were
Communists when they fought in Spain. 'Now – who knows?

I know some are, some aren't. Some guys I don't know but I'll tell you this. I'd cut my tongue out before I'd ask them.'[1]

Alvah Bessie claims that everything that happened to him personally after his return to America 'happened in one way or another because of Spain'. In a letter to me Bessie described his early experiences:

'I tried vainly to find work in my former field – newspaper editorial and critical work. I couldn't. I finally was given a job on the old *New Masses* as drama critic and remained there from January 1940 to December 1942 as drama, film and book critic and feature writer.

'In January 1943, much to everyone's astonishment, I was offered a job (contract) with Warner Brothers' pictures in Burbank, California, as a screenwriter and remained with them till January 1946 when my option was dropped because Warner (erroneously) thought that I – and one other man – was responsible for the 1945 strike of his workers. So I became a freelance writer throughout 1946 and 1947, until the subpoena arrived from the House of Representatives' Committee on Un-American Activities in October of that year. (Had "won" several screen-credits by then and was beginning to be noticed as a screenwriter.)'

There followed the famous Hollywood investigation by the Un-American Activities Committee and Bessie, with ten other writers, directors and producers, was blacklisted. On 29 June 1950 he appeared with Ring Lardner before the Committee for the last time and they repeated what they had pleaded in October 1947: that to be forced to answer questions about Communist Party affiliations would violate their constitutional guarantees. Lardner went further. He stated that there was only a minor difference between forcing a man to say what his opinions were and dictating what those opinions should be.

Once again the question was put by J. Parnell Thomas, the Republican Committee chairman: 'Are you or have you ever been a member of the Communist Party?' and once more they refused to answer. As one man said in court, 'This case occurs at a time when the nation's leading spokesmen are staking the

---

[1] *Esquire* magazine, 'The Abraham Lincoln Brigade', March 1962, Brock Bower, p. 65.

moral prestige of America on our alleged devotion to the cause of freedom.'

It was all of no avail. Bessie and Lardner were sentenced to one year in prison and $1,000 fine. Subsequently, J. Parnell Thomas found himself charged with conspiring to defraud the Government and went to prison.

Bessie continued his own story for me: 'Returning to Hollywood in April 1951, no work could, of course, be found. In August was offered job in San Francisco as public relations man and assistant editor to Harry Bridges's International Longshoremen's and Warehousemen's Union. Remained there five years until the International office of the union had to contract its staff and let me out.'

Today Bessie has a job as publicity man for six San Francisco movie houses but he doesn't know how long it will last. When I asked him whether he had changed his views he said: 'I have not changed my opinions, despite all the attempts to debunk that cause, to slander the Spanish Republican Government and the USSR's involvement in that fight.'

Unlike Bessie, another veteran found himself buffeted between the repulsions of a capitalist society which did not like this foreign body in its midst and the ruthlessness of a party from which he finally became a renegade.

When Sandor Voros first returned to the States he was escorted with all the pomp and ceremony of a returning hero to the offices of the Friends of the Abraham Lincoln Brigade. There, a woman secretary offered him the room of an absent comrade in Brooklyn for a couple of days, until he found a place of his own. 'She could let me have a a couple of dollars if I needed assistance desperately, she said. "Five dollars" – she eyed me speculatively – "ten dollars". That was absolutely the limit but the Party would get me on relief before I spent that ten if I was careful with it.'[1]

She left the room to see if there were any messages for him, and when she returned her attitude had changed completely. She had just discovered that she was dealing with none other than the Sandor Voros who wrote those articles in the *Daily Worker* which she had sometimes literally crowed over as she read. Now she offered him a beautifully furnished flat in

[1] Sandor Voros, *American Commissar*, p. 447.

Manhattan – just outside the Village – and her financial offer of help was suddenly inflated to 20 dollars. He turned down everything.

During the next few weeks Voros tried, first of all, to get his own report about the Spanish Civil War sent to the Central Communist Committee and thus to the Comintern. John Gates and Robert Minor had both returned to give accounts of a Republican Spain ready to fight to the death with   according to Voros – the highly romantic comment that if only the 'party concentrated all its efforts on lifting the arms embargo in the U.S. the victory of the Loyalists was certain'. Minor, on the evidence of Voros, had become a 'senile idiot', and Gates 'an over-ambitious careerist hellbent to make his way into the Party leadership'. When Voros insisted that Republican Spain could not continue to resist for long without trained French or Russian divisions to support them, equivalent to the divisions which Germany and Italy had poured into Nationalist Spain, he was told that such a message flatly contradicted the Party line. 'You know, Voros, that's impossible; you know the Comintern line is the line of Moscow. We can't go against that.'

Voros decided to break off discussion at this point. He walked the streets of New York for the rest of that day more depressed, he says, than he had ever felt in his life before. An embittered man, he now turned down jobs with the Party and gave up the idea of writing for the *Daily Worker*. Later he was offered the editorship of the Hungarian paper *Uj Elore*, but Peter Chaunt, the Party boss of the Hungarian section of the I.W.O., qualified the proposition with the words: 'Come to see me tomorrow morning and don't forget to bring your statement with you.'

'What statement?'

'A statement confessing your errors. . . . Stress particularly how right the Party was in making that nominal pact with Hitler and . . .'

The words flowed on until Voros at last interrupted. 'I am ready to start tomorrow. But I want to publish my statement as a two-column signed editorial on the front page.'

'Why on the front page?'

'Because my statement would open with the announcement that I am no longer a Party member.'[1]

[1] Sandor Voros, *American Commissar*, p. 471

Outside in the street again, New York seemed to go about its normal occasions with no sign of violence, but when Voros finally took a job with a furrier he quickly found himself fired again because the boss 'could not afford to have trouble with the unions'. This happened several times until he felt that it was part of a conspiracy. Finally he moved away from New York.

'I am still a materialist . . .,' he told me, 'a firm believer that Socialism is the only just social system to replace capitalism or communism, regardless of label.' But 'I would never again voluntarily put myself into any position where I'd have no right for dissent. I would again volunteer to fight against Franco – in Hungary I would have fought against Rakosi. In fact I tried to get there but was too late. I also volunteered for the American Marines in World War II, but was turned down twice. Selective service didn't take me because I was past draft age.'

Now he runs a small. furrier's business of his own – 'which allows me to buy a new car every other year,' but memories of Spain are ineradicable and alongside the incredible heroism and self-sacrifice he cannot forget the sycophancy of certain political commissars reduced by their faith to what he regarded as cretinous cyphers.

Fishman believes that memories of Spain are burnt into the minds of so many American volunteers because theirs was an act of personal conviction and individual commitment, not an involuntary response to conscription as it became for so many in World War II, but the ruling of the Subversive Activities Control Board makes it impossible for some to talk about Spain any more.

'A guy comes in here the other day all the way from California', Fishman says. 'Haven't seen him since Spain. . . . He's a TV repair man. "Do you want us to send you any mail?" He'd prefer not. I offered to send it in a plain envelope, but he feels no, the kids bring in their friends, you know how kids are, they might see something lying around the house. "Some people know," he says, "but we don't make a big thing of it that I fought in Spain. . . ." '[1]

James Norman is less worried. He fought in Spain because 'I was young and I believed in their republicanism', but he did not carry any direct Communist stigma. His beliefs today are

[1] *Esquire* magazine, March 1962, p. 65.

'more or less the same as those I held in Spain, although my attitudes have changed. I'm a rather fuzzy independent catholic anarchist now.'

When Bert (Yank) Levy returned to Canada, he travelled the country lecturing on Spain and then was seized by a series of asthmatic attacks which incarcerated him in Duke Fingard Hospital, Toronto, for seven months. When Germany attacked Poland he attempted to enlist in the Essex Fusiliers (Windsor, Ontario) and was turned down because of his political activities. In March 1940 he arrived in London and went to work as a template maker at a government-sponsored school for aeroplane construction. Later he joined Tom Wintringham's school in Osterley Park, wrote a book and lectured on guerrilla warfare. He returned to the States in 1943 and continued lecturing. After the war he went to work in a paper-box plant at Los Angeles and today, tragically, is crippled by arthritis which has made work impossible for the last twelve years. 'You ask', he says, 'whether I have the same political views I had then? If you mean one peaceful world with education, health, security in all facets . . . for the good of all – yes. But if you mean am I a blind adherent to others' thinking – no. My blinkers began falling off with the Saklatvala Battalion in Madrigueras.'

Edwin Rolfe died of a heart attack. Dr Edward K. Barsky, who set up the famous mobile medical unit of the Lincoln-Washingtons, was jailed for refusing to disclose details from the Joint-Anti-Fascist Refugee Committee, and has since become a leading surgeon in New York. William Carpenter is now a disillusioned radio-station technician.

There are many others who do not wish to be named. One who came through the battles of Jarama, Teruel and the Ebro with only minor wounds, had fifteen jobs in ten years and now finds himself restless, unhappy, as a wages clerk in a big store. The store does not know about his past. 'You get wised up after a bit. I got fired three times on account of shooting my mouth once too often. I don't talk any more.'

He has a wife and two children, and he never, at any point, embraced the Communist faith, but he has been through an infected organization and in the eyes of the trigger-happy Subversive Activities Control Board, who knows whether he isn't still a carrier? When he first came back from Spain there was an uneasy reception in his home town, half amazed at the audacity of anyone who could face a hail of bullets for his beliefs, half admiring someone who had survived a number of real battles, but no one seemed anxious to employ him. His old boss, who ran a gas station, had a sudden surplus of employees. He became a truck driver for the next three months, and then one night a spasm of memory recalled the Jarama battles and he launched into a vivid description to his buddy who listened, at first enthralled. Towards the end he eyed him anxiously and said: 'Are you a Commie?'

'No, I'm no Commie – I'm just a goddam revolutionary!' he said, meaning to be savagely funny. He was fired forty-eight hours later.

Now, at 52, a gaunt, grey-haired man, prematurely aged, he tries to concentrate on rows of figures for eight hours a day and 'it gets so's I could tear the goddam books into little pieces and shower them down on all those nice folk way down there. I wish something would happen in Spain again. I feel as of today just like going back and blasting hell out of somebody!'

Another veteran has a news-stand in New York and he is bitter about his Spanish experiences. 'We were a lot of dopes – dropped like a hot brick when it suited that bastard Stalin. I remember all that Pasionaria stuff – all that hooey about workers of the world fighting for freedom – fighting Fascism – but when it suited the Commies they shook the hand they asked us to bite – Hitler's! Jesus – I ask you – what sort of politics is that? Shit – that's what I call that game.'

It is chastening to reflect that in 1936–37 there was far less open hostility to Spanish veterans. A man with such impeccable lineage as Bernard Baruch gave $11,060 to help bring home a number of wounded veterans. Clare Boothe Luce and Henry Luce each contributed $250 to the same cause. Second thoughts of a serious kind only began to arise as the American Communist Party showed signs of growing strength if not power, until the final horror of McCarthy created that atmosphere of poisonous suspicion where the friend of a friend of a veteran might be victimized from guilt by association.

Today many veterans have found it hard to settle down to a 'permanent' job where they can freely admit their past. 'Wiser to keep the heroism out of it. Wiser to forget the old excitements. Defensive – yes – sure we're defensive. If we thought we'd get a fair hearing we'd talk. But one in a million gives you a fair hearing.'

One interesting question remains: If men were so eager and willing to volunteer to fight something indelibly labelled Fascism in Spain, why was it that when Britain stood alone in 1940 against the same enemy in a different guise, nothing comparable to the upsurge of volunteers for Spain poured into Britain from America? Of course, the climate of opinion had changed. The simple idealisms of the 1930s were already giving place to the vast cynicisms of the 1940s. No clarion call was any longer quite so convincing or clear-cut. But the Communist Party of America did not set up recruiting centres or propagand for volunteers. Nor did 3,000 Americans pour across the Atlantic to help Britain as they had done Spain. There were volunteers, of course, of a casual, unorganized kind, but their numbers were very limited and they had little to do with the Communist Party. The men of the Eagle Squadron were no substitute for the volunteers for Spain.

Now that the long, heroic and in some senses mistaken story is over, academic questions of this kind no longer matter. Any attempt at a statistical survey of the views of survivors of the Brigades is hopelessly complicated by the fact that in America they live under the shadow of the Un-American Committee, in England many of them are scattered to the four winds and in France many are difficult to trace. Some Germans now live in East Germany, but the organization which represents them does not seem over-anxious to divulge information. Similarly, the Volontaires Français en Espagne Republicaine is not very responsive to questioning. The fact is that Brigade Associations have diminished until, in most cases, one or two individuals give an occasional afternoon or evening to the work. Their limited resources make it difficult to respond to detailed inquiries and an atmosphere of suspicion and mistrust still tends to hamper researches.

However, certain statistical facts are worth recording. At least 85 per cent of those who volunteered came from the working classes, and well over half that number were Communists before volunteering. Comparison between the estimates of the various surviving associations seems to reaffirm Hugh Thomas's estimate of 60 per cent Communists at the outset. From propaganda, experience or sheer personal choice another 15 per cent became Communists while they were in Spain. Among the French many were unemployed when they volunteered, but it does not follow that they were, without exception, drifting, feckless types. A number had been driven into unemployment as a retaliation for political activities. Whatever stigma posterity has stamped on some of these men, no less than 25 per cent died in action, and a high proportion served an ideal, if the motives of some were mixed, occasionally neurotic and even in a number of cases pathological.

Despite a great deal of evidence to the contrary which has only come to light in the last ten years, many of those I corresponded or talked with were not disillusioned about their cause. They were different people. Their views had in many cases undergone modification or dramatic change, but whenever I succeeded in winning their confidence they still recalled that November day when the first battalions came marching splendidly into beleaguered Madrid, and the cold air rang to the Internationale, as the beginning of a great crusade, not for religious oppression or the will of an unknown divinity, but for the good of the common man in his age-long battle against despotism and exploitation. The whole experience was indelibly linked with an exciting sense of personal conviction and individual commitment which was lost in the vast divisions and enormous areas of World War II.

In the eyes of the historian, the picture is sadly different. This, which was probably the last crusade in the romantic meaning of that word, suffers sad inhibition in the full knowledge of Stalin's Machiavellian manœuvres and the resounding phrases of the Internationale echo emptily as each new piece of political chicanery falls into place. Something remains untouched in the crippling multiplication of qualification. It is never less than moving to witness a great upsurge of men from scores of alien parts of the world coming together to fight a common enemy and serve a common cause, when that cause arouses passionate beliefs in justice and freedom from oppression.

*   *   *

There are those ex-Brigaders who could not resist, years afterwards, setting foot in Spain again and going back to the old scenes, the old battlefields. Sometimes it was necessary to disguise identities, but there was, in fact, no law to prevent their returning. They found that the great metropolis of Madrid had obliterated most of the scars of war and the University City had recovered its academic symmetry, but it was otherwise elsewhere.

Peter Elstob went back a few years ago and penetrated once more into the small country town of Madrigueras, the training centre for the British. As he drove through the sandy countryside with its sentinel pine trees and turned down the rutted road, he came first upon a series of alien new houses which had spread from the old town. Driving slowly, he passed between them, through the outskirts into the small central square still unchanged, still with the two impossibly narrow exits, its iron balconies and cafés. The International Café they had always called the main one, and nothing much could be done locally by the Brigade Command until they had consulted its proprietor. There was the same ancient church, once the British Battalion's canteen, and the dilapidated hotel where the officers were billeted. Elstob went into the bars and the cafés, and talked to many people. Some remembered the International Brigades. Over many drinks they laughed about the crazy old horses, the out-of-date equipment and the struggle with the Spanish tongue. Someone said: 'They still call this town the Moscow of Spain!' and he remembered seeing Tito among the recruits although Tito never penetrated to Madrigueras.

Out in the Jarama battlefield near Madrid, Elstob found the same once-embattled church, its walls still scarred by shells and bullets. There was a blown bridge still unrepaired across the river. The fields were rich, burgeoning everywhere, and nature had swarmed over other scars and relics with a profusion of new life.

He drove on again looking for the farmhouse which had been Brigade Headquarters. As its outline came into view he felt his heart leap. But something was missing. The old stone cottage, the outpost which faced up to such appalling fire and witnessed terrible slaughter – where was that? It took him some time to find the cottage, or what was left of it – a heap of stones jumbled in an almost unidentifiable mound. He stood there, looking down at it for several minutes. There were no crosses: no memorials: nothing. The casual stranger passing here would have no hint, no inkling of what had marked this spot indelibly for so many men from alien lands, who came together to answer a call to arms in the tradition of another age. It was some time before he came back to life once more and drove away.

In the cafés of Madrigueras he talked again with casual Spaniards about the International Brigades, and now he noticed that men spoke of them with considerable reserve. Somewhere in the streets he seemed to hear the echo of the *vivas!* which had once greeted the volunteers – how long ago was it – thirty years – when they first poured into the town? Even the echo was almost gone now.

Select Bibliography

Acier, Marcel (ed.), *From Spanish Trenches*. Paris, 1937.
Ajzner, Seweryn, *Madryt-Saragossa*. Warsaw, 1961.
Azaña y Díaz, Manuel, *Memorias Intimas*. Madrid, 1939.
Aznar, Manuel, *Historia Militar de la Guerra España*. London, 1940.
Barea, Arturo, *The Clash*. London, 1946.
Bell, J. H., *Essays, Poems and Letters*. London, 1938.
Bessie, Alvah, *Men in Battle*. New York, 1939.
Borkenau, Franz, *The Spanish Cockpit*. London, 1937.
Borkman, Franz, *The Communist International*. London, 1938.
Brandt, Willy, *My Road to Berlin*. London, 1960.
Brome, Vincent, *Aneurin Bevan*. London, 1953.
Broué, Pierre and Terminé, Emile, *La Révolution et la Guerre d'Espagne*. Paris, 1963.
Calandrone, Giacomo, *La Spagna Brucia*. Rome, 1962.
Cleugh, James, *Spanish Fury – The Story of a Civil War*. London, 1962.
Cockburn, Claud, *In Time of Trouble*. London, 1956.
Cockburn, Claud, *Reporter in Spain*. London, 1939.
Colvin, I. G., *Chief of Intelligence*. London, 1951.
Copeman, F., *Reason in Revolt*. London, 1948.
Cox, Geoffrey, *Defence of Madrid*. London, 1937.
Dabrowsrwacy. Collection. Warsaw, 1956.
Dedijer, V., *Tito Speaks*. London, 1953.
Delaprée, L., *Mort en Espagne*. Paris, 1937.
Delmer, D. Sefton, *Black Boomerang*. London, 1962.
Delmer, D. Sefton, *Trail Sinister*. London, 1961.
De Wet, H. W. A. O., *Cardboard Crucifix*. London, 1938.
Dimitrov, Georgi, *The United Front*. Paris, 1938.
Dupré, Henri, *La Légion Tricolore en Espagne*. Paris, 1942.
Ehrenburg, Ilya, *Eve of War 1933–41*. London, 1944.
Elstob, Peter, *Spanish Prisoner*. London, 1939.
Fischer, Louis, *Men and Politics*. London, 1941.
Foote, A., *Handbook of Spies*. London, 1953.
Fox, R., *A Writer in Arms*. London, 1937.
Gillain, N., *Le Mercenaire*. Lille, 1937.
González, Valentín (El Campesino), *Listen Comrades*. London, 1956.
Graves, R., and Hodge, Alan, *The Long Week End*. London, 1940.
Guest, C. H., *David Guest: A Scientist Fights for Freedom*. London, 1938.
Guttmann, Alan, *American Neutrality and the Spanish Civil War*. New York, 1963.

Haldane, Charlotte, *Truth Will Out*. London, 1949.
Hemingway, E., *The Spanish War* ('Fact', July 1938). London, 1938.
Hemingway, E., *For Whom the Bell Tolls*. London and New York, 1940.
Junod, M., *Warrior Without Weapons*. London, 1951.
Koestler, A., *Spanish Testament*. London, 1937.
Johnstone, N. J., *Hotel in Flight*. London, 1939.
Joll, James, *Intellectuals in Politics*. London, 1960.
Kantorowicz, Alfred, *Spanisches Tagebüch*. Berlin, 1949.
Krivitsky, W. G., *I Was Stalin's Agent*. London, 1939.
Largo, Francisco Caballero, *Mis Recuerdos: Cartas a un Amigo*. Mexico, 1954.
Lindbaeck, Lise, *Bataljon Thaelmann*. Oslo, 1938.
Lizón Gadea, A., *Brigadas Internacionales en España*. Madrid, 1940.
Longo, Luigi, *Le Brigate Internationali in Spagna*. Rome, 1956.
Low, Mary, *Red Spanish Notebook*. London, 1937.
Macartney, W. F. R., *Walls Have Mouths*. London, 1936.
Macartney, W. F. R., *Zig-Zag*. London, 1937.
Madariaga, Salvador de, *Spain*. London, 1942.
Madem, Gina, *The Jews Fighting for Freedom*. New York, 1938.
Malraux, A., *Days of Hope*. London, 1938.
Martini, M., *La Bataglia dell' Ebro*. Paris, 1939.
Marty, A., *Volontaires d'Espagne*. Paris, 1938.
Mencken, H. L., *The Sage of Baltimore*. New York, 1952.
Mencken, H. L., *Heathen Days*. New York, 1940.
Mitford, Jessica, *Hons and Rebels*. London, 1960.
Muggeridge, Malcolm, *The Thirties*. London, 1940.
Murphy, J. T., *New Horizons*. London, 1941.
Nenni, Pietro, *Spagna*. Milan, 1958.
Nenni, Pietro, *Pagine di Diario*. Rome, 1947.
Orwell, George, *Homage to Catalonia*. London, 1938.
Pacciardi, Randolfo, *Il Battaglione Garibaldi*. Lugano, 1948.
Padev, M., *Marshal Tito*. London, 1944.
Payne, Robert, *The Civil War in Spain*. London, 1963.
Payne, S. R., *Falange – A History of Spanish Fascism*. London, 1963.
Péman, José María, *De la Entrada en Madrid: Historia de Tres Días*. Madrid, 1939.
Perucho, Arturo, *La Vida Heroica de Hans Beimler*. Madrid, 1938– .
Phillips, C. E. L., *The Spanish Pimpernel*. London, 1960.
Primo de Rivera, José Antonio, *Obras Completas*. Madrid, 1954.
Regler, G., *The Great Crusade*. London, 1940.
Regler, G., *The Owl of Minerva*. London, 1959.
Renn, Ludwig, *Der Spanische Krieg*. Berlin, 1955.
Riesenfeld, J., *Dancer in Madrid*. New York, 1938.
Rolfe, Edwin, *The Lincoln Battalion*. New York, 1939.
Romilly, E. M. D., *Boadilla*. London, 1937.
Rust, W., *Britons in Spain*. London, 1939.
Schlesinger, A. M., *The Age of Roosevelt*. London and New York, 2 vols. 1957–59.

Sedgwick, Frank, *The Tragedy of Manuel Azaña*. Ohio, 1964.
Seghers, Anna, *Ernst Thaelmann*. London, 1934.
Sloan, P. A., *John Cornford*. London, 1938.
Sommerfield, John, *Volunteer in Spain*. London, 1937.
Southworth, H., *Le Mythe de la croisade de France*. Paris, 1964.
Spender, Stephen, *World within World*. London, 1951.
Spender, Stephen, *Poems for Spain*. London, 1939.
Stackelberg, C. G. von, *Legion Condor*. Berlin, 1939.
Thomas, Hugh, *The Spanish Civil War*. London, 1961.
Thompson, Sir G. H., *Front Line Diplomat*. London, 1959.
Tinker, F., *Some Still Live*. London, 1938.
Toynbee, A., *Survey of International Affairs*. Vol. 1. Oxford, 1938.
Toynbee, P., *Friends Apart*. London, 1954.
Uhse, Die Bodo, *Lt. Bertram*. Berlin, 1961.
Vayo, Julio Álvarez del, *Freedom's Battle*. London, 1940.
Villarín, Jorge, *Guerra en España contra el Judaismo Bolchevigue*. Cadiz, 1937.
'Wayfarer', *The International Brigade*. London. No date.
Wecter, D., *The Saga of American Society*. New York, 1937.
Wintringham, T., *English Captain*. London, 1939.
Wish, Harvey, *Society and Thought in America*. 2 vols. New York, 1957.
Worsley, T. C., *Behind the Battle*. London, 1939.
Wullschleger, Max (ed.), *Schweizer Kämpfen in Spanien*. Zürich, 1939.
Wullschleger, Max (ed.), *Les Volontaires Suisses en Espagne*. Basle, 1939.

OTHER SOURCES

Spain, 1938. Report of Trade Union and Labour Party Members' Delegation to Spain, February 1938 – International Brigade Wounded and Dependants' Aid Committee.
Hansard. 1936–38.
In Spain with the International Brigade. Anonymous. 1936.
Documents of the International Committee for the Application of the Agreement Regarding Non-intervention in Spain. Unpublished.
Dokumenty Ministerstva Inostrannykh del Germanii (Documents of the Ministry of Foreign Affairs of Germany), vol. III.
Germanskaia politika i Ispaniia, 1936–43.
German Politics and Spain. 1936–43. Moscow, 1949.
The Book of the XV Brigade. The Commissariat of War, Madrid, 1938.
Documents on German Foreign Policy. Series D (1937–45). (Vol. III. Germany and the Spanish Civil War, 1936–39.) London, 1951.
League of Nations. *Official Journal*. 1936–39.
United States Government. *The Foreign Relations of the United States*

(State Department Papers USD). Vol. 2, 1936. Vol. 1, 1937.
Washington, 1952–54.
The General Cause. Mass Lawsuit brought by the Spanish Nationalist
Government (preliminary report). Madrid, 1953.
L'Épopée de l'Espagne: Brigades Internationales. 1936–38. Compiled by L'Amicale des Anciens Volontaires Français en Espagne
Republicaine. Paris, 1956.
The International Brigades. Madrid, 1953.

NEWSPAPERS AND PERIODICALS

Diario Vasca. Franco's publication in Pampeluna, 6 July 1937.
Journal des Nations. 6 February 1937. 9 April 1937.
Le Temps. 29 March 1937. 26 April 1937. 27 July 1937. 20 October
1937.
New York Times. 23 April 1937. 19 May, 25 May, 26 May, 13 June,
24 June, 17 July, 23 July, 3 September, 19 September, 3 October,
8 October, 31 October, 24 November, 28 December 1937.
16 January, 31 January, 4 April, 5 April, 23 May, 29 May, 8 June
1938.
Time Magazine. 10 March 1941.
L'Œuvre. 16 April, 23 July, 24 July, 26 October 1937.
Volkischer Beobachter. 22 July, 24 July, 13 October 1937.
Berliner Tageblatt. 24 July 1937.
Frankfurter Zeitung. 25 July, 3 August 1937.
Prage, Presse. 27 October 1937.
Il Giornale D'Italia. 6 February 1937. 5 February, 9 February,
12 February, 26 March 1938.
Il Popolo D'Italia. 6 March 1938.
The London Times and Daily Mail, 1936–1939.

LETTERS, ETC.

American letters from Alvah Bessie, James Norman, Moses Fishman,
Sandor Voros, Bert Levy, Paul Burns, Ben Leider, Arnold Krammer and Sheldon Jones. The unpublished diary of Alvah Bessie.
German letters from Ludwig Renn, the German-British Society,
Dr Ernst Adam and Hans Marchwitza.
English letters from Malcolm Dunbar, John Sommerfield, Walter
Greenhalgh, I. Königsberg, M. Stang, and Dr Tudor Hart.
Excerpts from the diaries of Miles Tomalin, Bob Elliot, Smrcka,
Laza Wovicky, Jock Cunningham, Kantorowicz, and Louis
Delaprée.
A collection of Hungarian letters and excerpts from a diary kept by
Dr George Tioli.

*A collection of material placed in the New York Public Library
by the Abraham Lincoln Veterans Association*

They did their part: let's do ours! Rehabilitate the veterans of the Abraham Lincoln Brigade. New York City: Rehabilitation department, Friends of the Abraham Lincoln Brigade [1939].

NORTH, Joseph. Men in the ranks; the story of 12 Americans in Spain, by Joseph North. With a foreword by Ernest Hemingway. [New York City: Friends of the Abraham Lincoln Brigade, 1939.]

ORNITZ, Louis. 1912– . Captured by Franco, by Lou Ornitz. New York City: Friends of the Abraham Lincoln battalion [1939].

The story of the Abraham Lincoln battalion, written in the trenches of Spain. [New York: Friends of the Abraham Lincoln battalion, 1937.]

WPA teachers in Spain; an appreciation of the work of those local 453 members who volunteered to serve in Spain with the Abraham Lincoln Brigade. With biographical sketches, letters and illustrations. [New York] WPA teachers union chapter of the Friends of the Abraham Lincoln brigade [1938].

A collection of material relating to the Spanish Civil war, International brigade, and the Abraham Lincoln Brigade, 1936–48.

Collection of newspaper clippings on the Spanish Civil war, International brigade, Veterans of the Abraham Lincoln Brigade, fascism, Spain, etc., 1937–47.

Veterans of the Abraham Lincoln Brigade, inc. [News bulletins, press releases, etc., 1937–47, on Spain and the Spanish Civil war.]

Veterans of the Abraham Lincoln Brigade, inc. Press releases, speeches, congratulatory messages, etc., concerning the fifth National convention, 21–22 September 1946 (first post-war convention. New York, 1946).

Veterans of the Abraham Lincoln Brigade, inc. Proceedings of the national convention. New York.

Veterans of the Abraham Lincoln Brigade, inc. [Releases, radio addresses, memoranda, etc., on Franco Spain, 1938–47, collected by the Veterans of the Abraham Lincoln Brigade. 1938–47.]

SMITH, Harold. Attack for victory. [New York, Veterans of the Abraham Lincoln Brigade, 1942.]

Spain and the Spanish Civil war; a miscellaneous collection of scattered issues of periodicals gathered by the Veterans of the Abraham Lincoln Brigade.

Spanish war pamphlets; material on the Spanish Civil war, Franco, fascism and anti-fascism, communism, and the economic, political, religious, and social aspects of Civil War Spain, collected by the Veterans of the Abraham Lincoln Brigade.

The Volunteer for Liberty; organ of the International Brigades. v. 1–2; 24 May 1937–7 November 1938. Madrid, etc., 1937–38. 2 vols.

The Volunteer for Liberty . . . [New York, 1949]. 2 v. in 1.

Volunteer for liberty. v. 1, no. 1, 3; v. 5, no. 1–3; v. 6, no. 5, 7–9,

11–12; v. 7, no. 1; v. 8, no. 2; v. 9, no. 6, January, December 1938, January–March 1946, January, September 1947. New York.

WOLF, Milton. Fascist Spain; menace to world peace. New York. Veterans of Abraham Lincoln Brigade, 1947.

WOLF, Milton. Western front now! [New York.] Veterans of the Abraham Lincoln Brigade [1941].

BESSIE, Alvah Cecil, 1904– . ed. The heart of Spain; anthology of fiction, non-fiction, and poetry. [New York.] Veterans of the Abraham Lincoln Brigade [1952].

RELACIÓN DE PERIÓDICOS DE LA HEMEROTECA NACIONAL

Le Volontaire de la liberté. Deutsche Ausgabe. Madrid 1937/8.

Le Volontaire de la liberté. Edizione Italiana. Madrid 1937/8.

Voluntario de la Libertad. Organo de las Brigadas Internacionales. Edición Polaca. Barcelona 1936.

Voluntario de la libertad. Organo de las Brigadas Internacionales. Edición Checoyugoeslava. Barcelona 1938.

Volontaire de la liberté. Organo delle Brigate internazionali. Bàrcelona 1938.

Volontaire de la liberté. Organe des Brigades Internationales. Ed. française. Madrid 1937/8.

Volunteer for Liberty. Organ of the International Brigades. Madrid 1937/8.

El Voluntario de la libertad. Edición Polaca. Madrid 1938.

Vers la liberté. Journal du Bataillon 'A Marty' de la 12ème Brigade Internationale. Madrid 1937. Este mismo después, en vez de la Brigada 12eme . . . se llama la Brigada Dabrowszack y después la Brigada Dombrowsky.

Le soldat de la République. Journal de la XIVème Brigade (luego llamada 'La Marseillaise'). Madrid 1937.

Our Fight. Organ of the Front of the XV Brigade. Madrid 1937 (primero aparece en multicopista, luego se publica en imprenta).

Nuestro Combate. (Editado en imprenta y con texto en Español, Inglés y Francés). Madrid 1937.

Venceremos. Organo de la Brigada Dombrowski. Madrid 1937/8.

NOTA:—Las colecciones no están completas, en muchos casos. Faltan generalmente algunos números, especialmente los primeros.

Index